GREAT WARSHIPS

GREAT WARSHIPS

AN ILLUSTRATED GUIDE TO GREAT SAILING SHIPS
FROM THE SIXTEENTH TO THE TWENTIETH CENTURIES

DAVID ROSS

METRO BOOKS
New York

METRO BOOKS
New York

An Imprint of Sterling Publishing
387 Park Avenue South
New York, NY 10016

Editorial and design by
Amber Books Ltd
74–77 White Lion Street
London N1 9PF
www.amberbooks.co.uk

Project Editor: Michael Spilling
Designer: Andrew Easton
Picture Research: Terry Forshaw

All artworks courtesy of Tony Gibbons © Amber Books
Photo credits: Dreamstime: 7 (Lee Snider), 9 (Martin Maun), 13 (Tamra Kulikova), 15 (Shutter 1970);
Library of Congress: 5, 8; Mary Evans Picture Library: 10; Photos.com: 11; Public Domain: 6, 12, 16, 17

ISBN: 978-1-4351-4852-9

For information about custom editions, special sales, and premium and corporate purchases,
please contact Sterling Special Sales at 800-805-5489 or specialsales@sterlingpublishing.com.

Manufactured in China

2 4 6 8 10 9 7 5 3 1

www.sterlingpublishing.com

Contents

Introduction

THE BEGINNINGS OF THE AGE OF SAIL GO FAR BACK INTO PRE-HISTORY. IT IS LIKELY THAT THE HARNESSING OF WIND POWER FOR SEA TRAVEL WAS DISCOVERED IN MANY DIFFERENT HUMAN COMMUNITIES, AT FIRST UNCONNECTED WITH ONE ANOTHER. COMPARED WITH THE ERAS OF THE STEAM AND INTERNAL COMBUSTION ENGINE, THE AGE OF SAIL WAS IMMENSELY LONG, AND OF COURSE HAS NOT FULLY ENDED.

This book takes as its subject what could be called the "great" age of sail, from the 16th to the 20th centuries. Many advances had been made in the century before 1500, and sailing ships had already passed the Cape of Good Hope and crossed the Atlantic Ocean. By around 1500, larger ships had become sophisticated wind machines. They could have several masts and a range of adjustable sails. Rudders, capstans, and windlasses helped to work them efficiently. Merchant ships were made larger and could carry more cargo, and warships were improved upon to make them more effective in sea battles. Merchant ships, often carrying a few guns for their own protection, could be rapidly converted for warfare, but also the specialized man of war, carrying cannons and soldiers, was in use, although in quite limited numbers as yet, providing flagships to lead a fleet.

IMPROVED TECHNOLOGY

The improvement of ships, in terms of their ability to travel farther from land, stay out at sea for longer, and to ride out storms, was matched by improved techniques of navigation and mapmaking. Charts were of high value, kept secret as part of the mariner's stock in trade. The compass had been known since the 12th century and the hourglass used to measure time was around since

RIGHT: *The 1514 warship* Henry Grace à Dieu, *as reconstructed after 1545, displays features of the time: a flat stern as found on caravels and galleys, and a massive forecastle projecting forwards over the bows, typical of large carracks.*

OPPOSITE: *The backdrop is modern Hong Kong, but the sailing junk in the foreground is timeless in its form. The oldest-known description of a ship of this type dates from 1298 A.D.*

ABOVE: *Conjectural images of Columbus's three ships,* Santa Maria, Pinta, *and* Niña, *are seen in the background. He referred to* Santa Maria *as a "nao", or ship, and to the two smaller craft as "caravels".*

OPPOSITE: *The remarkable state of preservation of Sweden's* Vasa (1628) *gives us authentic detail of the hull and elaborate decoration of an early 17th-century man of war. The remains can be seen in the Vasa Museum in Stockholm.*

the 1400s. Simple as these tools might appear, they revolutionized our ability to traverse the oceans.

With the use of the rudder, ships were steered by a tiller directly joined to the rudder. In the 16th century the whipstaff came into use, a pole pivoted to the end of the tiller enabling the helmsman to stand on deck and watch the sails while working the rudder, which might be one or two decks below. By the later 17th century this was being replaced by a far more effective mechanism, the ship's wheel, which, by operating ropes set in sheaves and pulleys, could turn the rudder. Even this could be a muscle-breaking job and several men were often needed to work the wheel of a big ship sailing close to the wind. These changes happened only gradually, and were slow to spread.

A technical base was needed where tools and stores could be kept, and experience gathered and put to use. The shipbuilding yard, in effect one of the first factories, became the place where a modern vessel was built and fitted out. One of the first great naval yards was the Arsenal at Venice, set up as early as the 12th century, which gave its name to many others, such as London's Woolwich Arsenal.

At first they were set up by kings and governments, but from the early 17th century there were also private companies who set up shipyards that, although primarily intended to construct merchant ships, could also build warships. These yards, like Buckler's

LEFT: *Lord Howard in the* Ark Royal *(right) attacks Medina Sidonia in the* San Martín *in a close-range exchange of broadsides off Portland Bill in the English Channel, August 2, 1588.* San Martín *carried 48 heavy guns, while* Ark Royal *was armed with 55 guns of various sizes.*

OPPOSITE: *English and Spanish ships exchange cannon-fire in a battle fought in the English Channel in May 1588. A large Spanish sailing galley is in the foreground.*

Hard in Hampshire, England, were often far from a town but close to oak forests.

TRADE ROUTES

The largest and most inventive seafaring nation of the Middle Ages was China, where many inventions long pre-dated those of Europe. After his 13th century journey to China, the Italian Marco Polo described a junk in terms that are still relevant today, with its interior partitions—the earliest known version of watertight compartments. It already had a single rudder at a time when European ships usually had two. With modern details and adaptations, the Chinese junk is still in use today, maintaining a strong resemblance to those of seven or eight hundred years ago.

Around the coasts of India and Arabia, a distinctive shipbuilding tradition grew up, with successive generations of traders and sailors who

crossed the Indian Ocean and reached as far as the Malay Peninsula. These waters were first visited by European ships from the late 15th century, initially from Portugal and Spain, then also from England and Holland. In the Middle East, shipbuilders created the lateen rig, a large triangular or four-sided sail mounted on an adjustable yard. The trade route to the Indies, once a laborious overland journey, was now a sea voyage.

Indeed, it was to find a shorter sea route that Christopher Columbus made his voyage of 1492, which reintroduced America to Europeans some four hundred years after Viking sailing ships had reached Vinland. To protect their trading stations—genesis of later colonies—and the long sea routes, the trading countries built armed ships, with heavy guns.

GALLEONS AND MEN OF WAR

Increasing wealth and technical skill and ambition encouraged the building of ever larger ships, especially those which reflected royal status. Vessels like *Henry Grace à Dieu* and *San Martìn* from the 16th century show a tendency to display that became even more elaborate in the 17th century, reaching a peak with such ships as *Vasa*, *Sovereign of the Seas*, and *Le Soleil Royal*. But these special ships might also show technical innovation, like the royal sails set above the topgallants on *Sovereign of the Seas*.

Meanwhile, in dozens of small ports local craftsmen were using native timbers and traditional methods to build far plainer and smaller ships that were capable of ocean voyages, like Sir Walter Raleigh's *Ark Royal*, built at Deptford,

OPPOSITE: *The preserved tea clipper* Cutty Sark *(1869) shows off its racing lines in dry dock at Greenwich, London. The mainmast is rigged to carry skysails.*

BELOW: *These scale drawings of the 1769 Spanish ship of the line* Santísima Trinidad, *when still a three-decker, were made to show how to erect a deck cover.*

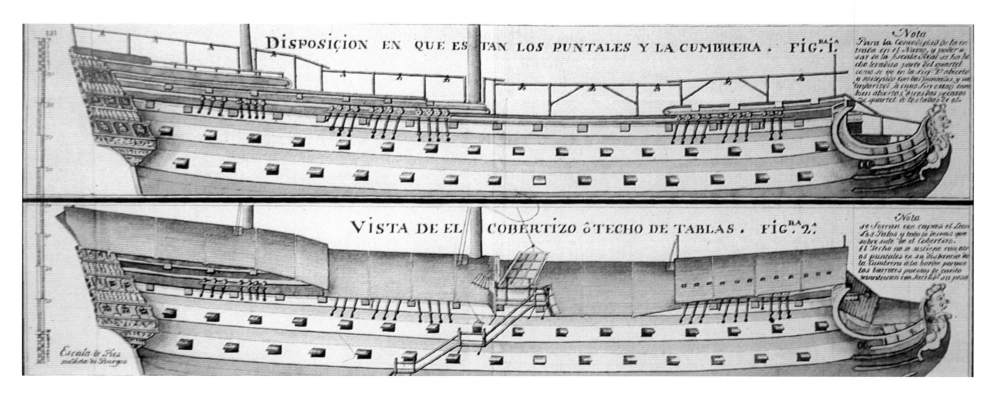

12

England, in 1587. This period is associated with the word "galleon" as a reference to the ships of the time, but it is not a very precise one. Essentially it describes a 16th-century ship with a low beak below the bowsprit, a raised forecastle, a central well-deck, and a high poop deck.

Normally three-masted, larger specimens might carry a fourth. Sometimes three masts were square rigged, sometimes only the fore and main masts. Size could vary from the relatively small, quick-handling English type of galleon to the much larger, more cumbrous but much more powerful (especially if it came to boarding) Spanish galleon. English captains had to be adept at keeping their distance.

Some shipwrights made notes and diagrams of ship hulls and frames for their own or their workmen's use, but by the early 17th century, manuals of shipbuilding were being printed and published, reflecting the growing size of the industry. This also promoted a growing degree of standardization in design. Ship types in the various European countries were gradually becoming more like one another. Innovations in rigging were introduced (sometimes reintroduced having been used on a limited basis a century or two before), like reef points, enabling a crew to quickly shorten sail on the topsail and topgallant, and with widened yards to accommodate the greater width of the reefed sail in its lower part.

SHIPS OF THE LINE

Improvements in ship handling, in gunmaking, and much scientific work in ship design all contributed to the emergence of the mighty ship of the line. Massive for their time, these vessels were intended to sail in line together against an enemy fleet and bombard it with "broadsides" from their two or three decks of cannon. At the same time they were built to withstand a certain amount of reciprocal battering from the cannonballs of the other side.

These ships were classified by a rating system (originally devised in England to define how much the sailors should be paid: the bigger the ship, the better the pay) but was transferred to the number of guns carried. By the 1790s a first-rate vessel carried 100 or more guns, a second-rate 80-plus, and a third-rate from 64 to 80. Fourth rate vessels and lower were not expected to join in the line of battle. Fourth and fifth rate ships had a single gun deck and it was from these that the frigate emerged as a distinct warship type.

To the casual eye, one 18th century man of war can look very like another: there is the hull, the gun deck or decks, the forecastle, the poop, the three masts with their rigging. But shipwrights and naval officers pored over the variations with eagle eyes, noting details and proportions. Every time a ship was seized in war from another navy, especially if it was still quite new, it was examined closely.

Many notable British warships of the Napoleonic period were floating tributes to the qualities of French ship design, such as HMS *Caesar* and *Minotaur*. Ever since the mid-1660s, French ships of the line had been built higher and broader than their British counterparts. In a sea battle, to have the main guns 4 ft (1.2 m) rather than 3 ft (.91 m) above the waterline was a considerable advantage.

SMALLER SHIP TYPES

Smaller sailing ships came in huge variety and, as they were often built in their home ports, local forms lasted longer than with larger ships constructed in purpose-built shipyards rather than on rough stocks above a beach. Luggers, cutters, Dutch jachts (yachts), pinnaces, galiots—there were many other terms—were used for coastal trading and fishing as well as more nefarious purposes like smuggling. Single- or two-masted and with a variety of rigs, they found their way into naval use, as shown in these pages by the *chasse-marée* and the naval cutter.

From a more specialized shipbuilding tradition came the gunboat, a shallow-draught small craft, again featuring no more than two masts, mounting a single cannon or several lighter guns. In the early years of the 19th century the U.S. Navy was largely composed of gunboats.

By the mid-18th century every kind of ship sail had been devised, including staysails, set between the masts, and studding sails extended on each side of the topsail on foremast and mainmast. Speed was important: a fast ship could escape a more powerful enemy or catch another ship in a chase. The American corvette *General Pike*, used on Lake Ontario in the War of 1812, carried six levels of sail on the foremast and the mainmast, with skysails above the royals.

Speed was also a pre-requisite for certain kinds of merchant ship, especially those carrying valuable or perishable cargo, and the clipper type developed on both sides of the Atlantic during the 19th century. Made most famous by the tea and wool races of the later years, the clippers worked on many sea routes. Other merchant ships were less speedy but might have greater cargo capacity and get by with smaller crews.

SAIL AND RIGGING

The naming and definition of ship types can be a complex and frustrating business. The shape of the hull and the form of rig were the key features, but size might also play a part. Ship types

RIGHT: *The British ironclad HMS* Warrior *(1861), still preserved here at Portsmouth, Hampshire, has retractable funnels and a propeller that could be raised when the ship was cruising under sail.*

had a tendency to be built larger as time went by—the frigate and the schooner are prime examples. A frigate of the 1840s was twice the size of a frigate of the 1740s, quite apart from the fact that it probably had a funnel and propeller as well as a full set of sails. But the basic schooner rig remains a fore-and-aft rig, without yards, whereas there never was such a thing as a frigate rig—frigates were ship-rigged with square sails just like the ships of the line.

These definitions, square, and fore-and-aft, refer to the position of the spars on which the sails are set. Square sails are mounted on yards set across the beam of the ship, whereas fore-and-aft sails are set on gaffs (above) and booms (below) running parallel to the length of the ship. By the 19th century merchant ship designations tended to focus on masts and sail-plan. A barque was a ship of three or more masts, with the first two carrying a square rig and the after masts a fore-and-aft rig. A barquentine was three-masted, and square-rigged only on the foremast. A brig had two masts, both carrying a square rig, while a brigantine also had two masts, with a square rig on the foremast

and a fore-and-aft sail on the mainmast. In American idiom a brigantine is referred to as a hermaphrodite brig. All types might carry topsails and staysails.

THE ADVENT OF STEAM POWER

Steam power was put to work on ships at first in a very small way from the beginning of the 19th century, and for a long time it was not seen as a rival to the long-distance sailing ship. Early marine engines were small and unreliable. When incorporated in seagoing ships they were regarded as auxiliary to the sails. Practical economics always played a major part in the building and running of merchant fleets (more so than in the management of navies) and shipbuilders and owners were well aware that the wind was free and that coal cost money and took up valuable cargo space.

Naval authorities were generally conservative by nature and did not relish the challenge put up by a

OPPOSITE: *The German flagship* König Wilhelm *(1869) at anchor. Gilded decoration at bow and stern was a feature of late 19th century German warships. The low bow was later heightened to deck level.*

change to steam propulsion. But the advantages of a self-powered ship were increasingly obvious, especially with new technologies including iron hulls, armor-piercing shells, and new types of gun. The Battle of Navarino, in 1827, between the Turkish fleet and those of Britain, France, and Russia, was the last naval battle fought exclusively by sailing ships. One British admiral complained that he had never seen a clean ship, or a clean officer, since steam was introduced. But commanders were more concerned with the possibility that another navy might seize on some technical innovation and produce a range of ships that would make all others obsolete. This is exactly what happened with the French *Gloire* and then the British *Warrior* at the end of the 1850s. Partly as a result of this sense of rivalry, and the technical advances that stemmed from it, from the 1850s onwards a fascinating range of warships, fully rigged but also steam-powered, appeared. The venerable French first-rate *Montebello*, launched in 1812, had an auxiliary engine installed in 1852. The American Civil War ships *Alabama* and *Kearsarge* were sail/steam

craft. Others included the ill-fated HMS *Captain*, one of the first ships to carry gun turrets, and the Italian and Austrian ships that fought at the Battle of Lissa in 1866. It was only in the late 1870s that navies began to de-rig their major ships.

That ended the great period of the Age of Sail as far as warships were concerned, although many navies continued to use sailing ships in training seamen far into the 20th century, as the example of *Amerigo Vespucci* shows. The merchant sailing ship had a longer life. With a capacious iron hull, four or five masts, and a comparatively small crew, the sailing ship could often undercut the steamship on price for the transportation of bulk cargoes. Tall masts and spars could be seen in harbors all over the world until the 1930s. It was in one such harbor, Falmouth in Cornwall, that Captain Dow saw the barque-rigged *Maria de Amparo* in 1922, and recognized in it the lines of the former (and future) *Cutty Sark*. *Archibald Russell* and *Herzogin Cecilie* also testify in this book to the usefulness and splendor, as well as the vulnerability, of tall ships in the 20th century.

RIGHT: HMS Inflexible *(1881) was the only turret ship to carry a full square rig, including upper topgallants. The two gun turrets weighed 680 tons (691 tonnes) each.*

Henry Grace á Dieu (1514)

NAMED FOR ITS ROYAL OWNER, KING HENRY VIII OF ENGLAND, THIS WAS A VERY LARGE SHIP FOR ITS TIME, INTENDED BOTH AS A MAN OF WAR AND AS A TRANSPORT VESSEL FOR THE KING AND HIS ENTOURAGE. AS SUCH, IT HAD TO CONVEY THE STATUS AND SPLENDOR OF MONARCHY IN ITS APPEARANCE AND FITTINGS AS WELL AS IN ITS FIGHTING POWER.

Constructed at the Woolwich Dockyard on the River Thames, where King Henry could watch its progress, this ship was of the carrack type, with the typical rounded hull shape, and with a carvel-built hull, with the planks set edge to edge rather than overlapping. The massive forecastle was also a usual feature, as was the squared-off stern. Soldiers and sailors lived at this end. The men-forward, officers-aft arrangement would be standard in future British Navy ships. Topgallant sails, providing a third tier of wind drive above the main yards, were still a recent innovation, dating from around 1500. It was a royal ship both in the sense that the King's funds paid for it and because it was designed only for warfare and for carrying the King himself with his attendants, at a time when most ships of war were hastily converted merchantmen. Its large guns were carried in the waist of the ship, helping stability but also ensuring that they could fire at the waterline of enemy vessels (encounters were always at close range at this time). The smaller guns were mounted on the high fore- and sterncastles, where they could be trained both on the rigging and on the decks of other ships.

Vessel in Action

Henry Grace à Dieu, also known as "Great Harry," carried Henry VIII to France in 1520 for a meeting with the French king where each tried to outdo the other in opulence and swagger. The ship was not engaged in military action until the Battle of the Solent in 1545, when the French attacked Portsmouth with a fleet consisting largely of galleys, and the unwieldy "Great Harry" found it difficult to counter their ability to execute swift turns and sudden stops. After Henry's death in 1547 it was renamed *Edward* for his successor, King Edward VI. It remained in commission, although not in active service, until August 23, 1553, when it caught fire at Woolwich and was totally destroyed.

SPECIFICATIONS

DISPLACEMENT: c. 1,500 tons (c. 1,524 tonnes)

DIMENSIONS: 190 ft x 50 ft (57.9 m x 15.2 m)

RIG: Four masts, square rig fore and main, lateen mizzens

ARMAMENT: 21 bronze cannons; 130 iron guns; 100 hand guns (1545)

CREW: c. 700

Henry Grace á Dieu

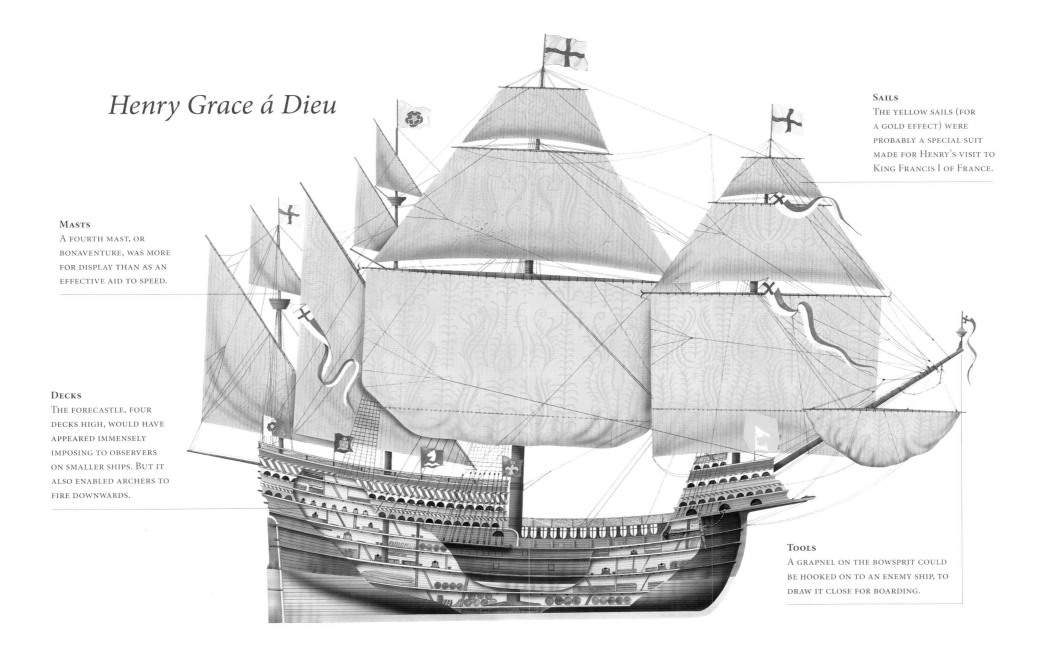

SAILS
THE YELLOW SAILS (FOR
A GOLD EFFECT) WERE
PROBABLY A SPECIAL SUIT
MADE FOR HENRY'S VISIT TO
KING FRANCIS I OF FRANCE.

MASTS
A FOURTH MAST, OR
BONAVENTURE, WAS MORE
FOR DISPLAY THAN AS AN
EFFECTIVE AID TO SPEED.

DECKS
THE FORECASTLE, FOUR
DECKS HIGH, WOULD HAVE
APPEARED IMMENSELY
IMPOSING TO OBSERVERS
ON SMALLER SHIPS. BUT IT
ALSO ENABLED ARCHERS TO
FIRE DOWNWARDS.

TOOLS
A GRAPNEL ON THE BOWSPRIT COULD
BE HOOKED ON TO AN ENEMY SHIP, TO
DRAW IT CLOSE FOR BOARDING.

19

San Martín (1580)

THIS CELEBRATED SHIP WAS ACTUALLY BUILT IN PORTUGAL AND BROUGHT INTO THE SPANISH NAVY IN 1580 WHEN PORTUGAL WAS ANNEXED BY SPAIN. APPRECIATING ITS SIZE AND QUALITIES, THE SPANISH ADMIRALTY MADE IT A *CAPITANA*, OR FLAGSHIP, AND IT LED THE VAST FLEET KNOWN AS THE "SPANISH ARMADA" AGAINST ENGLAND IN MAY 1588. THIS ILL-FATED EXPEDITION ENDED IN DISASTER, WITH ONLY HALF THE SHIPS RETURNING. *SAN MARTÍN* WAS ONE OF THEM, REACHING SANTANDER ON SEPTEMBER 23, 1588.

San Martín was a galleon, a term that covers quite a range of ship sizes. Typical features included a narrow ratio of length to beam and a low forecastle compared to earlier ships, with a beaklike prow extended in front.

Its career as a flagship began successfully, when it led the fleet at the Battle of Terceira, off the Azores, on July 25, 1582. In this engagement the Marqués de Santa Cruz defeated a French fleet of 75 ships, sinking 10 and losing none of his own fleet.

Six years later King Philip II of Spain planned an invasion of England, and assembled a fleet of some 130 ships of war, plus storeships and scouting vessels. It was one of the largest war fleets yet assembled, and certainly the most powerful.

Sailing against England

Commanded by the Duke of Medina Sidonia, with *San Martín* as his flagship, the fleet left La Coruña on July 22, 1588. The ensuing series of battles lasted between July 31 and August 8—a week in which the smaller, more maneuverable English ships, armed with longer-range guns, had the advantage.

San Martín was in the thick of the fighting, notably in an hour-long duel with the English flagship *Ark Royal* on August 3, and in a rearguard action off Gravelines on the French side of the English Channel on August 8.

The Armada was successfully fought off and the Spanish were forced to sail for home, taking the long way around, past the stormy coasts of Scotland and Ireland. Around 50 ships were lost.

Defeat and Retreat

Although *San Martín* returned safely to Spain, 180 men died on the homeward journey. By then the ship must have been in very poor condition. Although the war was not over, and Spain needed to re-form its fleet as quickly as possible, its subsequent history is not known.

SPECIFICATIONS

DISPLACEMENT: 1,000 tons (1,016 tonnes)

DIMENSIONS: 122 ft 3 in x 30 ft 9 in (37.3 m x 9.3 m)

RIG: Four masts, square rig fore and main, lateen mizzens

ARMAMENT: 48 heavy guns, including 17 cannons and culverins on lower deck and 17 lighter guns on upper deck

CREW: 350 seamen and gunners; 302 soldiers

San Martín

DESIGN
TWO GUN DECKS WERE
INCORPORATED INTO
THE DESIGN FROM THE
BEGINNING. THIS WAS A
SHIP PURPOSEFULLY BUILT
FOR FIGHTING.

GUNPORTS
GUNPORTS WERE FIRST USED IN
FRANCE, AROUND 1501, BUT WERE
QUICKLY COPIED BY OTHER NATIONS.

BOARDING
THE HIGH SIDES OF THE SPANISH
GALLEONS FAVORED "BOARDING"
AN ENEMY BY RUNNING ALONGSIDE,
BUT THIS TACTIC FAILED IN THE
ARMADA BATTLES.

Ark Royal (1587)

Laid down as *Ark Raleigh* at Deptford on the River Thames, the ship was built for Sir Walter Raleigh, courtier and explorer of North America, but taken over before completion as a royal vessel for the navy of Queen Elizabeth I. Flagship of the English fleet that defeated the Spanish Armada, *Ark Royal* also took part in the attack on Cádiz in 1596, and it remained in commission until 1636.

English warship design in the 1580s took a somewhat different course to that of Spain. Both countries built ships of the galleon type but the English vessels were generally smaller and easier to handle in battle conditions. They had high sterncastles but the galleon-type forecastles were relatively low. Their main guns were designed to fire over a longer range. This combination of maneuverability and long-range gunfire enabled them to stand off from an enemy ship and disable it from a distance. They were at their most vulnerable if the bigger vessel came close enough to grapple and board, but this could usually be avoided, as on August 2, 1588, when *Ark Royal* dodged the much bigger Spanish *Regazona*. It was also noted that Spanish cannonballs tended to fragment on impact, while the denser English ones had greater penetration.

Meeting the Armada

Ark Royal was the English flagship, under Lord Howard of Effingham, leading a fleet of 56 ships sent from Plymouth to meet the Armada. Howard called it "the odd (i.e. exceptional) ship in the world for all conditions" and declined to lead the fleet from a bigger vessel. His fleet was later reinforced to more than 100, and on July 31 *Ark Royal* was the first ship to engage the Spanish fleet, firing on the galleon *Santa Maria Encoronada*. For a time, on August 2–3, the two flagships were in combat, although relatively little damage was done.

After the retreat of the Armada, *Ark Royal* returned to port in triumph. Eight years later it participated in an English raid on Cadiz, and was readied for action again in 1599 to repel another threatened Spanish invasion. In 1608 it was rebuilt and renamed *Anne Royal* in honor of the consort of King James I. Although it saw no further action it remained part of the royal fleet until 1636, when it sank at Tilbury, on the Thames.

SPECIFICATIONS

DISPLACEMENT: 694 tons (705 tonnes)

DIMENSIONS: 140 ft x 37 ft x 15 ft (42.6 m x 11.2 m x 4.5 m)

RIG: Four masts, square rig fore and main, lateen mizzens

ARMAMENT: Four 60 pounders; four 30 pounders; twelve 18 pounders; twelve 9 pounders; six 6 pounders; 17 small guns (1599)

CREW: 304 sailors; 126 soldiers

Ark Royal

CARGO
ALTHOUGH SUCH SHIPS COULD UNDERTAKE VERY LONG VOYAGES, THEIR MANEUVERABILITY AGAINST THE ARMADA WAS HELPED BY NOT NEEDING TO CARRY LARGE SUPPLY STORES.

DESIGN
THE CUT-DOWN FORECASTLE MADE THE SHIP MORE "WEATHERLY"— EASIER TO HANDLE IN SIDE WINDS.

HULL
MUCH OF THE ARMADA FIGHTING WAS IN SHALLOW WATER WHERE THE LESSER DRAFT OF THE ENGLISH SHIPS WAS ANOTHER ADVANTAGE.

23

Vasa *(1628)*

THE PRIDE OF THE SWEDISH ROYAL FLEET, *VASA* WAS PLANNED AS PART OF A LARGE-SCALE STRATEGY TO ENSURE SWEDISH CONTROL OF THE BALTIC SEA AT A TIME WHEN THE COUNTRY, UNDER KING GUSTAVUS II ADOLPHUS, WAS HEAVILY ENGAGED IN WARFARE IN GERMANY AND POLAND. BUT ON ITS MAIDEN VOYAGE, APRIL 10, 1628, *VASA* HEELED OVER AND SANK ONLY A FEW MINUTES AFTER SETTING SAIL, AND LESS THAN A MILE FROM SHORE.

In the early 17th century, the Dutch were considered the best shipbuilders in Europe, and a Dutch architect, Henrik Hybertson de Groot, was employed to design and supervise construction of *Vasa*. Typically for the time, the ship was lavishly ornamented to emphasize the wealth and power of the Vasa, Sweden's ruling family, but it was intended for hard tasks in an era of international warfare. The Swedes were blockading the Polish harbor of Danzig (Gdańsk) with 34 ships, mostly small, and *Vasa* was intended to add power to this fleet.

The First and Last Voyage

Its departure from Stockholm was a gala occasion, with around 100 guests on board apart from the crew, intended to be transferred to shore boats before *Vasa* put to sea. It was warped out of the harbor by a longboat, because the wind was so light,

until it was in more open water. Then the fore and main topsails and courses were set to pick up what wind there was. Perhaps because of the calm, the gunports were left open. In a sudden gust of wind, *Vasa* was laid over to such a degree that the lower gunports went under water and the sea flooded in. Unable to right itself, the ship sank immediately in 115 ft (35 m) of water, and around 50 of the 250 people on board were drowned.

Salvage efforts began soon afterwards but to little effect until 53 bronze guns were lifted in 1663–64. The wreck then lay forgotten until it was located in 1956, found to be largely intact, and a major recovery operation was launched. On April 24, 1960, *Vasa* appeared again above the surface and since then has been preserved in a specially constructed museum building. Over 3,000 different artifacts have been recovered, including most of the fine wooden carvings which

adorned the ship as well as many more personal items that reveal the life of the early 17th-century mariner.

SPECIFICATIONS

DISPLACEMENT: 1,300 tons (1,321 tonnes)

DIMENSIONS: 226 ft x 38 ft 3 in x 15 ft 4 in (69 m x 11.7 m x 4.9 m)

RIG: Three masts, square rig

ARMAMENT: Forty-eight 24 pounders; eight 3 pounders; two 1 pounders; one 16 pounder; two 62 pounders; three 35 pounder guns

CREW: 145 sailors; 300 soldiers

Vasa

RIGGING
THE SOLID SEATING NEEDED FOR
THE MASSIVE BOWSPRIT, WITH ITS
SPRITSAIL AND TOPSAIL, IS CLEARLY
SHOWN.

ARMAMENT
VASA COULD FIRE 588 LB (267 KG) OF
SHOT FROM EACH SIDE, ALTHOUGH THE
MIXING OF CALIBERS WAS NOT HELPFUL
TO EFFICIENT GUNNERY.

GUNPORTS
IRONICALLY, THE GUNPORTS WERE OF
THE MOST UP-TO-DATE TYPE, HINGING
UPWARDS AND WITH INNER SEALS.

Sovereign of the Seas (1637)

MASTERWORK OF THE FAMOUS ENGLISH SHIPWRIGHT PHINEAS PETT, THIS "GREAT NEW SHIP" OF KING CHARLES I WAS LAUNCHED FROM WOOLWICH DOCKYARD, ON THE RIVER THAMES, IN 1637. IN MANY WAYS THE DESIGN BROKE WITH CONVENTION: IT HAD THREE DECKS OF GUNS, NEW-TYPE SAILS, AND WAS EXCEPTIONAL IN ITS SHEER SIZE. IN A LONG ACTIVE CAREER IT SAW CONSIDERABLE ACTION IN THE ANGLO-DUTCH WARS OF THE 17TH CENTURY BEFORE BEING ACCIDENTALLY DESTROYED BY FIRE IN 1703.

Critics were not lacking when the design of *Sovereign of the Seas*, ordered in 1634, was known: "the art or wit of man cannot build a ship fit for service with three tier of ordnance," wrote one. But Charles I was determined to have a ship that expressed England's claim to sea power. Like other capital ships of the time, the vessel was elaborately decorated with carvings, painted in gold and other colors, none of which had the slightest value in a fight but which looked magnificent. Indeed, much of its huge cost of £65,586 went into ornamentation.

Despite all that it was very much a man of war, with 30 gunports on the lowest deck, carrying demi-cannons (30-pounder) and whole cannons (60-pounder), 30 more on the middle deck, with culverins (20-pounder) and demi-culverins (10-pounder). The top tier had 26 ports for lighter guns, and there were 12 on the forecastle and 14 on the half deck. Altogether 102 guns were carried apart from "murdering pieces" intended to scatter fire on an enemy deck, and many musketry positions behind loopholes. For the 1630s this was a formidable battery, although it is unlikely that the ship could deliver a coordinated broadside.

Power Over Speed

By this time the bonaventure mast was a thing of the past, but a greater spread of sail was carried on three masts. This was the first, or one of the first, vessels to carry royals above the topgallants. Heavier and higher masts were needed, with a corresponding need for more substantial staying and rigging.

Sovereign of the Seas was comparatively slow and unwieldy, but its bulk and firepower made it effective in battle, and it featured in numerous conflicts in four decades of active duty between 1652 and 1692. During the Commonwealth period after Charles I's execution it was renamed *Sovereign*, and following the restoration of the monarchy in 1660 became *Royal Sovereign*, following a rebuild.

SPECIFICATIONS

DISPLACEMENT: 1,380 tons (1,522 tonnes)

DIMENSIONS: 127 ft x 46 ft 6 in (39 m x 14.17 m)

RIG: Three masts, square rig

ARMAMENT: 102 guns, including 60-pounders, 30-pounders (lower deck), 20-pounders, and 10-pounders (middle deck)

CREW: Not recorded

RIGGING
RIGGING HAD BECOME MORE
SUBSTANTIAL AND COMPLEX TO COPE
WITH LARGER AND HEAVIER SAILS.

Sovereign of the Seas

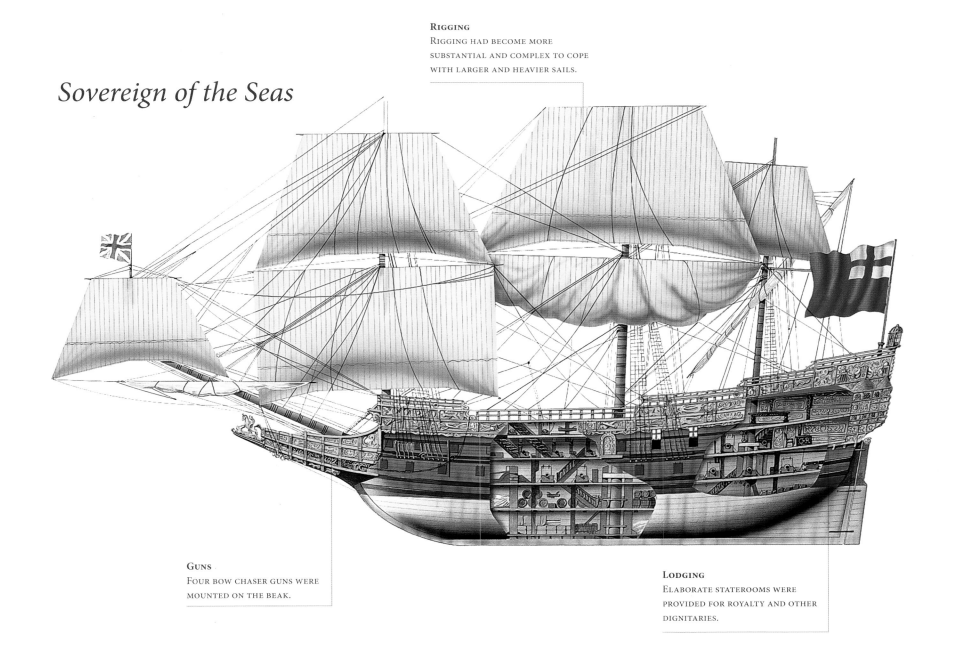

GUNS
FOUR BOW CHASER GUNS WERE
MOUNTED ON THE BEAK.

LODGING
ELABORATE STATEROOMS WERE
PROVIDED FOR ROYALTY AND OTHER
DIGNITARIES.

Le Soleil Royal *(1669)*

CLASSIFIED AS A *VAISSEAU*, OR FIRST-CLASS MAN OF WAR, *LE SOLEIL ROYAL* ("ROYAL SUN") WAS NAMED FOR LOUIS XIV OF FRANCE, THE "SUN KING," AND LIKE OTHER ICONIC SHIPS WAS DECORATED LIKE A FLOATING PALACE, ALTHOUGH CREW CONDITIONS WERE EVEN MORE SPARTAN THAN THOSE OF THE KING'S PALACE SERVANTS. AS FLAGSHIP OF FRANCE'S NAVY IT PARTICIPATED IN THE VICTORY AT BÉVEZIERS, BUT TWO YEARS LATER THE BATTLE OF BARFLEUR RESULTED IN ITS GROUNDING AND TOTAL DESTRUCTION.

L*e Soleil Royal* was the product of a modernization and revitalization of France's navy by the King's minister Jean-Baptiste Colbert. Only a very wealthy as well as ostentatious monarchy could have afforded to construct warships on such a sumptuous scale. Built at Brest by the King's master builder Laurent Hubac, it was launched on December 13, 1669 and commissioned in August 1670. In its first two decades of service the ship was not involved in any notable action.

A refit was done in 1689, with the number of guns increased to 104, and on completion *Le Soleil Royal* was made flagship of France's northern fleet, based at Brest in Brittany under the Comte de Tourville as Admiral. In 1690 France was at war with England and Holland, and the French fleet, 70-strong, met a Dutch-English fleet of 57 ships in the Battle of Béveziers off Beachy Head on England's

Channel coast. Eight English and Dutch ships were lost, while Tourville lost none.

Battle of Barfleur

On May 12, 1692, with a fleet reduced to 44 ships, the rest having been deployed to the Mediterranean Sea, Tourville again left Brest to protect an invasion fleet intended for England. A Dutch-English fleet of 88 ships had been mustered to prevent it, and on May 19 they met off the Pointe de Barfleur.

Leading the French central squadron of 16 ships of the line, *Le Soleil Royal* suffered severe damage in the course of a day-long battle and Tourville shifted his flag to *Ambitieux*. With two other large ships, *Admirable* and *Conquérant*, *Le Soleil Royal* was forced to take refuge in the Bay of Cherbourg, where they ran aground offshore. Still under attack, the masts were cut down. English fireships were sent in and *Le Soleil Royal* was

destroyed when its powder magazine exploded. Only 20 ships of Tourville's fleet returned safely to Brest.

SPECIFICATIONS

DISPLACEMENT: c. 1,200 tons (c. 1,219 tonnes)

DIMENSIONS: 180 ft 5 in x 51 ft 2 in x 24 ft 11 in (55 m x 15.6 m x 7.6 m)

RIG: Three masts, square rig

ARMAMENT: 104 bronze cannons (from 1689)

CREW: 1,200

Le Soleil Royal

STERN
BIG STERN LAMPS WERE THE
ONLY VISIBLE SIGN OF A SHIP
IN DARKNESS.

TOPS
WITH THE ADVENT OF
MUSKETRY, FIGHTING
TOPS BECAME IMPORTANT
PLACINGS FOR
SHARPSHOOTERS.

GUNS
FRENCH WARSHIPS
GENERALLY RODE HIGHER
IN THE WATER THAN
ENGLISH ONES, ENABLING
MORE EFFECTIVE USE OF
THE HEAVIEST GUNS.

HULL
THE HULL WAS PAINTED ROYAL
BLUE IN HONOR OF THE KING.

Renommée (1747)

A 30-GUN FRIGATE, CLASSIFIED AS A FIFTH-RATE, LAID DOWN AT BREST IN JANUARY 1744 AND COMMISSIONED JUST A YEAR LATER, *RENOMMÉE* ("FAME") HAD ONLY A SHORT CAREER IN THE FRENCH NAVY BEFORE BEING TAKEN AS A PRIZE BY A BRITISH FRIGATE AND SPENDING THE REST OF ITS CAREER UNDER THE BRITISH FLAG. RECOGNIZED AS AN EXCELLENT SAILER, IT GAVE DISTINGUISHED SERVICE FOR ALMOST A QUARTER OF A CENTURY BEFORE BEING BROKEN UP IN 1771.

Built by François-Guillaume Deslauriers in Brest, *Renommée* carried 30 guns, 26 of them 8-pounders, mounted on the upper deck. It was commissioned under Captain Guy Kersaint, who was succeeded by François de Saint-Alouarn. On September 23–34, 1747, it was carrying the new Governor of San Domingo out to the West Indies when it fell foul of the frigates HMS *Dover* and HMS *Amazon* (formerly the French *Panthère*).

Heavily outgunned, it surrendered and was taken as a prize. At first named as *Fame*, it was renamed *Renown* in January 1748, after a predecessor (see below), and was refitted at Plymouth Dockyard, with thirty British-made guns, twenty-four 9 pounders and six 4 pounders. As a Royal Navy frigate, it was captained first by Washington Shirley, who had been Captain of the *Dover*, and served in the West Indies.

The Seven Years' War

Between 1750 and 1756 it was laid up at the Hamoaze, Plymouth, but recommissioned when the Seven Years' War broke out in 1756, serving in the English Channel where it took part in operations against the harbors of Cherbourg and Saint-Malo, and captured the French frigate *Guirlande* on June 29, 1758; and also on occasions at Port Royal in the West Indies. In January 1759 it assisted at the attack on Martinique and the capture of Guadeloupe, and remained in the West Indies until late 1761. Early in 1762 it transported troops to Oporto, Portugal, and in March of that year captured four French privateers, three on the same day, off the coast of Brittany. Decommissioned again in 1766, it returned to service in 1767 and served continuously, mostly on the West Indies station, until its return to Britain in July 1770. A survey in April 1771 condemned

it, after which it was broken up at Woolwich Naval Arsenal.

Renommée was an unfortunate name in the French Navy: the first was captured by HMS *Nonsuch* in 1651 and renamed *Renown*; the second by HMS *Alfred* in 1796; and the third, captured in 1811 by the Royal Navy, was renamed HMS *Java* but later captured again by USS *Constitution* in 1812 and subsequently burned on January 1, 1813.

SPECIFICATIONS

DISPLACEMENT: 669 tons (679 tonnes)

DIMENSIONS: 126 ft 2 in x 34 ft 10.5 in x 11 ft 8 in (38.45 m x 10.63 m x 3.55 m)

RIG: Three masts, square rig

ARMAMENT: Twenty-six 8 pounders; four 4 pounder guns

CREW: 224

Renommée

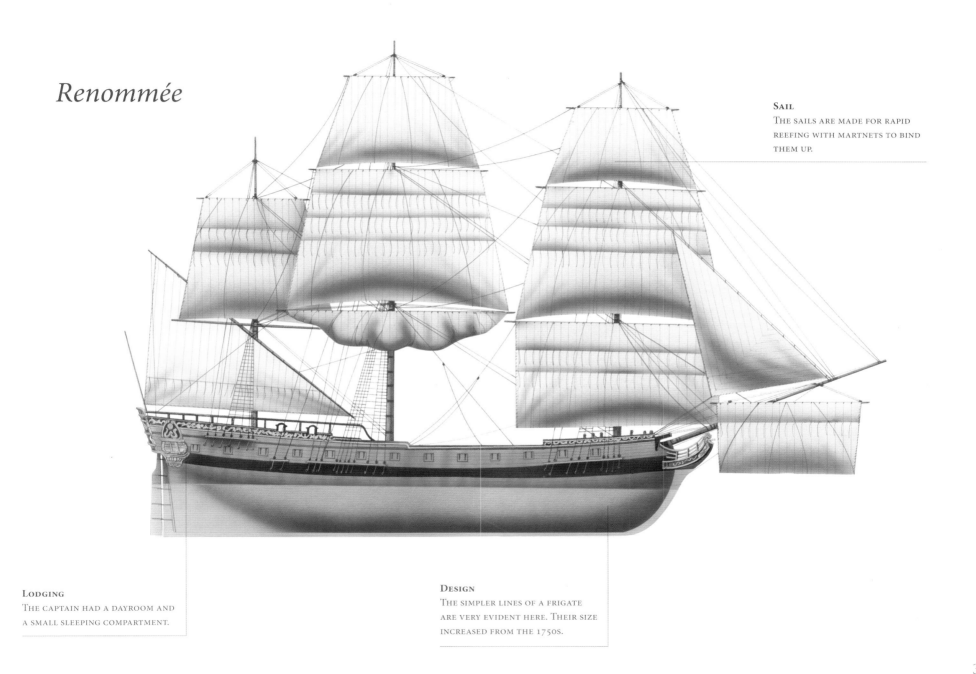

SAIL
THE SAILS ARE MADE FOR RAPID REEFING WITH MARTNETS TO BIND THEM UP.

LODGING
THE CAPTAIN HAD A DAYROOM AND A SMALL SLEEPING COMPARTMENT.

DESIGN
THE SIMPLER LINES OF A FRIGATE ARE VERY EVIDENT HERE. THEIR SIZE INCREASED FROM THE 1750S.

Fenix *(1749)*

Fenix WAS ORDERED IN 1747 AND LAID DOWN THAT YEAR AT THE SHIPYARD OF LA HABANA TO PLANS DRAWN UP BY JORGE JUAN, AND WAS CONSTRUCTED UNDER THE SUPERVISION OF PEDRO TORRES. A THIRD-RATE OF 74 GUNS, IT SPENT 30 YEARS IN THE SERVICE OF THE KING OF SPAIN BEFORE BEING CAPTURED BY THE BRITISH NAVY AND RENAMED AS HMS *GIBRALTAR*.

In 1750 *Fenix* left Havana for Cadiz, carrying gold bullion worth 15,847,423 pesos and a detachment of troops, and remained based at Cadiz. It was careened in April 1755 at La Carraca, and decommissioned until 1759. In August of that year it was flagship of a squadron sent to Naples to bring the new King Charles III of Spain from the Kingdom of the Two Sicilies to Barcelona, and gained the name *Real Fenix* ("Royal Phoenix"). Returned to Cadiz, it operated on routine patrols in the Mediterranean, the Straits of Gibraltar, and in the Atlantic, through to 1764. It was then held in ordinary until June 1779 when it was recommissioned under the command of Admiral de Córdoba.

From October 8 it was the flagship of Admiral Antonio de Ulloa, engaged in blockading the British naval base at Gibraltar; then of Commodore Juan de Lángara. This was a period of violent storms and in November the blockading squadron took refuge at Cartagena. Returning to station in January 1780 it encountered further storms, suffering damage. On January 16, 1780, in the first Battle of Cape St Vincent where 18 British ships of the line pursued and defeated a Spanish squadron of nine, it was captured by the British along with five others.

Under British Command

As HMS *Gibraltar*, the ship was second in the line of battle among 18 British ships of the line taking part in the indecisive Battle of Cuddalore (June 20, 1783) off the South Indian coast, between the British under Admiral Sir Edward Hughes and the French, with 15 ships of the line, under Admiral Pierre André de Suffren. It also participated in the victory of the "Glorious First of June" (1784), was in Egypt in 1801, and at the Basque Roads in 1809. Decommissioned in 1812, it was reduced to a powder hulk in 1813, and a lazaretto (quarantine ship) at Milford Haven in 1824. It was finally broken up in 1836.

SPECIFICATIONS

DISPLACEMENT: 2,184 tons (2,219 tonnes)

DIMENSIONS: 178 ft 10.75 in x 52 ft 11.75 in x 22 ft 1.75 in (54.53 m x 16.15 m x 6.75 m)

RIG: Three masts, square rig

ARMAMENT: Thirty 24 pounders; thirty-two 18 pounders; twelve 8 pounder guns (to 1780)

CREW: 450–750

Fenix

RIGGING
THE MAIN-YARD SPARS ARE EXTENDED
TO GIVE MAXIMUM WIDTH OF SAIL,
WELL BEYOND THE SHIP'S SIDES.

SAILS
BY THIS TIME THE SPRITSAIL AND
TOPSAIL WERE LONG OUT OF USE, AND
JIBS WERE FITTED TO THE BOWSPRIT.

DESIGN
ORNAMENTATION BY NOW IS FAR LESS
IN EVIDENCE. SHIPS OF THE LINE WERE
MORE NUMEROUS, BUILT FOR PRACTICAL
POWER RATHER THAN PRESTIGE.

Rayo *(1749)*

BUILT AT LA HABANA, CUBA, ALONGSIDE *FENIX*, AND SHARING THE SAME DESIGNER AND BUILDER, *RAYO* ("LIGHTNING") WAS LAID DOWN IN 1748, LAUNCHED ON JUNE 28, 1749, AND COMMISSIONED ON JANUARY 31, 1751. BASED AT CADIZ, IT HAD A LONG AND RELATIVELY UNEVENTFUL CAREER UNTIL OCTOBER 1805, WHEN IT TOOK PART IN THE BATTLE OF TRAFALGAR, WAS SUBSEQUENTLY CAPTURED, AND WRECKED IN A STORM ON OCTOBER 30.

On January 4, 1752, *Rayo* made a much delayed departure from Cuba for Cadiz, carrying tobacco, sugar, and timber for the La Carraca navy yard. From then its career was a typical blend of short active periods and long intervals of laying-up. In October 1757 it was remasted and careened. From May 1758 it was part of a fleet under the command of Admiral Reggio, but spent considerable time under repairs. In 1765 it sailed to Genoa, Italy, with a royal party. It saw active service from June 1779, with a French and Spanish fleet in the western approaches to the English Channel, but had to put into Brest because of disease among the crew.

On the way back to Cadiz, in January 1780, it was dismasted and repaired, and on August 9, 1780 it assisted in the capture of a British supply convoy of 51 vessels. Service off Brittany followed through 1782. In the brief peace of 1783 it was fitted with copper sheathing at La Carraca and recommissioned in December 1783, serving in the Mediterranean. Placed in ordinary again in November 1784, it was rearmed in January 1785. From mid-1785 to 1804 it remained mostly out of service. In 1805 it was reconstructed with an additional gun deck and reclassified as a second-rate of 100 guns.

Battle of Trafalgar

Once again placed in ordinary, *Rayo* was recommissioned on August 27, 1805 and joined the Combined Fleet at Cadiz, awaiting orders from the Emperor Napoleon. It was part of the line of battle at Trafalgar on October 21, 1805, commanded by Brigadier Don Enrique MacDonnell. *Rayo* survived the battle but was unable to get back to Cadiz. While at anchor off San Lucar, it was engaged by HMS *Donegal* on October 23 and captured. In the storm that followed the battle, under a prize crew, it broke its anchor cables and ran aground near Arenas Gordas. Most of those on board perished.

SPECIFICATIONS

DISPLACEMENT: 1,750 tons (1,778 tonnes)

DIMENSIONS: 180 ft 5 in x 51 ft 10 in x 28 ft 3 in (55 m x 15.8 m x 8.68 m)

RIG: Three masts, square rig

ARMAMENT: Thirty 24 pounders; thirty-two 18 pounders; eighteen 8 pounders; two 3 pounder guns (to 1803)

CREW: 453 (670 at Trafalgar)

Rayo

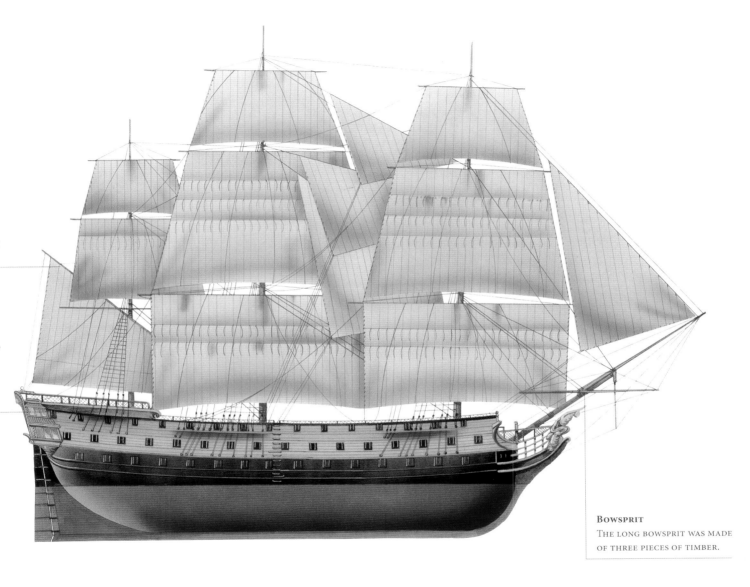

BOOM
AT TIMES THE SHIP WAS
FITTED WITH A SPANKER
BOOM EXTENDING ABAFT
THE TRANSOM.

POOP DECK
PRIOR TO THE 1803 REBUILDING,
RAYO CLEARLY SHOWED THE
FORM OF A MID-CENTURY SHIP
OF THE LINE, WITH A STEPPED-
UP POOP DECK.

BOWSPRIT
THE LONG BOWSPRIT WAS MADE
OF THREE PIECES OF TIMBER.

Venus (1755)

LIKE OTHER SPANISH WARSHIPS NOT NAMED AFTER SAINTS, *VENUS* HAD A SECOND "PROTECTIVE NAME," *SANTA BRÍGIDA*. BUILT AT LA CARRACA, CADIZ, TO DRAWINGS BY THE NAVAL ARCHITECT JORGE JUAN, ITS LONG CAREER SHOWS HOW BUSY A MEDIUM-SIZED SPANISH WARSHIP COULD BE WITHOUT EVER BEING INVOLVED IN A MAJOR BATTLE.

Launched on September 9, 1755, *Venus* was one of four almost identical frigates of twenty-six 12 pounder guns, the class leader being *Industria*, and all built at La Carraca. Its early years are not recorded and it may have lain in ordinary for some time. In August 1759, with Don José de Somaglia as captain, it formed part of the fleet sent to Naples to bring the new King Carlos III to Barcelona. It was based at Cadiz until 1762, undergoing a careen and coppering.

Transport Vessel

In 1763 it made the first of several voyages to South America, carrying artillery and ammunition to Buenos Aires, then the headquarters of a Spanish colony. After a second voyage to Buenos Aires it was deployed to the Philippines in 1769. On January 20, 1770, it picked up 24 Jesuits who had been expelled

from the Philippine colony. *Venus* was again in the Philippines in 1774–76, and on return to Cadiz was remasted at La Carraca in August 1776. At this time too it may have been rearmed, since it ultimately carried 30 guns: twenty-two 18 pounders on the gun deck, and eight 6 pounders on the upper deck. The ship then returned to the South Atlantic and Caribbean supply lines, based mostly at Montevideo, Uruguay, until 1788 but visiting numerous Spanish bases along the South American coast and in the islands, transporting troops, money, gold, and official passengers.

From 1788 *Venus* was based at Havana and Veracruz, and sailed on August 26, 1796 from Havana to Cadiz with sugar and tobacco. The employment of warships for transport of these high-value cargoes may reflect that they were for government use, or merely that no space was wasted on expensive voyages.

In 1805 *Venus* made its last transatlantic voyage, back to Cadiz, and was held there in ordinary until it was finally broken up in 1809.

SPECIFICATIONS

DISPLACEMENT: 505 tons (513 tonnes)

DIMENSIONS: 134 ft 8 in x 33 ft 5 in x 16 ft 9 in (41.14 m x 10.2 m x 5.1 m)

RIG: Three masts, square rig

ARMAMENT: Twenty-two 18 pounders; eight 6 pounder guns (final arrangement)

CREW: c. 230

Venus

CONSTRUCTION
THE SHIP'S LONGEVITY DESPITE MANY LONG
VOYAGES INDICATE NOT ONLY THAT IT WAS WELL
BUILT, BUT OF SEASONED HARDWOOD. SOME FIR-
BUILT FRIGATES BARELY LASTED 10 YEARS.

ARMAMENT
REPLACEMENT OF THE ORIGINAL TWENTY-TWO
12 POUNDER GUNS BY THE SAME NUMBER OF
18 POUNDERS, PLUS SIX 6 POUNDER GUNS, MUST
HAVE INCREASED OVERALL WEIGHT CONSIDERABLY.

HMS *Southampton* (1757)

WITH THE FOUR SHIPS OF THE *SOUTHAMPTON* CLASS, FOR THE FIRST TIME THE ROYAL NAVY HAD A CONSISTENT TYPE OF FRIGATE, WELL ARMED, WITH A SINGLE GUN DECK. THEY WERE CLASSIFIED AS FIFTH-RATES, NOT TO FORM PART OF THE LINE OF BATTLE BUT TO ACT AS SCOUTING AND RAIDING SHIPS.

HMS *Southampton*, the second Royal Navy ship to bear the name, was the first in the class to be ordered on March 12, 1756. The keel was laid in April at Robert Inwood's yard, Rotherhithe, on the Thames. It was launched on May 5, 1757, and completion followed on June 19, 1757 at Deptford. Three others followed: *Minerva*, *Vestal*, and *Diana*. *Southampton* was to be the longest-serving of the quartet. On its very first voyage, under Captain Gilchrist, taking pay money to the dockyard at Plymouth, it was attacked by the French frigates *Maréchal de Belle-Isle* and *Chauvelin*, both of 36 guns, off St Alban's Head, and fought them both off.

The Many Prizes of *Southampton*

Ordered to join Admiral Hawke's fleet off Brest, on September 21, 1757 *Southampton* captured the French frigate *Emeraude* (28 guns), and it was added to the British fleet as HMS *Emerald*. Two years later, in the North Sea, following another battle with two French frigates, *Southampton* captured the *Danaé*, which again was brought into the Royal Navy. Gilchrist, severely wounded, had to retire from the service.

Among other captures and prizes were the French privateer *Comte de Maurepas* (12 guns) sunk on August 3, 1780, and the corvette *Utile*, which was stormed by boarding on June 10, 1796 in a bold operation at Hyères. *Southampton* served in many parts of the world, including the Mediterranean under Nelson in mid-1795, on the usual frigate tasks of reconnaissance, convoy escort, and patrols off hostile territory.

Its final years were spent in the West Indies where it captured the French privateer *Hirondelle* on June 9, 1800. Captained by Sir James Lucas Yeo during the War of 1812–13, *Southampton* captured the French-manned pirate vessel *Améthyste* on February 2–3, 1812. Its last prize was USS *Vixen*, taken in the War of 1812, but both the frigate and its prize were wrecked, without loss of life, on an uncharted reef off Conception Island in the Crooked Island Passage, Bahamas, on November 27, 1812. The wreck site has been identified.

SPECIFICATIONS

DISPLACEMENT: 671 tons (681 tonnes)

DIMENSIONS: 124 ft 4 in x 35 ft x 12 ft 1 in (37.9 m x 10.67 m x 3.68 m)

RIG: Three masts, full square rig

ARMAMENT: Twenty-six 12 pounders; six 6 pounder guns

CREW: 210

HMS *Southampton*

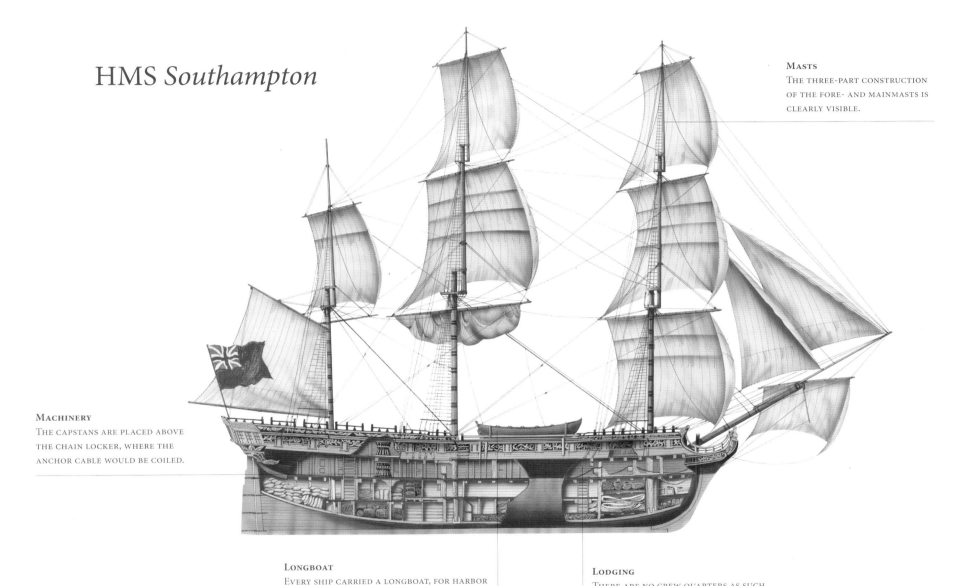

MASTS
THE THREE-PART CONSTRUCTION
OF THE FORE- AND MAINMASTS IS
CLEARLY VISIBLE.

MACHINERY
THE CAPSTANS ARE PLACED ABOVE
THE CHAIN LOCKER, WHERE THE
ANCHOR CABLE WOULD BE COILED.

LONGBOAT
EVERY SHIP CARRIED A LONGBOAT, FOR HARBOR
USE, TOWING, AND PASSING BETWEEN SHIPS. IT
WAS NOT CONSIDERED AS A LIFEBOAT.

LODGING
THERE ARE NO CREW QUARTERS AS SUCH.
SAILORS RIGGED THEIR HAMMOCKS ON
THE MAINDECK, FORWARD.

Mortar Ketch *(1760)*

KNOWN AS BOMB SHIPS OR JUST "BOMBS," MORTAR KETCHES WERE INTENDED FOR FIRING EXPLOSIVE SHELLS AT FIXED TARGETS LIKE SHORE STATIONS. ORIGINALLY MOUNTING A SINGLE GUN, 18TH- AND 19TH-CENTURY VERSIONS CARRIED TWO, WHICH COULD BE TRAINED AND ANGLED.

Mortars had been used in land war for decades, before the bomb ketch was first developed in France in the 1680s. By the mid-18th century British "bombs" carried two mortars, each a massive firing piece, mounted on the centerline: one of 13-in (33 cm) and the other of 10-in (25 cm) caliber. They could be swiveled and angled in order to bear on their targets.

Since the mortars had no recoil, the ships had to be built with exceptionally strong frames to absorb the shocks of discharge. They also had to be as stable as possible, and two anchors were provided to enable them to hold position, in order to fire as precisely as the gunners could achieve.

Bulwarks and embrasures could be hinged down for low-angle fire. Their specialized construction made the bomb ketches slow sailers, tending to wallow in anything other than a calm sea, and with the mortars lowered and concealed under hatch covers.

Vessels in Action

The Royal Navy had few mortar ketches until the 1790s. They were given explosive names, including *Explosion*, and also volcano names, such as *Vesuvius*. Mortars were not used in ship-to-ship combat, and the ketches normally only sailed under the protection of other vessels. Shore fortresses were the main target, but the British used mortars to attack concentrations of stationary ships, as in 1799 when five Spanish ships of the line, trapped in the Basque Roads, off La Rochelle, were bombarded by HMS *Explosion*, *Sulphur*, and *Volcano*.

Mortar firing was a tricky business, as the guns, if mishandled, had a tendency to burst. Incendiary as well as explosive missiles were fired. The vessel illustrated has a brig-type hull. Later "bombs," from the 1770s, were more tubby in plan, often converted merchant vessels. In later years, the massive internal structure of bomb vessels was made use of in the Antarctic explorations of the former "bombs" HMS *Erebus* and *Terror*.

SPECIFICATIONS

DISPLACEMENT: c. 100 tons (c. 101 tonnes)

DIMENSIONS: c. 115 ft x 32 ft 10 in x 9 ft 9 in (35 m x 10 m x 3 m)

RIG: Two masts, ketch rig

ARMAMENT: One 13 in mortar; one 10 in mortar

CREW: c. 36

Mortar Ketch

RIGGING
CHAIN RIGGING WAS SOMETIMES USED TO BETTER WITHSTAND THE BLAST FORCES.

FLAG
THE RED ENSIGN, LATER FLAG OF THE MERCHANT NAVY, INDICATED ONE OF THE ROYAL NAVY'S THREE MAIN DIVISIONS: WHITE, RED, AND BLUE.

ARMOR
AN EARLY VERSION OF THE BARBETTE FORMED THE MORTAR EMPLACEMENT BUT GAVE MINIMAL PROTECTION.

ARMAMENT
THE HEAVY SHELLS WERE STORED IMMEDIATELY BELOW THE MORTARS. THE BARRELS HELD GUNPOWDER.

San Carlos (1765)

THE ROYAL YARDS AT LA HABANA, CUBA, BUILT 69 SHIPS OF THE LINE FOR THE ROYAL
SPANISH NAVY IN THE 18TH CENTURY. SAN CARLOS WAS ONE OF SEVERAL BUILT BY THE
IRISH SHIPWRIGHT MATTHEW MULLAN TO PLANS DRAWN UP BY JORGE JUAN, AND THE
FIRST CONSTRUCTED ACCORDING TO JUAN'S "BRITISH SYSTEM." ORIGINALLY OF 80 GUNS,
IT WAS REBUILT WITH 112 GUNS IN 1801.

San Carlos was planned and built as a two-decker, launched on April 30, 1765 at a cost of 116,000 pesos. Its designer, Jorge Juan, was Chief of Naval Development between 1736 and 1754. Influenced by a visit to British shipyards in 1749, he inclined towards British rather than French design and techniques of construction. Havana was an ideal place for ship construction because of its proximity to hardwood forests and other sources of necessary materials such as hemp. Juan took care to use well-seasoned wood and as a result many of his ships, if they survived battle, had great longevity.

Voyages and Repairs

In 1766 San Carlos made a voyage to Cadiz and back to Havana, returning to Spain in the following year when it was based at Ferrol. Captained by Don Pablo Vicente Lasagna Cádiz, it formed a unit in the fleet under Admiral Luis de Córdoba, and patrolled off the western approaches to the British Isles, joined in the blockade of the British at Gibraltar, and made a further Atlantic crossing in 1787–88. From 1790–93 it was decommissioned, and probably at the end of this period its armament was increased to 94 guns. When Spain joined with Britain in war against France in 1793, San Carlos was one of 61 ships of the line in commission, serving in the Mediterranean Sea. In 1794 it returned again to Havana, under the command of Don Enrique MacDonnell.

Late in 1796 San Carlos was dismasted and lost its rudder in a storm. Repaired at Cartagena, it returned there in 1801, where a third deck was installed and its artillery increased to thirty 36 pounders, thirty-two 24 pounders, thirty-two 12 pounders, and eighteen 8 pounder guns—112 in all. The operation was completed in 1804. Based at Cartagena, San Carlos was not part of the Combined Fleet and was not present at Trafalgar. In 1808 the ship was disarmed and in 1810 was transferred to Cadiz. It was condemned and broken up in 1819.

SPECIFICATIONS

DISPLACEMENT: 1,714 tons (1,741 tonnes)

DIMENSIONS: 197 ft x 56 ft x 28 ft (60 m x 17 m x 8.5 m)

RIG: Three masts, square rig

ARMAMENT: Thirty 36 pounders; thirty 18 pounders; twenty 8 pounder guns (1765–1793)

CREW: c. 700–900

San Carlos

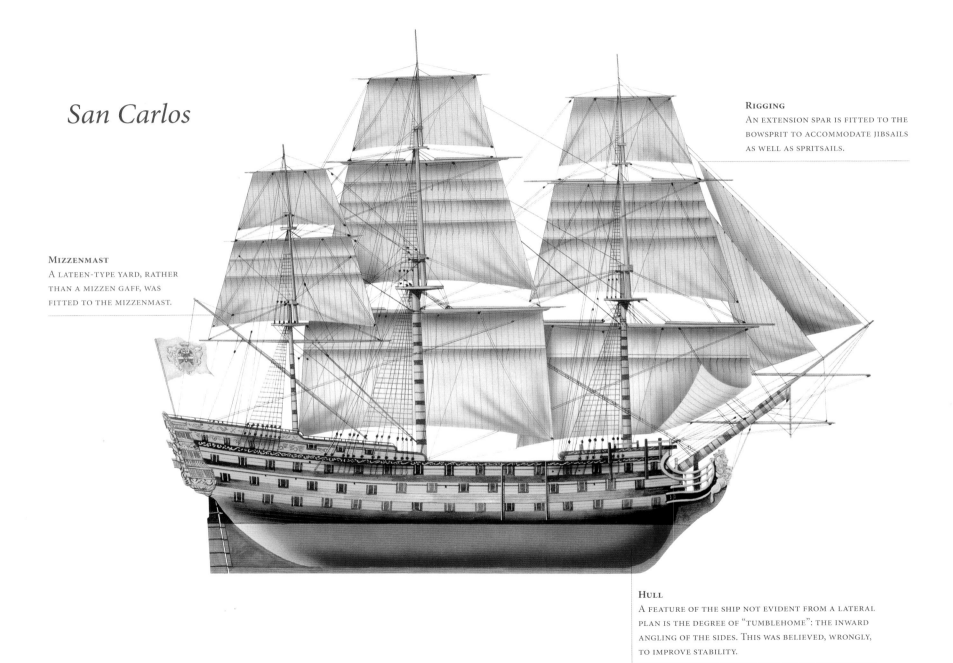

MIZZENMAST
A LATEEN-TYPE YARD, RATHER
THAN A MIZZEN GAFF, WAS
FITTED TO THE MIZZENMAST.

RIGGING
AN EXTENSION SPAR IS FITTED TO THE
BOWSPRIT TO ACCOMMODATE JIBSAILS
AS WELL AS SPRITSAILS.

HULL
A FEATURE OF THE SHIP NOT EVIDENT FROM A LATERAL
PLAN IS THE DEGREE OF "TUMBLEHOME": THE INWARD
ANGLING OF THE SIDES. THIS WAS BELIEVED, WRONGLY,
TO IMPROVE STABILITY.

HMS *Victory* *(1765)*

LAID DOWN AT CHATHAM NAVAL DOCKYARD AT A TIME OF WAR IN 1759, AND LAUNCHED IN 1765, HMS *VICTORY* WAS NOT COMMISSIONED UNTIL 1778, WHEN WAR WITH FRANCE WAS RENEWED AND THE ROYAL NAVY WAS HASTILY BROUGHT TO FULL OPERATIONAL STRENGTH. A FIRST-RATE, CARRYING (AT THE MAXIMUM) 102 GUNS, IT WAS INTENDED AS AN ADMIRAL'S SHIP, AND AS NELSON'S FLAGSHIP AT TRAFALGAR IT BECAME THE MOST ICONIC OF BRITISH WARSHIPS.

Victory was designed by Sir Thomas Slade, Surveyor of the Navy, at a cost of £63,176, and was of oak construction, 2 ft (60 cm) thick at the waterline, with a keel of elm. Copper plating, introduced in the Royal Navy in 1761, was applied in 1780 to protect the hull from shipworm and weed growth.

In July 1778 *Victory* was flagship of the Channel Fleet, under Admiral Keppel, then in 1782 Lord Howe's flagship at the relief of Gibraltar, but with the end of hostilities was held in ordinary at Portsmouth until 1791. From 1792–95 it was Vice Admiral Hood's flagship in the Mediterranean, then of Admiral Sir John Jervis at his victory in the Battle of Cape St Vincent on February 14, 1797.

In 1798–99 it was relegated to the role of a hospital ship at Chatham, but between 1800 and 1803 a major refit brought new masts, emplacements for 104 guns, and much internal rebuilding. The cost, at £70,933, exceeded that of the original construction.

Nelson at Trafalgar

On April 11, 1803, Vice Admiral Nelson hoisted his flag on board. Nelson had spent two frustrating years before the long-awaited encounter with the combined French and Spanish fleets took place off Cape Trafalgar on October 21, 1805.

Victory, leading the weather division, had to withstand 45 minutes of broadsides before bringing its own guns to bear. By 2:30 p.m., severely battered, it was out of the battle. Fifty-seven crew were killed and 102 wounded, the most notable death being that of Nelson himself, hit by a sharpshooter from the rigging of *Redoutable*. *Victory* was towed to Gibraltar and, after emergency repairs were made, returned to England with Nelson's body.

Victory returned to service as flagship of the Baltic Fleet, blockading Russia, protecting convoys of naval supplies from Sweden, and acting as escort to a military convoy to Spain. In 1812 the ship was paid off, but its association with Nelson saved it from the fate of most ships. From 1824 it was designated as flagship of the commander in chief at Portsmouth, and although now a museum ship, remains in commission.

SPECIFICATIONS

DISPLACEMENT: 2,162 tons (2,197 tonnes)

DIMENSIONS: 226 ft 6 in x 52 ft x 28 ft 9 in (69 m x 15.8 m x 8.76 m)

RIG: Three masts, full square rig

ARMAMENT: Thirty 32 pounders; twenty-eight 24 pounders; forty-four 12 pounder cannons; two 68 pounder carronades (1805)

CREW: c. 850 sailors and marines

Sails
FULL SAIL EXTENT WAS 6,510 SQUARE
YARDS (5,440 SQ M), MAKING SHIPS OF
THIS TYPE BOTH FASTER AND MORE
MANEUVERABLE THAN OLDER VESSELS.

HMS *Victory*

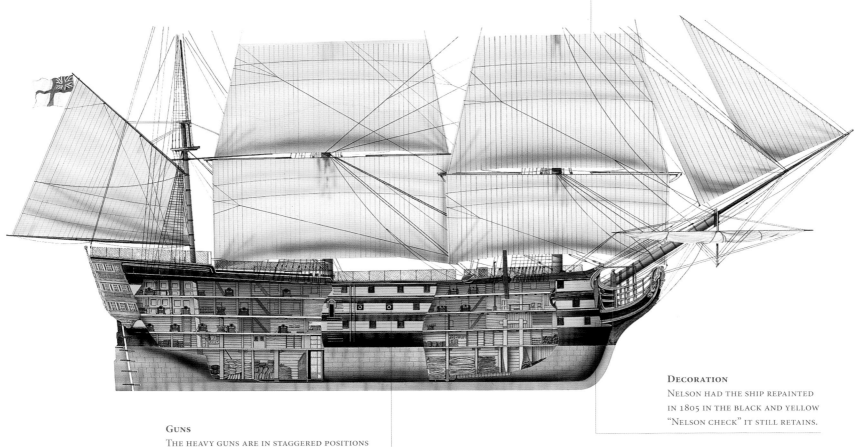

Decoration
NELSON HAD THE SHIP REPAINTED
IN 1805 IN THE BLACK AND YELLOW
"NELSON CHECK" IT STILL RETAINS.

Guns
THE HEAVY GUNS ARE IN STAGGERED POSITIONS
FROM THE CENTERLINE, AND ALTERNATE PLACINGS
ON EACH DECK, RATHER THAN STACKED RIGHT
ABOVE ONE ANOTHER.

San Genaro (1766)

A Spanish third-rate of 74 guns, *San Genaro* was laid down at the Cartagena naval base on September 12, 1764 to plans made by Jorge Juan, and launched on December 23, 1765. Eleven successive captains commanded it, and it was flagship to two admirals, seeing varied service, including the Battle of Cape St Vincent, before being handed over to France in 1801.

Today, "third rate" implies inferior, but for warships it merely defined their gun numbers. The great majority of ships of the line were third-rates of 74–80 guns. *San Genaro* was the third Spanish warship to bear the name, both predecessors having been captured or destroyed by the British. Its first cruise was to Naples in April–June 1766, and from July 1766 to October 1767 it was engaged on transport, escort, and patrol duties from Cadiz, then transferred to Ferrol. Careened and disarmed between May 1771 and June 1772, it remained at Ferrol until March 14, 1774, when it returned to Mediterranean waters, based primarily at Cartagena.

Atlantic Crossings and Engagement Battles

In January 1780 *San Genaro* was part of the blockading force off Gibraltar, then made its first Atlantic crossing from April 28, participating in the Florida campaign of 1780–81, carrying gold between Veracruz and Havana, and returning to Cadiz on July 20, 1783. It lay decommissioned at Cartagena from September 1783 to June 1790, when it was back in service as a troop transport, and transferred to Ferrol at a time of hostility with Britain in the Nootka Sound incident, when Spanish ships seized British vessels off British Columbia.

From the end of 1790 to January 1793 it was again in ordinary at Cartagena, then careened and rearmed, and restored to active service in the Mediterranean from October 1795 to March 1797. It was involved in the Battle of Cape St Vincent, on February 14, 1797, but its performance in the battle was so poor that its captain was court-martialed and dismissed.

On March 3, 1797 *San Genero* arrived in Cadiz and was disarmed in October, while the British blockade was on. A royal order transferred the ship to the French squadron of Admiral Dumanoir on March 31, 1801, and it was renamed *Ulysse*, then later *Tourville*. It was stricken from the French Navy list in 1822.

SPECIFICATIONS

DISPLACEMENT: 1,591 tons (1,616 tonnes)

DIMENSIONS: 175 ft x 47 ft 8 in x 23 ft (53.35 m x 14.54 m x 7 m)

RIG: Three masts, full square rig

ARMAMENT: Twenty-eight 24 pounders; thirty 18 pounders; sixteen 8 pounder guns

CREW: 568

San Genaro

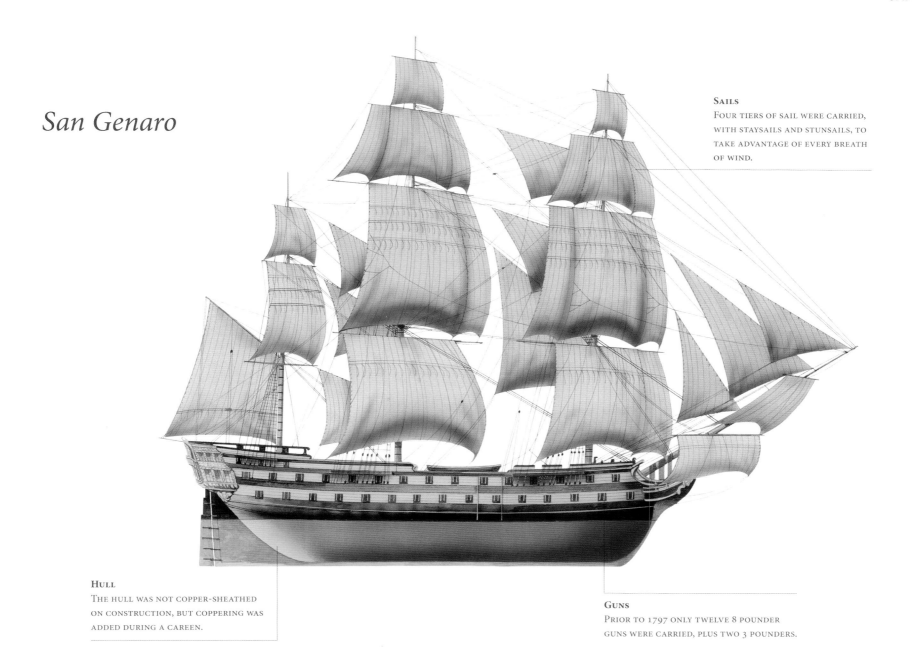

SAILS
FOUR TIERS OF SAIL WERE CARRIED,
WITH STAYSAILS AND STUNSAILS, TO
TAKE ADVANTAGE OF EVERY BREATH
OF WIND.

HULL
THE HULL WAS NOT COPPER-SHEATHED
ON CONSTRUCTION, BUT COPPERING WAS
ADDED DURING A CAREEN.

GUNS
PRIOR TO 1797 ONLY TWELVE 8 POUNDER
GUNS WERE CARRIED, PLUS TWO 3 POUNDERS.

Flore (1768)

THIS HANDSOME FRIGATE WAS THE THIRD *FLORE*, BUILT AT BREST AND COMMISSIONED IN 1769. IN 1771–72 IT WAS EMPLOYED ON A VOYAGE OF SCIENTIFIC RESEARCH FROM THE ANTILLES TO ICELAND, TESTING NAVIGATIONAL AND SCIENTIFIC INSTRUMENTS, INCLUDING THE MARINE CHRONOMETERS MADE BY LEROY AND BERTHOUD.

French ship designers paid a great deal of attention to frigates, and it was in France that the type really evolved, although the British and then the Americans quickly followed and improved. In the course of the 18th century, the caliber of frigate guns rose from 6- to 8-pounder, then to 12-pounder, and finally to 18-pounder. Frigates were big enough to conduct long-range operations, cheaper to build than ships of the line, and in periods of peace they were the main strength of the fleets, while the majority of ships of the line would be laid up in reserve.

Built for Speed

The plan of *Flore* was drawn up by the designer Antoine Groignard. The French Navy had been experimenting with two-deck frigates but had settled for a single-deck type, partly in the interest of speed. *Flore's* 4:1 ratio between length and beam was intended to ensure a good turn of speed, and records of the time show that it could make the best speed close-hauled to the wind of any of the ships at Toulon, although it needed a fresh to strong wind for best performance. By this time the 8-pounder frigates were classified as *frégates du deuxième ordre*, although forming numerous subclasses and with anything from 24 to 32 guns. They were supplanted by the *frégate de douze*: mounting 12-pounder guns, of which France built 104 in the 50 years between 1748 and 1798. *Flore's* six 4 pounder guns were mounted on the forecastle and poop decks.

In 1773 *Flore* was based at Bayonne, then at Toulon in 1775. It made a voyage to America and back in 1778. Back in the Mediterranean, it was engaged in operations in the eastern area, then participated in the capture of Minorca in November 1781. Withdrawn from the active list at Toulon in 1785, it was sold in 1787. This *Flore* should not be confused with another ship, sometimes called "American Flore," of 28 guns, built in America and in the French fleet from 1784.

SPECIFICATIONS

DISPLACEMENT: 400 tons (406 tonnes)

DIMENSIONS: 136 ft 6 in x 34 ft 9 in x 14 ft 1 in (41.6 m x 10.6 m x 4.3 m)

RIG: Three masts, square rig

ARMAMENT: Twenty-six 8 pounders; six 4 pounder guns

CREW: Not known

Flore

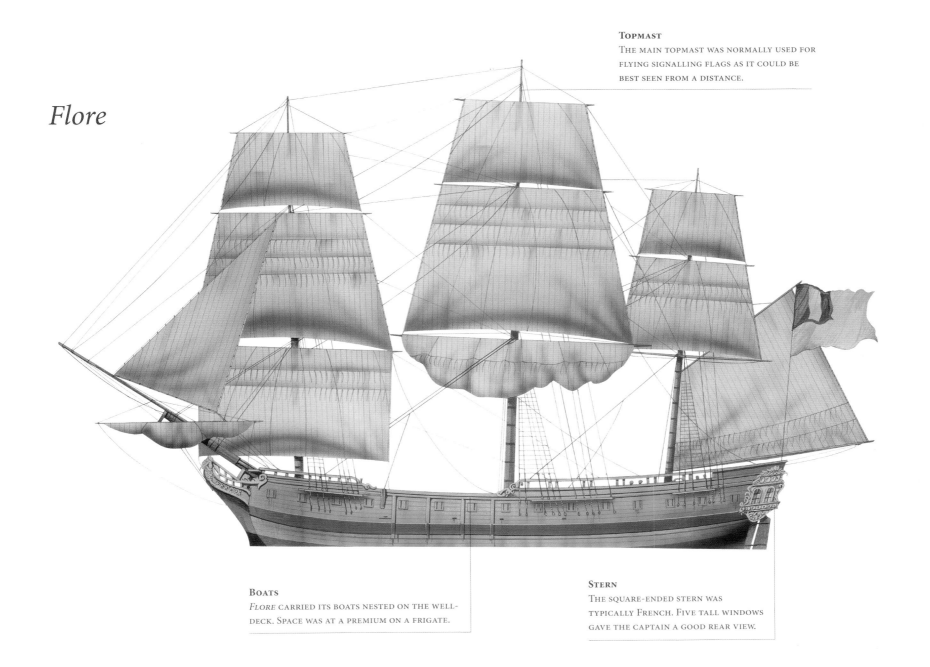

TOPMAST
THE MAIN TOPMAST WAS NORMALLY USED FOR
FLYING SIGNALLING FLAGS AS IT COULD BE
BEST SEEN FROM A DISTANCE.

BOATS
FLORE CARRIED ITS BOATS NESTED ON THE WELL-
DECK. SPACE WAS AT A PREMIUM ON A FRIGATE.

STERN
THE SQUARE-ENDED STERN WAS
TYPICALLY FRENCH. FIVE TALL WINDOWS
GAVE THE CAPTAIN A GOOD REAR VIEW.

Santísima Trinidad (1769)

SANTÍSIMA TRINIDAD, THE SEVENTH SPANISH WARSHIP OF THE NAME, WAS CONFIRMED BY A ROYAL ORDER ON MARCH 12, 1768. SOMETIMES CLAIMED AS THE LARGEST WARSHIP OF THE 18TH CENTURY, WITH FOUR DECKS OF GUNS, AND KNOWN AS THE "ESCORIAL (ROYAL PALACE) OF THE SEAS," IT WAS BUILT AT THE ROYAL SHIPYARDS AT LA HABANA, CUBA, AND FOUGHT IN TWO OF HISTORY'S GREAT NAVAL BATTLES AT CAPE ST VINCENT AND TRAFALGAR.

Built by the Irish shipwright Matthew (or Mateo) Mullan, *Santísima Trinidad* was launched as a three-decker. Spanish ships were strongly built and generally of larger size for their gun rating than British vessels, which made them both more stable as gun platforms and better able to withstand attack. This tradition of size and strength gave the builders of 1769 confidence to construct the largest warship of the time. In its first years *Santísima Trinidad* was probably not in commission. With the declaration of war by Spain on Britain in July 1779, it entered service as flagship of the Spanish fleet, under Admiral Luis de Córdova y Córdova, operating with allied French ships in the English Channel and the western approaches. In August 1780 it led an action that resulted in the capture of 55 British merchant vessels from a convoy. In 1782 it participated in the second siege of Gibraltar.

Cape St Vincent and Trafalgar

Back in service in 1797, *Santísima Trinidad* was the Spanish flagship at the Battle of Cape St Vincent on February 14, and suffered major damage, striking its colors to HMS *Orion*, but before the British could take possession it was rescued by *Pelayo* and *Príncipe de Asturias*, and limped back to Cadiz for repair.

After the construction of the fourth deck, giving a high exposure to side winds, *Santísima Trinidad* gained the nickname "El Ponderoso." In the course of its more than 38-year career, the ship was refitted three times, and spent almost 20 of those years out of service.

At Trafalgar, captained by Francisco Javier Uriarte and carrying the pendant of Rear Admiral Baltasar de Cisneros, it was in the thick of the central battle. After four hours, by 2:12 p.m., all three masts were gone and the ship was compelled to surrender. After the battle it was taken in tow by HMS *Prince*, but in the storm which followed, the tow could not be held, and *Santísima Trinidad* was scuttled on October 22.

SPECIFICATIONS

DISPLACEMENT: c. 4,750 tons (c. 4,826 tonnes)

DIMENSIONS: 200 ft x 62 ft 9 in x 26 ft 4 in (60.1 m x 19.2 m x 8.02 m)

RIG: Three masts, square rig

ARMAMENT: Thirty 36 pounders; thirty-two 24 pounders; thirty-two 12 pounders; eighteen 8 pounder guns (1768)

CREW: 950

Santísima Trinidad

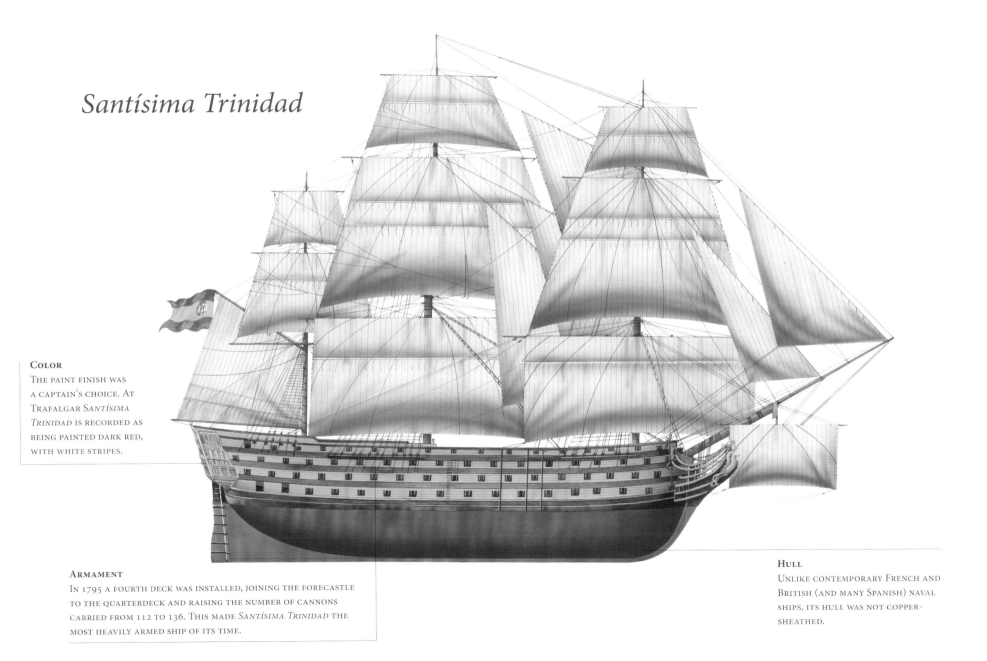

COLOR

THE PAINT FINISH WAS
A CAPTAIN'S CHOICE. AT
TRAFALGAR *SANTÍSIMA
TRINIDAD* IS RECORDED AS
BEING PAINTED DARK RED,
WITH WHITE STRIPES.

ARMAMENT

IN 1795 A FOURTH DECK WAS INSTALLED, JOINING THE FORECASTLE
TO THE QUARTERDECK AND RAISING THE NUMBER OF CANNONS
CARRIED FROM 112 TO 136. THIS MADE *SANTÍSIMA TRINIDAD* THE
MOST HEAVILY ARMED SHIP OF ITS TIME.

HULL

UNLIKE CONTEMPORARY FRENCH AND
BRITISH (AND MANY SPANISH) NAVAL
SHIPS, ITS HULL WAS NOT COPPER-
SHEATHED.

USS *Hancock* *(1776)*

SECOND SHIP TO BE NAMED FOR THE FIRST SIGNATORY OF THE DECLARATION OF INDEPENDENCE, *HANCOCK* WAS ONE OF THE 13 "CONTINENTAL FRIGATES" ORDERED BY THE U.S. CONGRESS ON DECEMBER 13, 1775. THE AMERICAN FRIGATES OF THE LATER 1770S WERE ACCLAIMED AS FINE SAILERS AND EXCELLENT WARSHIPS DESPITE THEIR RELATIVELY SMALL SIZE, AND *HANCOCK* WAS CONSIDERED THE MOST HANDSOME, AS WELL AS THE MOST EFFECTIVE, OF THE 1775 SHIPS.

Laid down at Greenleaf & Cross's yard, Newburyport, Massachusetts, in 1776, it was launched on July 10 that year. John Manley had been named as captain from April 17, but fitting out and finding a crew was a slow process and the ship was not commissioned until May 1777.

From May 21 *Hancock* and sister ships were deployed along the New England coast to look out for British merchantmen and warships. Evading the 74-gun HMS *Somerset*, on May 29 *Hancock* and *Boston* captured a British supply vessel, and a month later on June 21 forced the 28-gun HMS *Fox* to surrender, taking it into the U.S. squadron.

But on 7 July, *Hancock*, *Boston,* and *Fox* were intercepted by the British frigates HMS *Rainbow* (44 guns), *Flora* (32), and the sloop *Victor* (10). *Hancock* was forced to surrender and the British also reclaimed *Fox*.

Renamed HMS *Iris*, the ship was taken into the Royal Navy, where its sailing qualities were greatly admired, and for which it was used to capture numerous American vessels. A fierce battle with the French 26-gun frigate *Hermione* (which had just brought the French General Lafayette to Boston) on June 7, 1780, was broken off when a second French frigate appeared.

On August 29, 1781 it encountered one of its original sister ships, USS *Trumbull*, which had been partially dismasted in a storm, and after a brief battle captured it and towed it to New York.

Under a New Flag

On September 11 of that year, however, *Iris* was captured by the French after the Battle of the Virginia Capes. Now under a third flag, it retained the name of *Iris* and served in the French Navy. Eventually it was hulked at the Toulon naval base and used as a gunpowder store. The British and Spanish occupied the port in the second half of 1793, and as they withdrew in December they blew up *Iris*.

SPECIFICATIONS

DISPLACEMENT: 763 tons (775 tonnes)

DIMENSIONS: 136 ft 7 in x 35 ft 6 in x 11 ft 0.5 in (41.6 m x 10.8 m x 3.38 m)

RIG: Four masts, square rig

ARMAMENT: Twenty-four 12 pounders; ten 6 pounder guns

CREW: 290

USS *Hancock*

RIGGING
A SHORT STERNPOST MAST WITH
LATEEN-TYPE SAIL WAS FITTED.

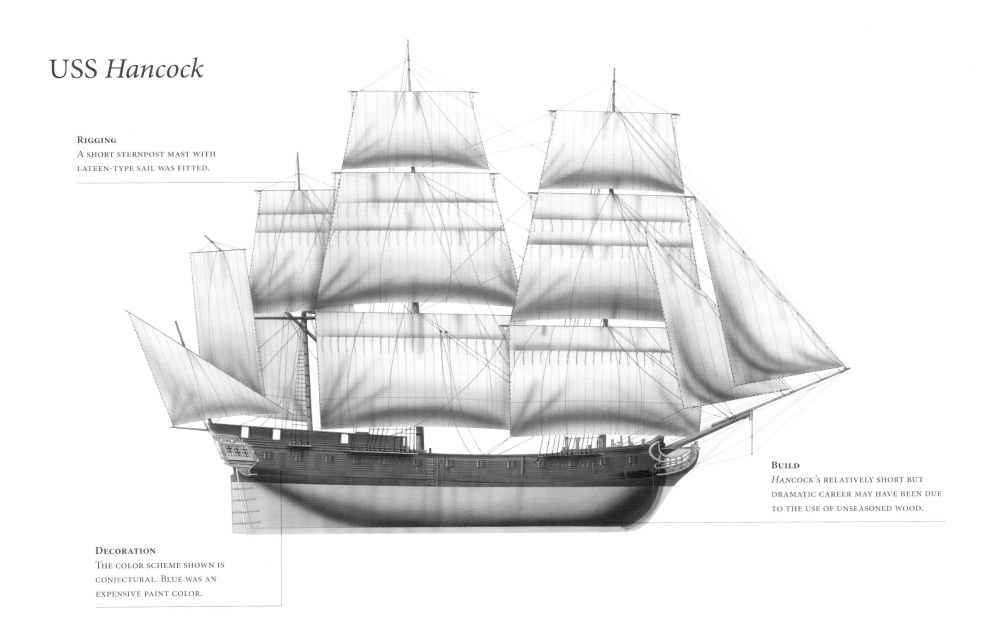

BUILD
HANCOCK'S RELATIVELY SHORT BUT
DRAMATIC CAREER MAY HAVE BEEN DUE
TO THE USE OF UNSEASONED WOOD.

DECORATION
THE COLOR SCHEME SHOWN IS
CONJECTURAL. BLUE WAS AN
EXPENSIVE PAINT COLOR.

USS *Ranger* (1777)

Designated as a sloop of war, *Ranger* was completed for the Continental Congress in June 1777 and John Paul Jones was appointed Captain. A crew recruitment poster for "gentlemen seamen and able-bodied landsmen" claimed that "No vessel yet built was ever calculated for sailing faster." As a U.S. warship it had an eventful career until captured by the British on the fall of Charleston in May 1780.

Ranger was built by James Hackett at Portsmouth, New Hampshire. Originally to be named *Hampshire*, it was launched on May 10, 1877. Crewing new ships was not easy, since the Americans could hardly use the British press-gang method, and the recruitment posters extolled *Ranger's* merits as "one of the best Cruizers in America." On November 1 it sailed for France, ally of the newly established United States, with dispatches from Congress. On the way it captured two prizes, reaching Nantes on December 2.

Transferring to the main French naval base at Brest, *Ranger* received the first official salute to the new Stars and Stripes flag on February 14, 1778. Leaving Brest on April 11, Jones conducted sea and shore raids, boldly attacking a fort at Whitehaven, Cumberland (from where *Ranger's* captain, then known as John Paul, had left for America at age 13), capturing the 20-gun HMS *Drake*. Jones then took command of *Bonhomme Richard*, and his lieutenant, Thomas Simpson, took *Ranger* back to America, in company with *Boston* and *Providence*, reaching Portsmouth with three captured vessels on October 16, 1778. With other U.S. warships, *Ranger* then cruised the Atlantic coast, capturing 18 ships between February and November 1779, with a value calculated at over $1 million.

Siege of Charleston

On November 23, 1779 *Ranger* was assigned to Commodore Whipple's squadron bound for the defense of Charleston, South Carolina. Three British transports were captured by *Ranger* and *Providence* off Tybee Island on January 24, 1780. But with the fall of Charleston on May 11, *Ranger* and other ships were caught in the Cooper River.

Commissioned into the Royal Navy as HMS *Halifax*, it was sold off for use as a merchant vessel in 1781.

SPECIFICATIONS

DISPLACEMENT: 308 tons (313 tonnes)

DIMENSIONS: 116 ft x 28 ft x 13 ft 6 in (35.3 m x 8.5 m x 4.1 m)

RIG: Three masts, sloop rig

ARMAMENT: Eighteen 6 pounder guns

CREW: 140

USS *Ranger*

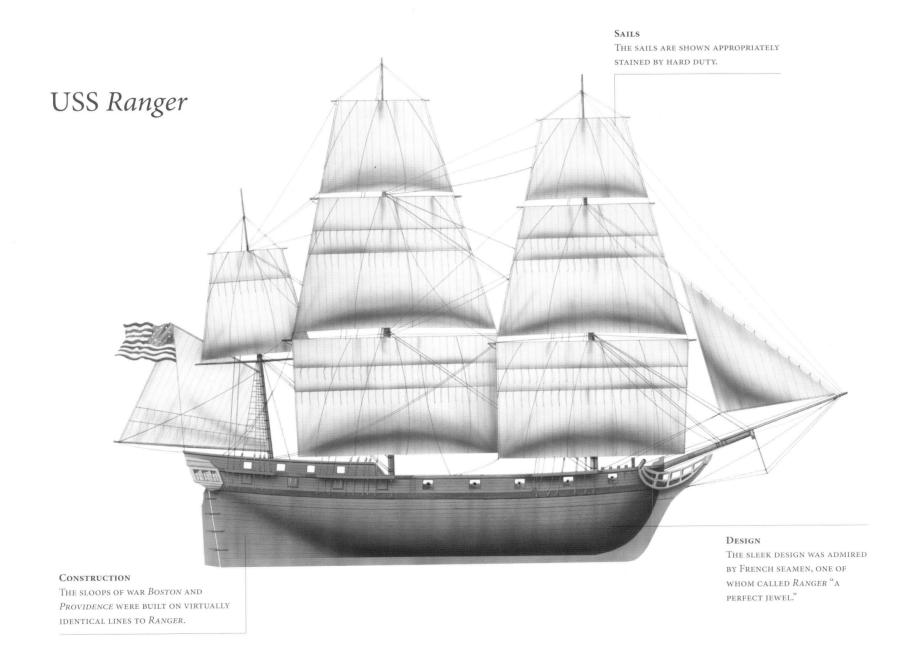

SAILS
THE SAILS ARE SHOWN APPROPRIATELY STAINED BY HARD DUTY.

DESIGN
THE SLEEK DESIGN WAS ADMIRED BY FRENCH SEAMEN, ONE OF WHOM CALLED *RANGER* "A PERFECT JEWEL."

CONSTRUCTION
THE SLOOPS OF WAR *BOSTON* AND *PROVIDENCE* WERE BUILT ON VIRTUALLY IDENTICAL LINES TO *RANGER*.

L'Indien (1778)

IN 1777 THE UNITED STATES COMMISSIONERS IN FRANCE PLACED AN ORDER FOR A LARGE SHIP TO ADD TO THE SMALL AMERICAN NAVY THAT WAS FACING THE MIGHTY ROYAL NAVY OF GREAT BRITAIN. FIRST NAMED *L'INDIEN*, INTERNATIONAL DIPLOMACY AND FINANCIAL PROBLEMS DELAYED ITS DELIVERY. IT EVENTUALLY REACHED AMERICA AS *SOUTH CAROLINA*, BUT HAD ONLY A BRIEF CAREER BEFORE BEING SEIZED BY THE BRITISH.

The Staats Yard in Amsterdam was contracted to build the vessel (the largest yet built in the port), to the design of a French naval architect, Jacques Boux. It was to be heavily armed, with twenty-eight 36 pounder guns on the main gun deck and twelve 12 pounders on the forecastle and quarterdeck. Ordered from Sweden, they were long-barrelled, weighty, and expensive. The Dutch were neutrals in the American War of Independence and strong pressure was applied from London to prevent the ship being handed over to the rebel colony.

Instead the French royal government purchased the vessel. It was not added to the French Navy, and remained uncommissioned until May 30, 1780, when King Louis XVI of France granted it to the Duke of Luxembourg, who immediately chartered it on a three-year contract to Commodore Alexander Gillon for the Navy of South Carolina. Renamed *South Carolina*, it was commanded by John Joyner.

War with Great Britain

By the time *South Carolina* sailed in late 1781, Charleston was still in British hands and course was diverted to Cuba. On the way to Havana it took five British ships on the way back from Jamaica as prizes (this was important: the ship had to earn its keep, and Luxembourg got a quarter of the prize money), reaching port on January 12, 1782.

In May it formed part of a Spanish expedition to capture the British colony of New Providence in the Bahamas, then sailed for Philadelphia, at last docking in the continental United States on May 28. With the Royal Navy blockading the harbor it remained there for six months before breaking out, along with three smaller craft. But the British HMS *Diomede* (44 guns) with the 32-gun frigates *Quebec* and *Astraea*, chased *South Carolina* into the Delaware River and, after a two-hour exchange of fire, forced Joyner to surrender. It was taken as a prize to New York and sold as a merchantman. Its last known use was in evacuating British troops after American independence had been conceded, in 1783.

SPECIFICATIONS

DISPLACEMENT: 1,430 tons (1,453 tonnes)

DIMENSIONS: 170 ft x 43 ft 3 in x 16 ft 6 in (52 m x 13.18 m x 5.03 m)

RIG: Full square rig

ARMAMENT: Twenty-eight 36 pounders; twelve 12 pounder guns

CREW: 550

L'Indien

CONSTRUCTION
SOUTH CAROLINA WAS SAID TO HAVE
BEEN ERECTED ON THE SCANTLINGS OF
A FOURTH-RATE 74-GUN VESSEL.

GUNS
THE WEIGHT OF THE GUNS
WAS SUCH THAT THE SHIP
SAGGED IN THE MIDDLE.

KEEL
SOME OFFICERS BELIEVED THAT THE SHIP'S KEEL WAS
PERMANENTLY WEAKENED BY GROUNDING WHILE BEING
DRAGGED THROUGH THE SHALLOW CANALS BETWEEN
AMSTERDAM AND THE OPEN SEA.

USS *Bonhomme Richard* (1778)

BUILT AS *DUC DE DURAS* AT LORIENT, FRANCE, IN 1765, THIS WAS AN ARMED MERCHANTMAN OF THE FRENCH EAST INDIA COMPANY. IN 1778 IT WAS GIVEN TO JOHN PAUL JONES AND LED AN AMERICAN SQUADRON THAT RAIDED THE BRITISH COASTS. IN A CELEBRATED BATTLE WITH HMS *SERAPIS*, *BONHOMME RICHARD* SANK BUT JONES CAPTURED THE ROYAL NAVY SHIP.

The French government had allied itself with the new American Republic and had promised Jones a warship to help the Revolutionary cause. In 1778, with the help of wealthy sympathizers, this was arranged. The ship, which had made two voyages to China and a third as a troopship to the West Indies, was refitted as a frigate, with twenty-eight 12 pounder and six 78 pounder cannons, and ten 3 pounder swivel guns.

It was named *Bonhomme Richard* ("Poor Richard") by Jones—a tribute to founding father Benjamin Franklin, author of *Poor Richard's Almanack*. On August 14, 1779 it led a seven-strong squadron, including *Alliance* (32 guns) on commerce and coastal raids on both the west and east coasts of Britain, including a venture into the Firth of Forth which scared the city of Edinburgh, chief city of Scotland.

Battle of Flamborough Head

On September 23 off Flamborough Head the squadron encountered a convoy of 41 ships coming from the Baltic Sea, escorted by HMS *Serapis*, a 44-gun two-decked fifth-rate, and a furious two-ship duel at close range ensued. Two of *Bonhomme Richard's* 18-pounder guns exploded and the ship was heavily raked by broadsides from *Serapis*. Jones brought his ship alongside *Serapis* in what was effectively a death grapple. Both ships were severely damaged and both had lost half their crew.

Alliance, under Captain Pierre Landais, stood off at first but after two hours fired broadsides of canister and grapeshot that inflicted as much injury on *Bonhomme Richard's* crew as on *Serapis's*. Invited to surrender, Jones made the reply, "No, I'll sink, but I'll be damned if I strike," and Captain Pearson of the *Serapis*, reckoning his convoy was now safe, surrendered to spare further bloodshed. Of the 322 crewmen on *Bonhomme Richard*, 140 were killed. Jones sailed the *Serapis* to Texel in the Netherlands, leaving the battered, half-burnt hulk of *Bonhomme Richard* to sink in 600 ft (183 m) of water. Despite efforts to locate the remains it has never been found.

SPECIFICATIONS

DISPLACEMENT: 998 tons (1,014 tonnes)

DIMENSIONS: 152 ft x 40 ft x 19 ft (46 m x 12 m x 5.8 m)

RIG: Three masts, square rig

ARMAMENT: Twenty-eight 12 pounders; six 18 pounders; eight 9 pounder guns

CREW: 380

USS *Bonhomme Richard*

OLD SHIP
AS *DUC DE DURAS*, THE SHIP WAS
ALREADY 14 YEARS OLD AND WELL-
TRAVELLED WHEN JONES TOOK IT OVER.

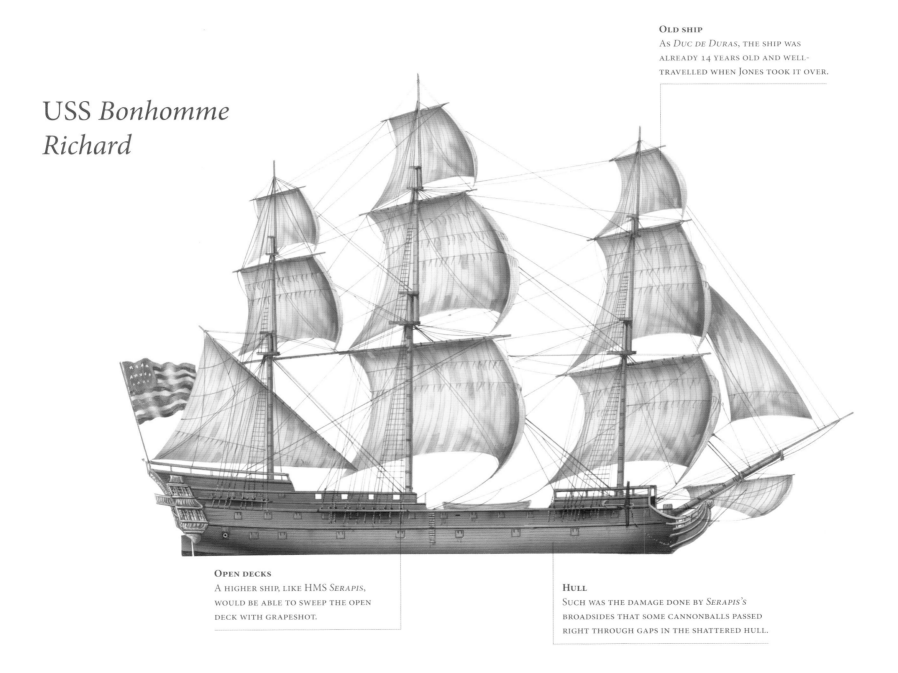

OPEN DECKS
A HIGHER SHIP, LIKE HMS *SERAPIS*,
WOULD BE ABLE TO SWEEP THE OPEN
DECK WITH GRAPESHOT.

HULL
SUCH WAS THE DAMAGE DONE BY *SERAPIS'S*
BROADSIDES THAT SOME CANNONBALLS PASSED
RIGHT THROUGH GAPS IN THE SHATTERED HULL.

Santa Ana (1784)

FLAGSHIP OF THE SPANISH FLEET AT TRAFALGAR, THE 112-GUN *SANTA ANA* WAS IN THE MIDDLE OF THE FRENCH–SPANISH LINE AND FOUGHT A TREMENDOUS BATTLE AGAINST BRITISH FIRST-RATES. DISMASTED, IT WAS FORCED TO SURRENDER AND WAS TAKEN AS A PRIZE, BUT IT WAS RECLAIMED IN A BOLD OPERATION BY FRENCH SHIPS ON OCTOBER 23.

A first-rate *navío de línea*, *Santa Ana* was constructed by José Romero y Fernández de Landa to the design of Miguel de la Puente, its keel laid in June 1783, and launched at Ferrol Navy Yard on September 29, 1784. Sea tests were found to be highly satisfactory and it was commissioned under Captain Felix de Tejada on February 28, 1785.

Lead Vessel

Although built on similar lines to Landa's *Purísima Concepcion*, it is usually taken as lead vessel of the eight first-rates known as the *Meregildos*, built at Ferrol and Havana between 1786 and 1794. *Santa Ana* was used for testing six large-caliber carronade guns from the Carron factory in Scotland, and also for testing explosive shells in 1785. In peacetime its 36-pounder guns were replaced by 24-pounders. Based at Cadiz, like other capital ships it had lengthy spells out of commission—five years out of its 21-year career. The hull was coppered in September 1798 and the ship re-keeled in 1800.

Fight at Trafalgar

Over the course of 1805 it was careened and rearmed at La Carraca, with a total of 120 guns. At Trafalgar, under Captain Gardoqui, it was the flagship of Admiral Don Ignacio Alava at the head of the Spanish division. Engaged by Admiral Collingwood's 112-gun *Royal Sovereign* at the head of the British lee division, *Santa Ana* suffered a double-shotted broadside through the vulnerable stern, putting seven guns out of action, and a furious two-hour battle went on between the two ships, with other British ships also firing on *Santa Ana*.

Finally, dismasted and battered, with 97 men killed and 141 wounded, Gardoqui was forced to strike his colors. *Santa Ana* was claimed as a prize and taken in tow. But on October 23 it was recaptured by Captain Julien Cosmao-Kerjulien's French squadron and brought back to Cadiz.

It remained out of commission for several years before repairs were completed. In 1810 it was transferred to Havana, Cuba, and sank at the anchorage there in 1816; its remains could be seen for another 20 years or so.

SPECIFICATIONS

DISPLACEMENT: 2,543 tons (2,803 tonnes)

DIMENSIONS: 184 ft 2 in x 50 ft x 23 ft (56.14 m x 15.5 m x 7.4 m)

RIG: Full square rig with staysails and studding sails

ARMAMENT: Thirty 36 pounders; thirty-two 24 pounders; ten 8 pounder cannons; ten 48 pounders; two 32 pounders; six 24 pounder howitzers; four 4 pounder swivel guns (1805)

CREW: 1,048 (wartime)

Santa Ana

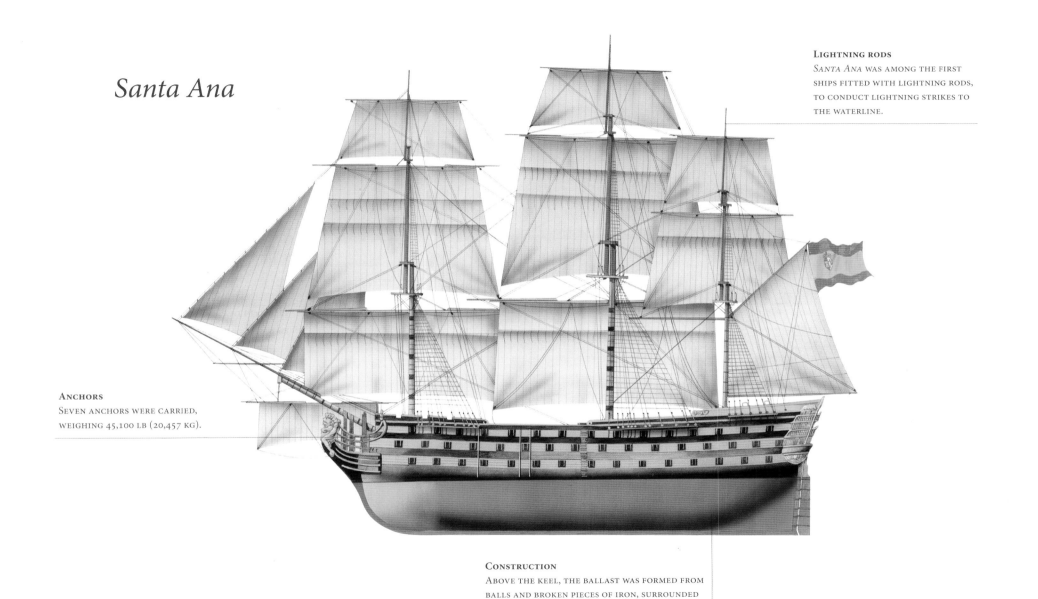

LIGHTNING RODS
Santa Ana WAS AMONG THE FIRST
SHIPS FITTED WITH LIGHTNING RODS,
TO CONDUCT LIGHTNING STRIKES TO
THE WATERLINE.

ANCHORS
SEVEN ANCHORS WERE CARRIED,
WEIGHING 45,100 LB (20,457 KG).

CONSTRUCTION
ABOVE THE KEEL, THE BALLAST WAS FORMED FROM
BALLS AND BROKEN PIECES OF IRON, SURROUNDED
BY STONE AND CEMENTED INTO PLACE.

HMS *Saturn* *(1786)*

LAUNCHED AS A 74-GUN THIRD-RATE IN 1786, *SATURN* SAW VARIED SERVICE BEFORE BEING REDUCED TO A LARGE FRIGATE IN 1812–13. IT CONTINUED IN ACTIVE NAVAL OPERATIONS UNTIL 1817 WHEN IT WAS LAID UP IN MILFORD HAVEN, FIRST AS A QUARANTINE SHIP, THEN AS A DRILL AND TRAINING SHIP, UNTIL 1864.

Saturn was one of the ten-strong *Edgar* class, designed by Sir Thomas Slade and built at the Northam Yard, Portsmouth. Laid down in August 1782, it was not launched until November 22, 1786 and commissioned on February 5, 1787. Its total cost was £39,549.

Battles and Blockades

On May 25, 1795 *Saturn* was deployed to the Mediterranean Sea and was present at the battle of Hyères on July 13. Between February 1797 and January 1799 it spent much time in dock at Plymouth and Portsmouth and was with the Channel Fleet in 1799. In 1801–02 it served in the Baltic, participating in the Battle of Copenhagen on April 2, 1801, although it was held in Sir Hyde Parker's reserve fleet rather than with Nelson's attacking squadron; it was later deployed to the Leeward Islands. In 1808 it was with the fleet blockading Lorient, and returned to the Baltic in 1810.

In 1813, with three other 74-guns (*Elephant*, *Excellent*, and *Goliath*), it was reduced to 58 guns in order to combat American frigates. Re-classed as a fourth-rate frigate, it was sent in August of that year first to Bermuda, then to Halifax, Nova Scotia, where the main task was to blockade the port of New York. On November 5, 1814 *Saturn* captured the two American brigs *Charles* and *Theodore*. In August 1815 it carried Mr. G. Robertson, Agent for Prisoners of War in the United States, from New London to Halifax.

Saturn had 13 captains in its time. One of them, Thomas Totty, had it as his flagship in 1802 after promotion to Rear Admiral of the Blue in 1801. From 1817 the ship was based at Pembroke Dock, Milford Haven, and from 1825 was used, like many other larger vessels, essentially for land purposes, first as a quarantine ship for fever patients, then for the drilling of new recruits. It was finally broken up at Pembroke Dock in 1868.

SPECIFICATIONS

DISPLACEMENT: 1,617 tons (1,643 tonnes)

DIMENSIONS: 168 ft 2 in x 46 ft 11 in x 19 ft 10 in (51.26 m x 14.3 m x 6 m)

RIG: Three masts, square rig

ARMAMENT: Twenty-eight 32 pounders; twenty-eight 18 pounders; eighteen 9 pounder guns (1790)

CREW: 550

HMS *Saturn*

HULL
SATURN AFTER 1813. THE
HULL WAS CUT DOWN, FORE-
AND-AFT, TO THE CLAMPS
OF THE QUARTERDECK AND
FORECASTLE.

ARMAMENT
THE MAIN BATTERY OF TWENTY-EIGHT
LONG 32 POUNDERS WAS RETAINED.

GUNS
THE UPPER GUN DECK NOW HELD TWENTY-EIGHT 42 POUNDER
CARRONADES, PLUS TWO LONG-BARRELLED 12 POUNDERS AS
CHASE GUNS.

HMS *Captain* (1787)

HMS *CAPTAIN* WON FAME AS NELSON'S SHIP FROM JUNE 1796, DOING MUCH TO COMPLETE THE BRITISH VICTORY IN THE BATTLE OF CAPE ST VINCENT ON FEBRUARY 14, 1797. IT SAW MUCH FURTHER ACTIVE SERVICE DURING THE NAPOLEONIC WARS, BEFORE BEING RELEGATED TO HARBOR SERVICE IN 1809.

Ordered on November 14, 1782, and laid down in May 1784, *Captain* was built at Limehouse Yard on the River Thames and launched on November 26, 1787.

A 74-gun third-rate, with *Majestic* and *Orion* it was one of three modified versions of the *Canada* class, which dated from the mid-1760s. First commissioned in June 1790 under Captain Archibald Dickson, it was only briefly in service before being paid off until May 1793, when it was deployed to the Mediterranean Fleet.

On October 11, 1793 it captured the French frigate *Modeste*, and took part in the action off Genoa on March 14, 1795 when, under Captain Samuel Reeve, it was first in the British-Neapolitan battle line in a victory over a French fleet commanded by Admiral Pierre Martin.

The French fell back on the Hyères Islands where a further battle took place on July 13, considered a British victory although both fleets withdrew.

Cape St Vincent

In 1797, under Nelson, by then a Commodore, it was in the second battle of Cape St Vincent, where Admiral Jervis's 15 ships confronted Admiral de Córdoba's fleet of 27. Nelson, most junior of Jervis's three flag officers, independently made the decision to take *Captain* out of the line of battle and cross the Spanish line. His unorthodox maneuver assured a decisive victory. *Captain* took the surrender of the third-rate *San Nicolás de Bari* and the first-rate *San José*, but was heavily damaged and virtually unmanageable, and Nelson transferred to *Irresistible*.

After major repairs at Plymouth *Captain* returned to the Mediterranean in May 1799, then was part of the fleet attacking Ferrol, in northeastern Spain, in August 1800. From 1802–05 it was out of commission, then served in the Baltic, Mediterranean, and West Indies theaters until December 1809 when it was unrated, disarmed, and converted into a receiving ship at Plymouth.

On March 22, 1813 *Captain* accidentally caught fire and sank. The wreck was raised and broken up in July of that year.

SPECIFICATIONS

DISPLACEMENT: 1,639 tons (1,665 tonnes)

DIMENSIONS: 170 ft x 46 ft 10 in x 18 ft 10 in (51.8 m x 14.3 m x 5.74 m)

RIG: Three masts, full square rig

ARMAMENT: Thirty-six 32 pounders, thirty 18 pounders, ten 9 pounder guns

CREW: 550

HMS *Captain*

RUDDER
ALL SHIPS OF THIS PERIOD
HAD "UNBALANCED"
RUDDERS, WITH THE WHOLE
BLADE AREA BEHIND THE
TURNING AXIS, AND FIXED
AT THE TOP TO THE TILLER
INSIDE THE HULL.

DOUBLE WHEEL
BIGGER SHIPS SINCE THE MID-CENTURY WERE
STEERED BY A DOUBLE WHEEL, MOUNTED JUST
FORWARD OF THE MIZZENMAST.

LOWER DECKS
ON THE LOWER DECKS, A SAILOR WAS ALLOWED ONLY
14 IN (35 CM) SPACE TO SLING HIS HAMMOCK.

San Telmo *(1788)*

THE SHIP WAS LAUNCHED AT FERROL ON JUNE 20, 1788, THE SECOND OF A LINE OF 74-GUNS INITIATED WITH *SAN ILDEFONSO* (1785) AND KNOWN AS THE *ILDEFONSINOS*. THEIR PLANS WERE DRAWN BY DON JOSÉ ROMERO Y FERNÁNDEZ DE LANDA AND BUILT UNDER THE SUPERVISION OF JORGE JUAN, WHO INCORPORATED NUMEROUS BRITISH SHIPBUILDING TECHNIQUES IN ORDER TO PRODUCE A SHIP THAT COULD MATCH THE BRITISH NAVY'S 74-GUNS IN SPEED.

While the main hull, coppered during construction, was still made of oak, lighter woods like pine and cedar were used in the upper parts, and the dimensions were less than those of traditional Spanish 74-gun ships. *San Telmo's* first captain was Juan José Ruiz de Apodaca, future Captain General and Head of the Spanish Navy. Records of its sea trials survive and indicate how important these were for getting the right positioning of the hull in the water.

San Telmo was launched with a draft of 17 ft 8 in (5.4 m) aft and 12 ft 4 in (3.76 m) forward; after trials its most effective draft was established at 22 ft 4 in (6.8 m) aft and 20 ft 2 in (6.15 m) fore, using 6,000 quintals (300 tons; 305 tonnes) of stone ballast and 6,300 quintals (315 tons, 320 tonnes) of iron. Heeling the ship in a strong side wind brought the gun deck freeboard down from 6 ft 4 in (1.92 m) to 3 ft 3 in (1 m) on the leeward side.

Performance Testing

These trials taught valuable lessons and were followed by *San Telmo's* participation in a testing squadron, under Admiral Tejada, comparing the performance and key features of different designs, both ships of the line and frigates. The Spanish Navy took a scientific approach to the design and maintenance of its ships. It was known that every two months spent at sea would reduce the life of a hull by one month: hence the periods of disarming and holding in ordinary, with guns removed to minimize stresses on the hull, whenever conditions allowed a ship's services to be dispensed with.

In the Nootka Incident crisis of 1790, *San Telmo* was one of 14 ships held in readiness at Ferrol against a possible war with Great Britain. Little is known of its career until 1819, when under Captain Rosendo Porlier it left Cadiz for Lima on May 11 to strengthen colonial forces fighting the independence movement in Peru. Of its two accompanying ships, the frigate *Test* got through, and the supply ship *Alejandro* turned back, but *San Telmo* was wrecked with all hands off Cape Horn. Pieces of wreckage were later found on Livingston Island, Antarctica.

SPECIFICATIONS

DISPLACEMENT: 1,640 tons (1,666 tonnes)

DIMENSIONS: 170 ft 7 in x 47 ft 6 in x 23 ft (52 m x 14.5 m x 7 m)

RIG: Three masts, square rig

ARMAMENT: 74 guns

CREW: 644

San Telmo

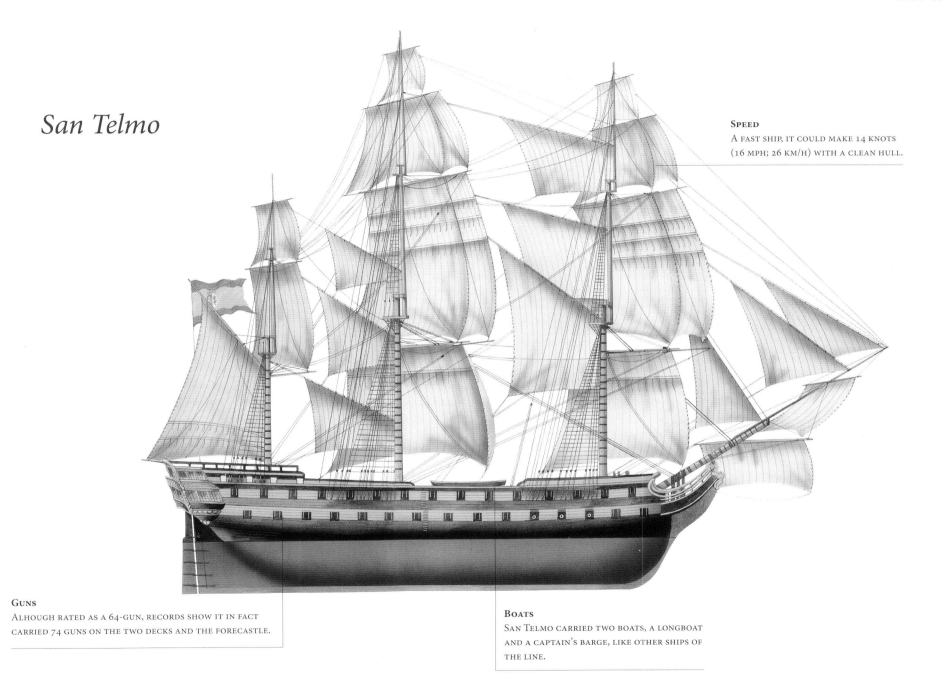

SPEED
A FAST SHIP, IT COULD MAKE 14 KNOTS
(16 MPH; 26 KM/H) WITH A CLEAN HULL.

GUNS
ALHOUGH RATED AS A 64-GUN, RECORDS SHOW IT IN FACT
CARRIED 74 GUNS ON THE TWO DECKS AND THE FORECASTLE.

BOATS
SAN TELMO CARRIED TWO BOATS, A LONGBOAT
AND A CAPTAIN'S BARGE, LIKE OTHER SHIPS OF
THE LINE.

Commerce de Marseille (1788)

IN THE EARLY 1790S THE FRENCH NAVY POSSESSED MORE FIRST-RATES THAN GREAT BRITAIN, WITH FIVE OF 110 GUNS AND THREE OF 118. AMONG THEM WAS *COMMERCE DE MARSEILLE* WITH ITS MASSIVE LOWER-TIER BATTERY OF 36-POUNDER (CLOSER TO 40 LB/18 KG IN BRITISH WEIGHT) CANNONS—PROBABLY THE WORLD'S LARGEST WARSHIP AT THE TIME.

The name was owed to donations from the Marseilles chamber of commerce, which financed its building at the Toulon Arsenal. Laid down in September 1786, it was launched on September 7, 1788 and completed in October 1790, after the French Revolution.

Design

The design was produced by Jacques-Noël Sané, and a further 15 first-rates of the class were to follow, including *Océan* and *Orient*. Its hull was built of oak, at a time when a smaller ship of three decks required 5,740 cartloads of wood (each equivalent to a fully grown tree). The guns were of iron. Its color scheme is known to have been dark gray up to the main battery, yellow ochre on the second and top tiers of guns, and marine blue on the bulwarks and topsides. The decks were scrubbed white. The undersea hull was copper-plated from the start.

Commerce de Marseille was intended as the flagship of France's Mediterranean fleet and so based at Toulon, which was held in 1793 by French royalists. On August 29, 1793 a British force under the command of Admiral Samuel Hood entered the naval base, taking the ships inside by surprise. Only four put up a fight. One was *Commerce de Marseille*, whose officers were not on board but whose crew resisted the invaders.

When the French republicans took Toulon in December, the British left, burning the arsenal and nine warships, but taking away three including *Commerce de Marseille*. At Plymouth it was greatly admired for its sailing qualities as well as its size. But it was considered too structurally weak for the long-term seakeeping required of British ships of the line, and not taken into the Royal Navy. Instead it was turned into a storeship and departed in this capacity for the West Indies before being turned back to Plymouth by a violent gale.

From 1798 it was used as a prison ship. On June 22, 1806 the order to break it up was given, and this was completed by 1808.

SPECIFICATIONS

DISPLACEMENT: 2,746 tons (2,790 tonnes)

DIMENSIONS: 208 ft 4 in x 54 ft 9 in x 26 ft 6 in (63.5 m x 16.7 m x 8.1 m)

RIG: Three masts, full square rig

ARMAMENT: Thirty-two 36 pounders, thirty-four 24 pounders, thirty-four 12 pounders, eighteen 8 pounder guns

CREW: 1,079

Commerce
de Marseilles

RIGGING
ITS FULL RIG COMPRISED 21 SAILS,
WITH A SAIL AREA OF 34,444 SQUARE
FT (3,200 SQ M).

SIZE
THIS SHIP RIVALED AND
PERHAPS EXCEEDED
SANTÍSIMA TRINIDAD AS
THE LARGEST WARSHIP OF
ITS TIME.

Éole (1789)

THIS FRENCH SECOND-RATE WAS ONE OF A LARGE CLASS OF 107 SHIPS BUILT BETWEEN 1782 AND 1813, DESIGNED BY JACQUES-NOËL SANÉ, WITH *TÉMÉRAIRE* (1782) AS THE FIRST. BUILT TO STANDARD DIMENSIONS, THEY WERE MEANT TO HAVE INTERCHANGEABLE PARTS THAT COULD BE PRODUCED IN QUANTITY, AT A TIME WHEN MANY SHIPS WERE ONE-OFFS REQUIRING SPECIALLY MADE AND THUS MORE EXPENSIVE FITTINGS.

French 74-guns were generally larger and roomier than their British counterparts. Numerous examples of the class were captured and used by the British Navy, where their comparative spaciousness as well as their good handling qualities were appreciated. Their sail surface amounted to 26,748 square ft (2,485 sq m). Examination often found that their drafts were by no means identical, but with ships built at different times in different yards, even to the same specifications, this is not surprising. *Éole* (named after Aeolus, mythical ruler of the winds), second bearer of the name, was launched at Lorient in 1789. From 1791 to 1793 it was based at Santo Domingo.

The Glorious First of June

Éole was one of eight ships of the line in the vanguard of Admiral Villaret-Joyeuse's fleet at the Battle of "The Glorious First of June" (as the British Navy called it) in the Atlantic in 1794, when 23 ships of the line, with 16 frigates, escorting a grain convoy, were intercepted by 25 British ships. Many experienced officers had been purged in the Revolutionary years after 1789 and the fleet's effectiveness suffered as a result. But under Captain Bertrand Keranguen, *Éole* played a vigorous part, joining with *Trajan* (74 guns) in disabling HMS *Bellerophon*. Although the result was considered a British victory, the convoy got safely through to France. *Éole* suffered serious damage and was repaired in the winter of 1794 at Brest.

In 1796–97 it was part of the fleet sent in support of a failed attempt to invade Ireland. *Éole's* final years were spent primarily in the West Indies, and in the imperial service of Napoleon I it was awarded an Eagle in 1804. On August 19, 1806 it was dismasted in a violent storm off the coast of Martinique, and was towed to Annapolis, Maryland, by two American ships. It lay there until 1811 when it was stricken from the active list. Its guns were unshipped and used in American shore forts, and *Éole* was broken up at Baltimore in 1816.

SPECIFICATIONS

DISPLACEMENT: 2,966 tons (3,013 tonnes)

DIMENSIONS: 183 ft 4 in x 48 ft 11 in x 23 ft 10 in (55.87 m x 14.9 m x 7.26 m)

RIG: Three masts, full square rig

ARMAMENT: Twenty-eight 36 pounders, thirty 18 pounders, sixteen 8 pounder guns; three 36 pounder carronades

CREW: 705 (wartime)

Éole

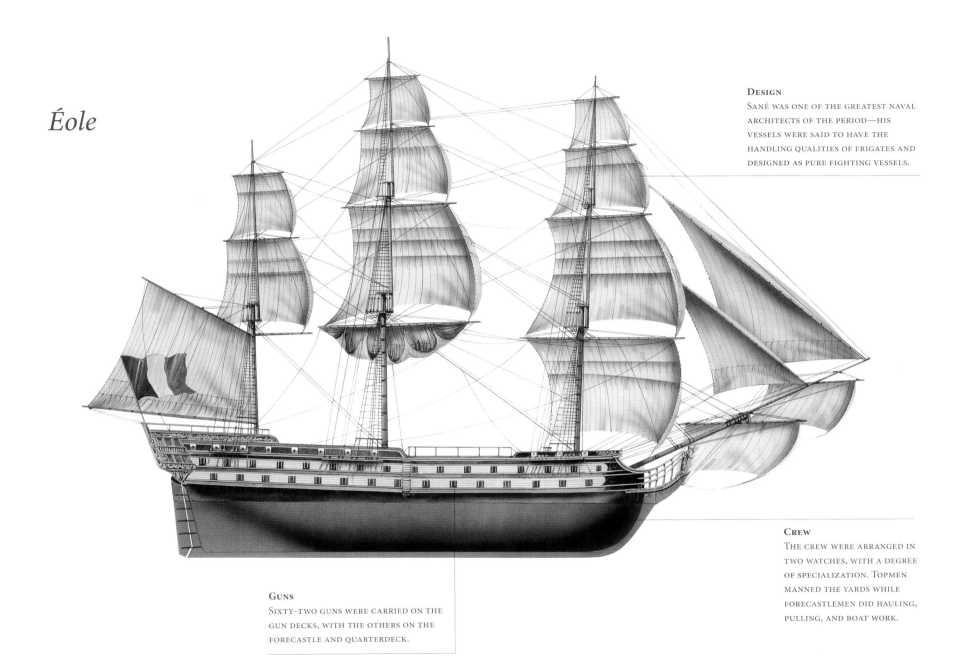

DESIGN
SANÉ WAS ONE OF THE GREATEST NAVAL ARCHITECTS OF THE PERIOD—HIS VESSELS WERE SAID TO HAVE THE HANDLING QUALITIES OF FRIGATES AND DESIGNED AS PURE FIGHTING VESSELS.

CREW
THE CREW WERE ARRANGED IN TWO WATCHES, WITH A DEGREE OF SPECIALIZATION. TOPMEN MANNED THE YARDS WHILE FORECASTLEMEN DID HAULING, PULLING, AND BOAT WORK.

GUNS
SIXTY-TWO GUNS WERE CARRIED ON THE GUN DECKS, WITH THE OTHERS ON THE FORECASTLE AND QUARTERDECK.

HMS *Boyne* (1790)

THIRD TO CARRY THE NAME, HMS *BOYNE* WAS LAUNCHED AT DEPTFORD IN 1790. WITH 98 GUNS, IT WAS A SECOND-RATE. THE SECOND-RATE THREE-DECKER WAS A DISTINCTIVELY BRITISH TYPE, WITH A FIREPOWER, JUDGED IN TERMS OF BROADSIDE WEIGHT, LESS THAN THAT OF A TWO-DECK FRENCH 80-GUN SHIP—1,012 LB (459 KG) AGAINST 1,287 LB (584 KG)—BUT THE BRITISH SECOND-RATES, ALTHOUGH OFTEN POOR AND SLUGGISH SAILERS, WERE UNDOUBTEDLY MORE SOLID IN BATTLE THAN THE TWO-DECKERS.

The backbone of the British battle fleet was the 74-gun third-rate, of which there were 58 in sea service in 1799, with a further 11 in ordinary or under repair. By contrast there were only four first-rates in the fleet, with two repairing. The number of second-rates in the Royal Navy was also never very great, at its maximum in 1799, with 15 on service and two in ordinary or under major repair. In fact there were not enough of the largest classes to provide flagships for the admirals.

Boyne was not among the ships listed in 1799. It was laid down at Woolwich Naval Dockyard on November 4, 1783, launched six years later on June 27, 1790, and commissioned in August of the same year. Its active service began in 1793 when it captured a French privateer, *Guidelon*, in the English Channel.

As flagship of Vice Admiral Sir John Jervis, captained by George Gray, it led a fleet from England on November 26, 1793 on a mission to capture the island of Martinique from the French. Gray's father, Sir Charles, was General in command of the invasion troops. Possession of the island was accomplished by March 4, 1794, but a French squadron arrived on June 5 with reinforcements, and the British gains were rapidly lost. Jervis was recalled, and *Boyne* returned to Portsmouth in February 1795.

Fire at Anchor

On May 1, 1795, while lying at anchor in Spithead, off Portsmouth, *Boyne* caught fire, perhaps through a hot stovepipe setting light to papers in the admiral's cabin. It burned for seven hours, drifting aground, until finally the forward powder magazine exploded, making the ship a total wreck. Its guns, kept ready loaded, discharged, making help operations difficult. Most of its crew were rescued, but 11 men were killed. In a crude salvage operation from 1840–41, a few artifacts were brought up.

SPECIFICATIONS

DISPLACEMENT: 2,021 tons (2,053 tonnes)

DIMENSIONS: 182 ft x 50 ft 4.5 in x 21 ft 9 in (55 m x 15.36 m x 6.63 m)

RIG: Three masts, full square rig

ARMAMENT: Twenty-eight 32 pounders, thirty 18 pounders, forty 12 pounder guns

CREW: c. 800

HMS *Boyne*

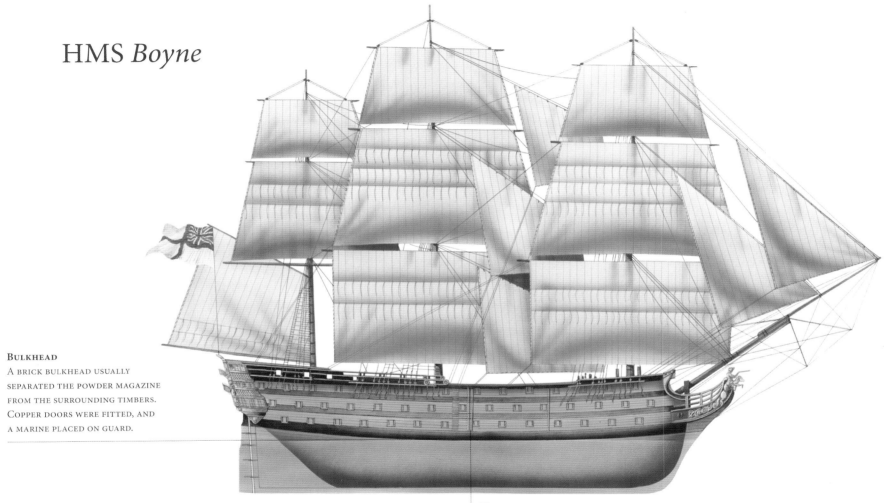

BULKHEAD

A BRICK BULKHEAD USUALLY
SEPARATED THE POWDER MAGAZINE
FROM THE SURROUNDING TIMBERS.
COPPER DOORS WERE FITTED, AND
A MARINE PLACED ON GUARD.

HULL

A SET OF PROTRUDING RIBS AMIDSHIPS WAS A STANDARD FEATURE
OF LARGER SHIPS, ENABLING MEN TO SCRAMBLE UP THE HULL
SIDE. IN A SECURE ANCHORAGE, AN ACCOMMODATION LADDER
WOULD BE SLUNG FOR OFFICERS AND VISITORS.

Diana *(1792)*

THE *MAHONESAS* WERE A CLASS OF SIX 34-GUN FRIGATES BUILT AT MAHÓN, ON THE ISLAND OF MINORCA, BETWEEN 1789 AND 1797, BEGINNING WITH *LA MAHONESA* ITSELF. CONSTRUCTION WAS SUPERVISED BY HONORATO DE BOUYÓN, AND THE PLANS WERE DRAWN UP BY JULIÁN MARTÍN DE RETAMOSA. THEY WERE DISTINGUISHED BY THEIR SPEED AND EASE OF HANDLING.

Diana, third in the class, was ordered on September 22, 1790 and launched on March 10, 1792. Its first captain was Baltasar Hidalgo de Cisneros y la Torre. Tests against the frigate *Nuestra Señora de la Soledad*, built by Landa Romero at Cartagena between August 8 and 29, showed *Diana's* speed and sailing qualities to be superior.

At the start of war with France in March 1793 it carried Spanish troops to Roussillon and from the Balearic Islands to Cartagena. That summer Cisneros was put in command of a squadron of frigates, xebecs, and galleys operating off the southern French coast, then joined with Admiral Lángara's fleet at Toulon, still under the control of French royalists. After further service in the Mediterranean, *Diana* was transferred to Cadiz at the end of September 1794 but returned to the Mediterranean fleet by March 1795.

It was with the Spanish fleet at the Battle of Cape St Vincent on February 14, 1797, although as a frigate it was not in the line of battle. On December 20, 1798 it made the first of several transatlantic voyages, to Suriname, carrying troops. Its armament was increased in 1800 by six 6 pounder cannons.

Escort Duties

In 1805 *Diana* was laid up in ordinary at Ferrol, leaving that port in August 1808 for Cadiz, from where it sailed as a convoy escort to Veracruz. Escort duties were always its main function, including a convoy of 200 vessels with 7,000 soldiers, to Tarifa at the end of February 1811. From 1812 to 1817, long-range escort duty took it to Havana, Cuba, Montevideo, Uruguay, and Veracruz, Mexico; to Valdivia, Chile, in 1818, and again to Havana on several occasions through the 1820s. Between these missions it served

with Mediterranean squadrons patrolling the Spanish and North African coasts.

After a long and useful career, *Diana*, which should not be confused with a Spanish corvette of the same name and era, was broken up in Cartagena Naval Yard in 1833.

SPECIFICATIONS

DISPLACEMENT: 900 tons (914 tonnes)

DIMENSIONS: 143 ft x 34 ft 5 in x 11 ft 2 in (43.6 m x 10.5 m x 3.4 m)

RIG: Three masts, square rig

ARMAMENT: Twenty-six 12 pounders, six 8 pounders (to 1800)

CREW: 265

Diana

ARMAMENT
BY 1817 *DIANA*'S ORIGINAL
ARMAMENT WAS AUGMENTED BY SIX
6 POUNDER GUNS, SIX 24 POUNDERS,
AND THREE 3 POUNDER HOWITZERS.

SPEED
THE 'MAHONESAS' WERE BUILT FOR SPEED,
WITH FINE UNDERWATER LINES PARTICULARLY
NOTICEABLE TOWARDS THE STERN.

Pompée (1792)

NAMED FOR THE ROMAN GENERAL POMPEIUS MAXIMUS, *POMPÉE* WAS CONSTRUCTED AT TOULON NAVAL SHIPYARD AS A 74-GUN FRENCH SHIP OF THE LINE OF THE TÉMÉRAIRE CLASS, BUT AFTER THE FRENCH REVOLUTION IT WAS HANDED OVER BY FRENCH ROYALISTS TO THE BRITISH NAVY AT TOULON, AND ITS ENTIRE ACTIVE SERVICE WAS SPENT FLYING THE BRITISH FLAG.

Pompée, laid down in January 1790 and launched on May 28, 1791, was commissioned in February 1793 and handed over to the British in August of the same year. Like other French ships, it was closely examined and the design was copied in HMS *Superb* and *Achilles,* both launched in 1798.

Pompée was entered on the list as a British warship on October 29, 1794, and in May 1795 it was assigned to the Channel Fleet. Based at Portsmouth, it was one of the ships affected by the mutiny of many crews at Spithead during April–May 1797, spreading to other ports, in protest against the atrocious conditions of the naval service.

Mediterranean Action

In 1801, under Captain Charles Stirling, *Pompée* was one of Saumarez's ships in the Battle of Algeciras, fighting in shallow water and suffering serious damage from the French flagship *Formidable.* Eventually it had to be towed by ships' boats from the bay to receive hasty makeshift repairs at close-by Gibraltar. It continued to serve with the Mediterranean Fleet, and was flagship of Rear Admiral Sir Sydney Smith in the Sicilian campaign of 1806.

Pompée was one of eight ships of the line in the action at the Dardanelles when it appeared that Turkey might be about to renew its alliance with France, on February 19, 1807, exchanging fire with Turkish shore forts and capturing two small warships; it then moved on to the occupation of Alexandria, Egypt, in March. In 1808 it was with the Atlantic fleet, participating in the capture of Martinique in January 1809.

In the winter of 1810–11 it was fitted out as a prison hulk at Portsmouth, at first for British naval offenders, and later for French prisoners of war. It appears to be a true story that Portsmouth's nickname of "Pompey," used by generations of Royal Navy personnel, stems from the presence of *Pompée* at the base. It was finally towed to Woolwich on the Thames and broken up there in early 1817.

SPECIFICATIONS

DISPLACEMENT: 1,901 tons (1,931 tonnes)

DIMENSIONS: 182 ft 2 in x 49 ft x 21 ft 10 in (55.52 m x 14.94 m x 6.6 m)

RIG: Three masts, full square rig

ARMAMENT: Thirty 32 pounders, thirty 18 pounder guns; sixteen 32 pounders, eight 18 pounder carronades

CREW: 640

Pompée

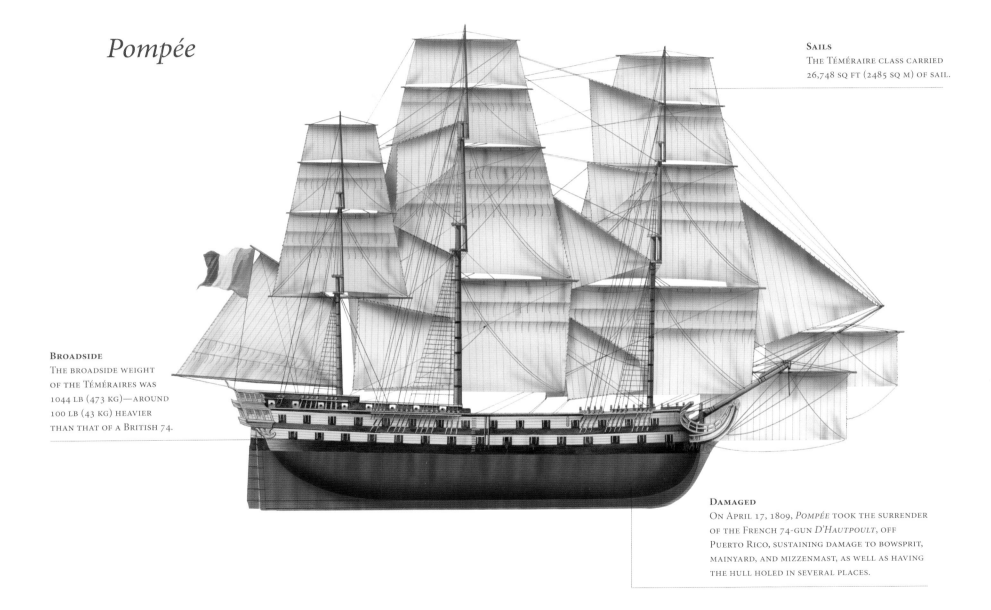

SAILS
THE TÉMÉRAIRE CLASS CARRIED
26,748 SQ FT (2485 SQ M) OF SAIL.

BROADSIDE
THE BROADSIDE WEIGHT
OF THE TÉMÉRAIRES WAS
1044 LB (473 KG)—AROUND
100 LB (43 KG) HEAVIER
THAN THAT OF A BRITISH 74.

DAMAGED
ON APRIL 17, 1809, *POMPÉE* TOOK THE SURRENDER
OF THE FRENCH 74-GUN *D'HAUTPOULT*, OFF
PUERTO RICO, SUSTAINING DAMAGE TO BOWSPRIT,
MAINYARD, AND MIZZENMAST, AS WELL AS HAVING
THE HULL HOLED IN SEVERAL PLACES.

HMS *Minotaur* (1793)

ITS DESIGN BASED ON A FRENCH 74-GUN, *MINOTAUR* WAS A THIRD-RATE OF THE ROYAL NAVY, WHICH WAS HEAVILY ENGAGED IN THE WARS AGAINST REVOLUTIONARY AND NAPOLEONIC FRANCE. IT SURVIVED THREE MAJOR BATTLES ONLY TO RUN AGROUND ON THE DUTCH COAST IN 1810 AND BECOME A TOTAL WRECK.

The French 74-gun ship *Courageux* was captured in 1761 by HMS *Bellona* and its structure was closely studied by British naval designers, who modeled four ships on it. *Minotaur* was the fourth, laid down at Woolwich in January 1788 and launched on November 6, 1793. From 1794 to 1802 Captain Thomas Louis commanded it. In August 1798 it was with Nelson's fleet at the Battle of the Nile, catching the 74-gun *Aquilon* between itself and HMS *Theseus*, and forcing its surrender and capture.

It remained with the Mediterranean Fleet, and on the French surrender of Rome on September 29, 1799 Captain Louis was rowed up the Tiber by his barge crew and hoisted the Union flag over the Capitol. After further service in the Mediterranean *Minotaur* was deployed in the Atlantic Ocean, and on May 28, 1803, with HMS *Thunderer*, it captured the French frigate *Franchise*.

Under Captain John Mansfield *Minotaur* was once again part of Nelson's fleet, and served at Trafalgar, tenth in line in the Weather column led by HMS *Victory*, capturing the Spanish *Neptuno* of 80 guns, although in the storm following the battle *Neptuno* was retaken by its crew before being wrecked.

At the second battle of Copenhagen, August 16–September 5, 1807, *Minotaur* was the flagship of Rear Admiral Essington, joining Admiral Gambier's fleet on August 7; it was then deployed into the Baltic Sea during the naval war of 1807–12 with Russia, and was one of the British ships whose boats were in combat with Russian gunboats off the Finnish coast on July 25, 1809.

Shipwreck

On December 22, 1810 while sailing from Gothenburg, Sweden, to Britain, *Minotaur* came too close to the Dutch coast and grounded on a mudbank off the island of Texel, where it was dismasted and began to break up. At least 370 men were lost, the others being taken prisoner, as Holland was then controlled by France.

SPECIFICATIONS

DISPLACEMENT: 1,723 tons (1,750 tonnes)

DIMENSIONS: 172 ft 3 in x 47 ft 9 in x 20 ft 9 in (52.5 m x 14.55 m x 6.2 m)

RIG: Three masts, full square rig

ARMAMENT: Twenty-eight 32 pounders, twenty-eight 18 pounders, fourteen 9 pounder guns

CREW: 700

HMS *Minotaur*

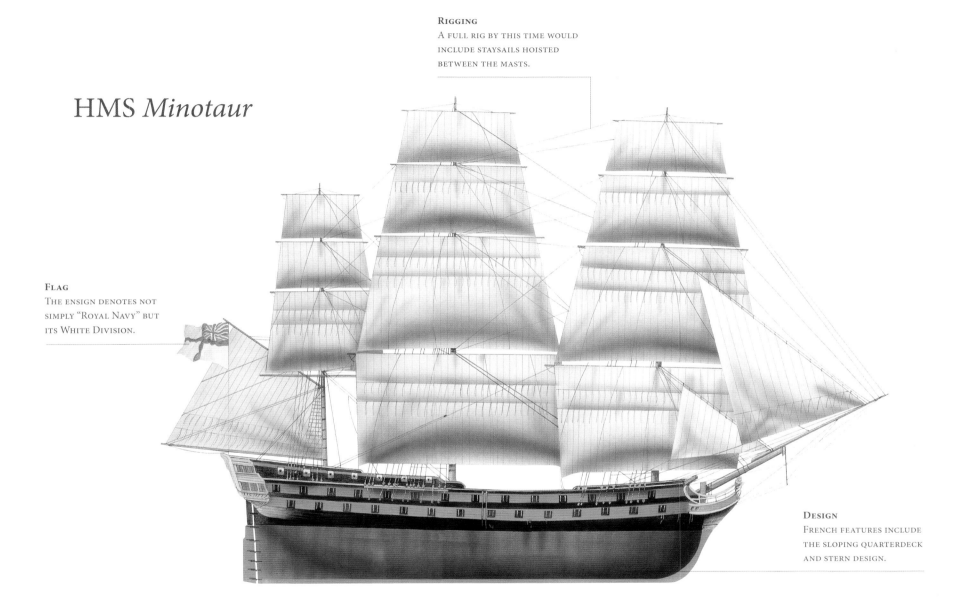

RIGGING
A FULL RIG BY THIS TIME WOULD INCLUDE STAYSAILS HOISTED BETWEEN THE MASTS.

FLAG
THE ENSIGN DENOTES NOT SIMPLY "ROYAL NAVY" BUT ITS WHITE DIVISION.

DESIGN
FRENCH FEATURES INCLUDE THE SLOPING QUARTERDECK AND STERN DESIGN.

HMS *Caesar* (1793)

AN 80-GUN SHIP WAS A RARITY IN THE ROYAL NAVY, WITH ONLY TWO IN SERVICE BETWEEN 1793 AND 1815 (THE OTHER BEING *FOUDROYANT*, OF 1798), AND *CAESAR*—CLASSED AS A THIRD-RATE— WAS A ONE-OFF DESIGN. IT WAS INVOLVED IN NUMEROUS BATTLES AND WAS THE FLAGSHIP OF SOME OF BRITAIN'S MOST DISTINGUISHED ADMIRALS, INCLUDING LORD HOWE, SIR JAMES SAUMAREZ, AND SIR RICHARD STRACHAN.

Designed by Sir Edward Hunt, with a French two-decker as his original model, *Caesar* was laid down at Plymouth Naval Dockyard on January 24, 1786 and launched on November 16, 1793. Under Captain Molloy it was the lead ship in Howe's fleet at the Battle of "The Glorious First of June" in 1794, but in the opening stages Molloy failed to obey the order to engage the enemy and was subsequently court-martialed and dismissed.

The *Caesar* was Admiral Cornwallis's flagship in the winter of 1794, and gave its best service as the flagship of independent squadrons. In 1801 it was engaged under Saumarez in the blockade of Brest, then deployed on the same duty off Cadiz where it fought with distinction in the two-stage action of Algeciras, against the French-Spanish ships of Admiral Linois, between July 6 and 13, 1801. In this battle Saumarez retrieved a British setback

in a night action on the 12th, and it resulted in the destruction of the 112-gun *Hermengildo* and *Real Carlos*.

Action against France

During a refit in 1803 additional bracing was applied to the hull, to reduce its tendency to hogging. Despite this Caesar had a reputation as a good sea boat. After Trafalgar, in November 1805, with a "flying squadron" of three other ships of the line under Commodore Strachan, it pursued Admiral Dumanoir's four ships of the line, and captured all of them on November 4, completing the rout of the Trafalgar campaign.

Caesar was then returned to blockading duties, off Rochefort, under Admiral Stopford. On February 23, 1809 it was engaged in the indecisive action against three French frigates known as the Battle of Les Sables-d'Olonne, and claimed as a victory by both sides.

In 1813 *Caesar* was withdrawn from active service and converted to an army clothing storeship at Plymouth. It was broken up in 1821.

SPECIFICATIONS

DISPLACEMENT: 1,992 tons (2,024 tonnes)

DIMENSIONS: 181 ft x 50 ft 6 in x 22 ft 11 in (55.1 m x 15.4 m x 7 m)

RIG: Three masts, full square rig

ARMAMENT: Thirty 32 pounders, thirty-two 24 pounders, eighteen 9 pounder guns

CREW: 719

HMS *Caesar*

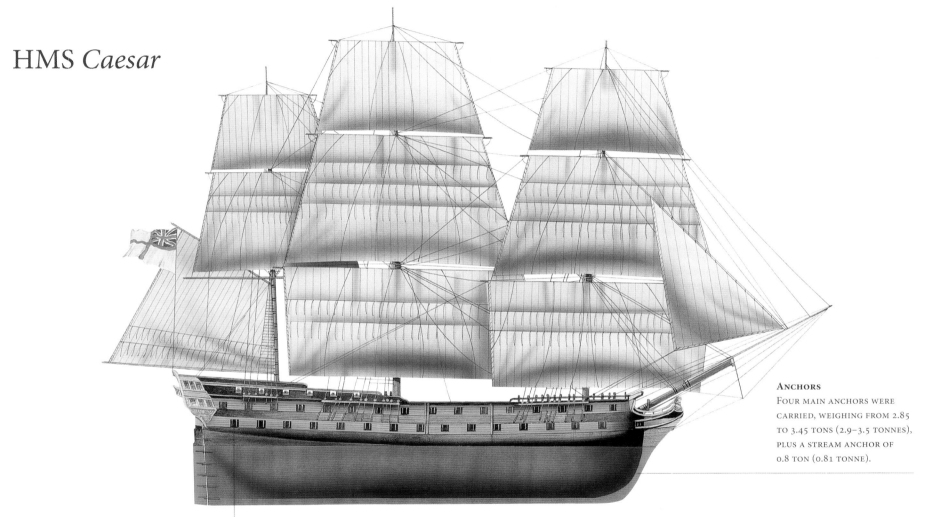

ANCHORS
FOUR MAIN ANCHORS WERE
CARRIED, WEIGHING FROM 2.85
TO 3.45 TONS (2.9–3.5 TONNES),
PLUS A STREAM ANCHOR OF
0.8 TON (0.81 TONNE).

GUNS
THE GUN ARRANGEMENT WAS: MAIN GUNDECK,
THIRTY 32 POUNDERS; UPPER GUNDECK, THIRTY-
TWO 24 POUNDERS; QUARTERDECK, FOURTEEN
9 POUNDERS; FORECASTLE FOUR 9 POUNDERS.

Montañes (1793)

LEADER OF A CLASS OF FOUR 74-80 GUN SHIPS OF THE LINE, ALL OF WHICH FOUGHT AT TRAFALGAR, *MONTAÑES* WAS FINANCED BY MONEY RAISED AMONG HILLTOWNS AND VILLAGES, HENCE THE NAME. AS USUAL WITH SPANISH SHIPS, IT HAD A SAINT'S NAME AS WELL: *SANTO TORIBIO DE MOGROBEJO.*

Julián Martín de Retamosa designed and supervised construction of *Montañes* at Ferrol, where the keel was laid in 1793 and launching was on November 24, 1793. Following the usual period of trials and shaking down, it was deployed to Mahón in the Balearic Islands to join Admiral Lángara's fleet. On March 30, 1795 it was one of the ships in action against eight French ships of the line and two frigates off Cape San Sebastian, and in June was assigned to Admiral de Alava's fleet at Cadiz.

On November 11 *Montañes* left Cadiz with a squadron bound for Callao, Peru, by way of Cape Horn: a dangerous voyage but successfully accomplished. In 1796 it crossed the Pacific to Manila. On leaving the Philippines on April 20, 1797 the squadron was struck by a hurricane, forcing its return to the Cavite base. In 1798 it was back at Cadiz, but made a further voyage to the Philippines in

1802–03, returning via the Cape of Good Hope and so being one of the comparatively few vessels of the period to circumnavigate the globe.

Refitted for Battle

Between March 16 and June 24, 1805, *Montañes* was given what was doubtless a much needed careen and the hull was coppered. It was also re-gunned, with 36 pounders replacing the twenty-eight 24 pounder cannons on the lower gun deck: the short time taken in the refit is expressive of the urgency of the times. Spain was under pressure from Napoleon to get its battle fleet into readiness.

On August 20, 1805, *Montañes* joined Villeneuve's Combined Fleet at Cadiz, and fought at Trafalgar on October 21. It successfully regained Cadiz but left again to help stragglers coming in, before entering La Carraca for repairs. On June 9, 1808 it took part in the Battle

of Cadiz and, after a run to Ferrol and back, was about to depart from Cadiz for Puerto Rico when its cable parted in a storm on March 7, 1810. It ran ashore and was set on fire by French troops. What remained of the *Montañes* was sold off on March 12, 1822.

SPECIFICATIONS

DISPLACEMENT: 2,763 tons (2,807 tonnes)

DIMENSIONS: 173 ft 6 in x 47 ft 3 in x 21 ft 10 in (52.9 m x 14.4 m x 6.65 m)

RIG: Three masts, full square rig

ARMAMENT: Twenty-eight 36 pounders, thirty 18 pounders, eight 8 pounder guns; ten 30 pounder obuses (1805)

CREW: 686

Montañes

CABINS
SOME ILLUSTRATIONS OF THE SHIP
SHOW A CABIN CONSTRUCTED ON
THE POOP DECK, BUT THIS WAS NOT
AN ORIGINAL FEATURE.

CAPSTAN
A CAPSTAN USUALLY EXTENDED THROUGH
TWO DECKS, ENABLING IT TO BE TURNED BY
MORE MEN: UP TO 200 MIGHT BE NEEDED.

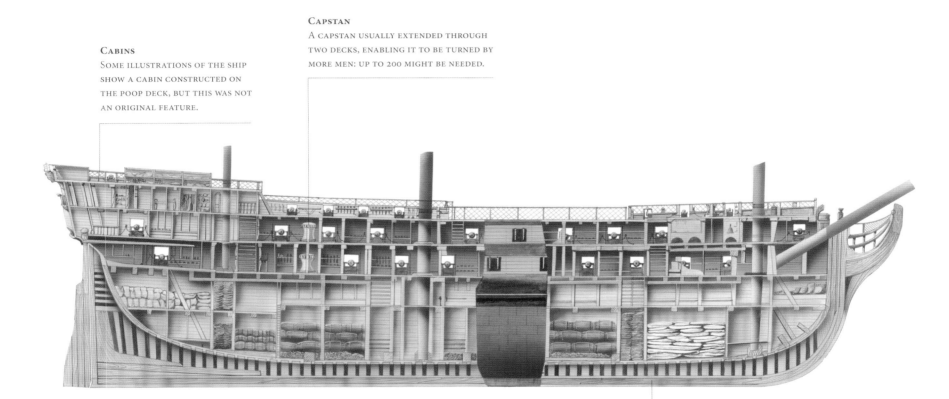

BEAM
MAXIMUM BEAM WAS AT WATERLEVEL, WITH A
DISTINCT TUMBLEHOME REDUCING TO ALMOST
VERTICALITY AT THE LEVEL OF THE BULWARKS.

HMS *Monmouth* (1796)

A 64-GUN THIRD-RATE, THE *MONMOUTH* OF 1796 WAS FOURTH TO CARRY THE NAME, MADE DISTINGUISHED BY THE SECOND, WHICH WAS LAUNCHED IN 1667 AND BROKEN UP 100 YEARS LATER. DURING AN ACTIVE CAREER IT WAS INVOLVED IN VIRTUALLY EVERY THEATER IN WHICH THE ROYAL NAVY WAS ENGAGED, FROM NORTH AMERICA TO INDIA. ITS LAST YEARS WERE SPENT AS A FLOATING WORKSHOP.

Monmouth was laid down as an East India Company ship, *Belmont*, built by Randalls of Rotherhithe but acquired for the Admiralty on July 14, 1795 and launched on April 23, 1796, with completion on October 31 of that year at Deptford. Like the previous *Monmouth*, a design modeled on that of HMS *Intrepid*, designed by Sir John Williams, it was a two-decker of 64 guns, but somewhat longer. Its first captain was William Carnegie, Earl of Northesk, who resigned his commission after the ship's crew was involved in the mutiny at the Nore anchorage in the Thames in May 1797.

Battles and Expeditions
Commander James Walker took over and *Monmouth* was with Admiral Duncan's fleet at the Battle of Camperdown on October 11, 1797, where it played a distinguished part, capturing the Dutch ships *Delft* and *Alkmaar*. *Monmouth* continued to serve with the North Sea fleet, patrolling the Dutch coast and capturing numerous small vessels, and in the summer of 1799 it gave support to the "Helder Expedition," an Anglo-Russian land campaign in North Holland.

In 1801 *Monmouth* was transferred to the Mediterranean Fleet for a year, then returned to the North Sea. On September 15, 1806 it left with a convoy for the East Indies, returning with another convoy in September 1808. Held in ordinary until August 1809, it was again in action against Holland in the Walcheren Expedition, and until 1815 continued on service in the southern North Sea, usually as an admiral's flagship.

Monmouth was laid up in ordinary at Woolwich in 1815, then converted to a sheer hulk or pontoon at Deptford, and was broken up in 1834. This ship should not be confused with its predecessor,

launched in 1772 and converted to a prison ship with the unlovely name HMS *Captivity*, which held prisoners of war (mostly French seamen) and which was broken up at Portsmouth in January 1818.

SPECIFICATIONS

DISPLACEMENT: 1,369 tons (1,391 tonnes)

DIMENSIONS: 173 ft 1 in x 43 ft 4 in x 19 ft 8 in (52.76 m x 13.2 m x 5.9 m)

RIG: Three masts, full square rig

ARMAMENT: Twenty-six 24 pounders, twenty-six 18 pounders, ten 4 pounders, two 9 pounder guns

CREW: 491

HMS *Monmouth*

SAILS
FIVE TIERS OF SAIL ARE NOW EVIDENT ON FORE- AND MAINMASTS OF SHIPS OF THE LINE.

ARMAMENT
THE TWO 9 POUNDER GUNS WERE MOUNTED IN THE FORECASTLE AS BOW-CHASERS.

CONVERSION
UNUSUALLY, MONMOUTH WAS LAID DOWN AS AN EAST INDIAMAN, AND BOUGHT AS A WARSHIP WHILE BUILDING. BUT EAST INDIAMEN WERE ARMED VESSELS, READILY CONVERTIBLE TO WARSHIPS.

USS *Constitution* (1797)

USS *CONSTITUTION* WAS SOLIDLY BUILT, BUT AT A TIME WHEN THE LIFE OF A MAN OF WAR WAS TWO OR THREE DECADES AT BEST—EVEN IF IT AVOIDED DESTRUCTION IN BATTLE OR SHIPWRECK— ITS CONSTRUCTORS WOULD HAVE BEEN AMAZED TO KNOW THAT THE SHIP WOULD STILL BE A COMMISSIONED VESSEL IN THE U.S. NAVY MORE THAN 200 YEARS AFTER ITS COMPLETION.

One of six frigates authorized by Congress on March 27, 1794, *Constitution* was designed by Joshua Humphreys and built by the Hartt Shipyard, Boston. It was a large frigate of 40 guns, twice the size and gunpower of mid-century frigates. Launched on October 21, 1797, it first put to sea on July 22, 1798 under Captain Samuel Nicholson, patrolling against French shipping between Cape Henry and the Florida coast.

It was then deployed as flagship on the Santo Domingo station until the end of the French War, when it was laid up in ordinary at Charlestown Navy Yard. Recommissioned in 1803, it sailed under Captain Edward Preble as flagship of a Mediterranean Squadron on August 14. The piratical activities of certain North African ports had affected U.S. shipping, and the squadron bombarded Tripoli on August 3–7, 1804. *Constitution* remained in the Mediterranean until November 1807, then returned to Boston for a refit and was decommissioned until August 1809 when it returned to service as flagship of the Atlantic Squadron. In 1811 it carried the U.S. Minister Joel Barlow to France, and in the course of the War of 1812–15 took five warships, including HMS *Guerrière* (49 guns), *Java* (38 guns), and *Cyane* (22 guns), as well as nine merchantmen as prizes or destroyed. A long period in ordinary followed until it was recommissioned in May 1821 for two Mediterranean cruises, ending in July 1828.

Rebuilt and Recommissioned

Inspection in 1830 found "Old Ironsides" unseaworthy and it was rebuilt at Boston in 1833. From 1833–55 it was on active service and circumnavigated the globe between March 1844 and September 1846. Decommissioned 1855–60, it was then used for training, and a further rebuild was undertaken at Philadelphia in 1871, after which it was again a training ship from 1877–82, then made a receiving ship at Portsmouth, New Hampshire. Scrapping was narrowly avoided in 1905. On July 1, 1931 *Constitution* was recommissioned and sailed around both U.S. coasts, returning to Boston on May 7, 1934. It is preserved at the former Charlestown Navy Yard, Boston.

SPECIFICATIONS

DISPLACEMENT: 2,200 tons (2,235 tonnes)

DIMENSIONS: 175 ft x 43 ft 6 in x 22 ft 6 in (53.3 m x 13.3 m x 6.9 m)

RIG: Three masts, square rig

ARMAMENT: Twenty-eight 24 pounders, ten 12 pounder guns

CREW: 450

USS *Constitution*

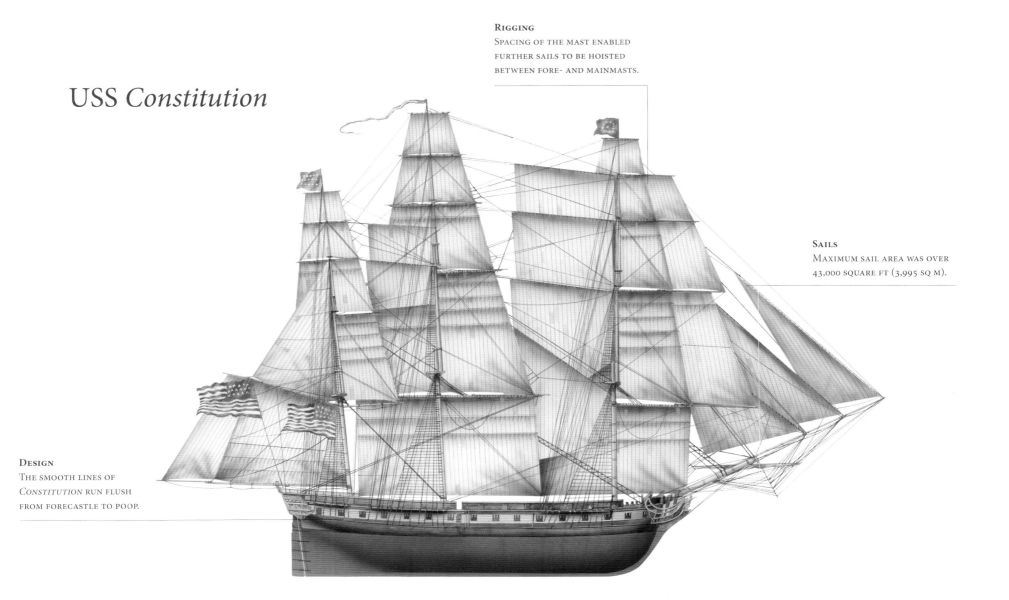

RIGGING
SPACING OF THE MAST ENABLED FURTHER SAILS TO BE HOISTED BETWEEN FORE- AND MAINMASTS.

SAILS
MAXIMUM SAIL AREA WAS OVER 43,000 SQUARE FT (3,995 SQ M).

DESIGN
THE SMOOTH LINES OF *CONSTITUTION* RUN FLUSH FROM FORECASTLE TO POOP.

HMS *Foudroyant* (1798)

FOUDROYANT ("THUNDERER") BECAME A ROYAL NAVY NAME WITH THE CAPTURE OF THE FRENCH *FOUDROYANT* BY HMS *MONMOUTH* IN 1758 AND ITS INCORPORATION INTO THE BRITISH FLEET. LIKE ITS PREDECESSOR, THE BRITISH-BUILT SECOND-RATE OF 1798 WAS OF 80 GUNS ON TWO DECKS, ONE OF ONLY TWO SUCH SHIPS IN THE ROYAL NAVY AT THAT TIME.

Laid down at Plymouth Navy Yard in May 1789 and launched on March 31, 1798, the ship was commissioned on May 25 under Captain Thomas Byard. It was designed by Sir John Henslow, Surveyor of the Navy, on similar lines to its namesake. At 184 ft 8 in (56.3 m) it was longer than most British first-rates.

Its active service began with the action off Donegal, Ireland, on October 12, 1798, when the French ship of the line *Hoche* (74 guns) and four frigates were captured. *Foudroyant* was then deployed to the Mediterranean as Admiral Lord Keith's flagship, then from June 1799 it was Nelson's flagship, captained by Thomas Hardy, taking part in the recapture of Naples and Malta from the French. In 1800 it participated in the capture of *Le Généreux* and *Guillaume Tell* on February 18 and March 31, both of which had escaped the Battle at Aboukir Bay.

Blockade and Escort Duty

After a major refit at Plymouth, it remained in ordinary for a few months before being recommissioned on June 11, 1803, when it joined the Channel Fleet, engaged primarily on blockading the ports of Brest and Rochefort. This was not entirely successful as two French divisions broke out from Brest in December 1805.

From March 1808 *Foudroyant* was the flagship of Admiral Sir Sydney Smith on a convoy-escort cruise to Argentina and Brazil. Paid off in Plymouth on November 30, 1812, it was used as a depot ship then converted as a training ship in 1862 and used in this form until 1892.

Foudroyant was due to be broken up in 1892 but was bought as a private speculation for £20,000 as a memento of Nelson's time and as a training ship for boys, but was wrecked off the northwest coast of England near Blackpool on June 16, 1897. It was unsalvageable, but much of its wood and copper was retrieved and sold as souvenir items.

SPECIFICATIONS

DISPLACEMENT: 2,054 tons (2,087 tonnes)

DIMENSIONS: 184 ft 8 in x 50 ft 6 in x 23 ft (56.3 m x 25.4 m x 7 m)

RIG: Three masts, full square rig

ARMAMENT: Thirty 32 pounders, thirty-two 24 pounders, eighteen 12 pounder guns; two 32 pounders, six 18 pounder carronades

CREW: 650

HMS *Foudroyant*

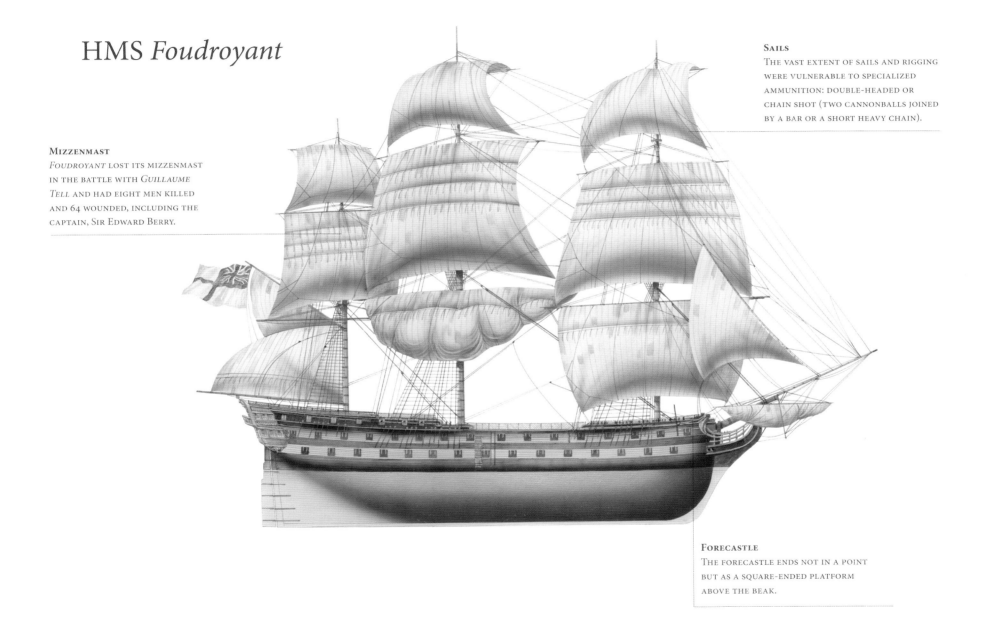

SAILS
THE VAST EXTENT OF SAILS AND RIGGING WERE VULNERABLE TO SPECIALIZED AMMUNITION: DOUBLE-HEADED OR CHAIN SHOT (TWO CANNONBALLS JOINED BY A BAR OR A SHORT HEAVY CHAIN).

MIZZENMAST
FOUDROYANT LOST ITS MIZZENMAST IN THE BATTLE WITH *GUILLAUME TELL* AND HAD EIGHT MEN KILLED AND 64 WOUNDED, INCLUDING THE CAPTAIN, SIR EDWARD BERRY.

FORECASTLE
THE FORECASTLE ENDS NOT IN A POINT BUT AS A SQUARE-ENDED PLATFORM ABOVE THE BEAK.

USS *Essex* (1799)

THE FAR-TRAVELED USS *ESSEX* WAS THE FIRST AMERICAN WARSHIP TO PASS THE EQUATOR AND THE CAPE OF GOOD HOPE. IT SERVED IN THE MEDITERRANEAN SEA AGAINST THE BARBARY PIRATES AND PLAYED A DISTINGUISHED PART IN THE WAR OF 1812–15 UNTIL IT WAS CAPTURED AT VALPARAISO, CHILE, BY BRITISH FRIGATES AND SUBSEQUENTLY BROUGHT INTO THE ROYAL NAVY.

Named for Essex County, Massachusetts, which raised the necessary $139,362, *Essex* was built at Salem by Enos Briggs and launched on September 30, 1799. Presented to the U.S. Navy on December 17, it was first captained by Edward Preble. Sent to escort a convoy home from Indonesia, it passed the Cape of Good Hope in March and August 1800. Its next cruise, under Commander William Bainbridge, was to the Mediterranean in the campaign against pirate ships and, with a return for refitting at Washington Navy Yard in 1802, was engaged there until 1806. Between April 27 and May 13, 1805, under Commodore Samuel Barron, it lent support to land forces in the Battle of Derne against pirates. From 1806 to February 1809 it was held in ordinary at Washington.

Recommissioned in 1809 and equipped with forty 32 pounder carronades, it served in home waters until the War of 1812, when it saw much action in the Atlantic before rounding Cape Horn into the Pacific, under Captain (future Admiral) David Porter. In total *Essex* took 23 prizes.

War of 1812 and Capture

In January 1814, lying in Valparaiso Roads, *Essex* was blocked by the British frigate *Phoebe* (36 guns) and sloop *Cherub* (18 guns). Porter attempted to break out but was forced back by a storm. Following him into Chilean territorial waters, *Phoebe* and *Cherub* opened fire and a stiff battle ensued. After two-and-a-half hours, with 155 men lost, Porter struck his flag.

Repaired by the British, *Essex* was sailed to England and taken into the Royal Navy as HMS *Essex*, re-gunned with twenty-six 18 pounders on the gun deck and twelve 32 pounder carronades on the quarterdeck, also two 9 pounder long guns and two 32 pounder carronades on the forecastle. In October 1823 it was hulked at Cork, Ireland, as a prison ship, and from 1833 it served the same purpose at Kingston (now Dun Laoghaire). It was sold on June 6, 1837.

SPECIFICATIONS

DISPLACEMENT: 850 tons (864 tonnes)

DIMENSIONS: 140 ft x 31 ft x 12 ft 3 in (42.7 m x 9.4 m x 3.73 m)

RIG: Three masts, full square rig

ARMAMENT: Twenty-six 12 pounders, ten 6 pounder guns (1799)

CREW: 300

USS *Essex*

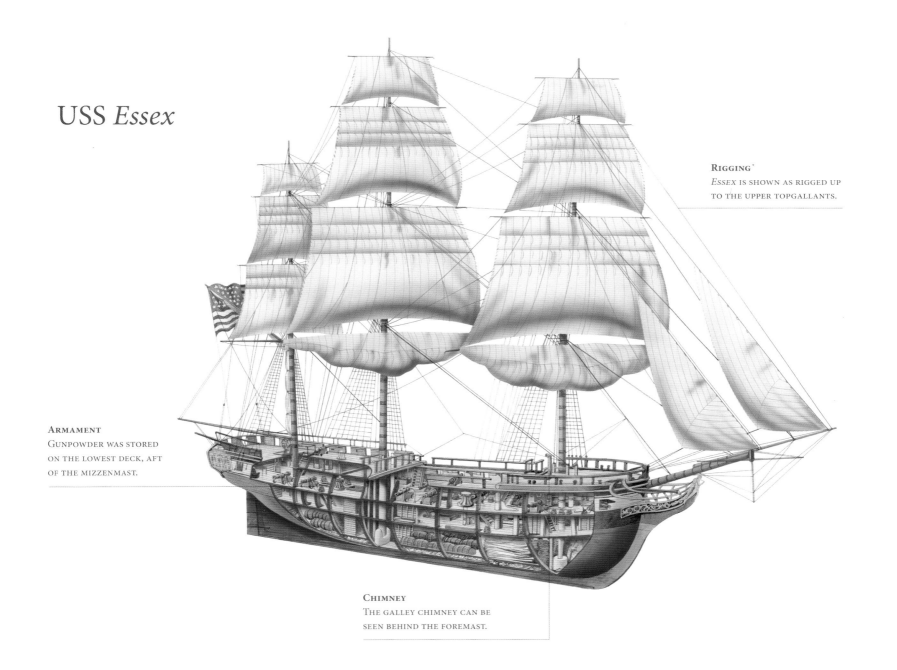

RIGGING
ESSEX IS SHOWN AS RIGGED UP
TO THE UPPER TOPGALLANTS.

ARMAMENT
GUNPOWDER WAS STORED
ON THE LOWEST DECK, AFT
OF THE MIZZENMAST.

CHIMNEY
THE GALLEY CHIMNEY CAN BE
SEEN BEHIND THE FOREMAST.

Chasse-marée *(1800)*

CARRYING A LARGE EXTENT OF SAIL ON THREE OR SOMETIMES TWO MASTS, THE *CHASSE-MARÉE* ("TIDE-CHASER") WAS THE FRENCH EQUIVALENT OF THE AMERICAN SCHOONER AND THE BRITISH CUTTER. CAPABLE OF GREAT SPEED, WHICH MADE IT EXTREMELY SUITABLE AS A SMUGGLERS' BOAT, IT COULD ALSO OPERATE AS A PRIVATEER, WHICH COULD CAPTURE MERCHANT VESSELS BUT WAS FAST AND AGILE ENOUGH TO ESCAPE MOST WARSHIPS.

As the name suggests, the privateer was a private-enterprise vessel that could legally operate against an enemy in time of war by obtaining a certificate, or letter of marque, from the relevant Admiralty.

The attraction for its owners and crew was the value of prize money that could be obtained by capturing a ship and bringing it into port. They were especially numerous where concentrations of shipping could be found, as in the English Channel, off the Dutch coast, and at the entry to the Kattegat.

Military Use

The *chasse-marée* had developed as a fast vessel to carry fresh-caught fish to port, but its value as a swift, elusive craft led to its conversion to military use, with bracing in the prow to support a cannon. A relatively large crew was needed to work the ship and to provide a prize crew on a captured vessel. Sometimes a chasse-marée could be used in subtle tactics, as when *Rebecca*, of Brest, with four light swivel guns and seven men, was caught by the British privateer *Black Joke* on April 27, 1799. A naval officer on board had letters about a fleet deployment to Ireland, but these turned out to be a ruse to divert British attention from a French break-out to the south.

Adaptations for War

By around 1798 the old fishing craft had been adapted to use in war. The masts were raked back, with a long bowsprit and a bumpkin boom at the stern, to maximize the extent of sail. The largest *chasse-marées* carried a lug topsail on the mainmast.

Sailing into the wind, the weatherly qualities of a *chasse-marée* made it hard to beat, but with a following wind it could be run down by a frigate or sloop of war.

Their shallow draft and crews' familiarity with the coastline also helped survival against more powerful ships.

SPECIFICATIONS

DISPLACEMENT: 50 tons (50 tonnes)

DIMENSIONS: c. 75 ft x 20 ft x 4 ft (c. 22.8 m x 6 m x 1.2 m)

RIG: Three or two masts, lug rig, often with topsails

ARMAMENT: From one to six light cannons, usually 3 pounders

CREW: c. 50–60

Chasse-marée

STERN
A LONG BUMPKIN OR
SPANKER-BOOM WAS FITTED.

LODGING
VIRTUALLY NO ACCOMMODATION WAS
PROVIDED: THESE VESSELS WERE INTENDED
FOR QUICK IN-AND-OUT ACTIONS.

ARMAMENT
SMALLER BOATS HAD A CANNON FITTED
IN A REINFORCED PROW; LARGER ONES
MIGHT HAVE LATERAL GUNS.

Dhow *(1800)*

NOT KNOWN IN ARABIC, THE TERM "DHOW" FIRST APPEARS IN ENGLISH AROUND 1802, APPLIED TO A SMALL SAILING VESSEL, USUALLY SINGLE-MASTED, AND WITH A LATEEN OR SETTEE RIG, WORKING IN THE PERSIAN GULF, RED SEA, AND INDIAN OCEAN. SOME MADE VOYAGES FROM AS FAR AS ZANZIBAR TO MALAYA. BUT CRAFT OF THE DHOW TYPE HAD BEEN IN EXISTENCE FOR HUNDREDS OF YEARS.

Indigenous to the coasts of the Arabian Peninsula, India, and East Africa, the earliest dhows were simple dugouts with teak planks sewn to their sides to form a hull. Gradually, larger vessels evolved, based on a keel to which additional planking was sewn, and originally steered by a steering oar until the rudder came into use. Dhow types are generally defined by their hull shape. They include the *ghanjah*, a large vessel with a curved stem and a sloping, ornately carved transom.

This type of stern is believed to have been introduced from the 1500s when Portuguese and other European ships began to appear in these waters. Prior to that, dhows had pointed sterns as well as sharply raked stems. The *baghlah*, common through the 19th century, was the traditional deep-sea vessel, and by 1800 would often have a raised poop deck. The *boum* or boom was of more traditional build, double-ended with both stem- and sternposts (later versions often had bowsprits), as was the *sambuk*, a smaller variant often used as a platform by pearl divers.

Masts were relatively short, raked forwards, stepped into the keel timber, and fitted with a very wide yard normally built up from four or five separate pieces. Coir rope was used for the rigging. The lateen sail was of quadrilateral, not triangular, form and is more correctly termed a settee sail. Iron nail fastenings began to supplant sewn planks from the mid-16th century, although sewn hulls were still found in the 19th century.

Merchant Vessels

Dhows were often built on open beaches rather than in yards, using basic tools. Larger dhows could be used for military purposes, carrying troops and light guns, but essentially they were merchant vessels, engaged in the import-export trade along the Gulf and Indian Ocean coasts, and carrying cargoes of timber, fish, dates, cloves, grain, and general goods. They may still be seen, but no longer in the many hundreds visible around 1800.

SPECIFICATIONS

DISPLACEMENT: c. 125–150 tons (c. 127–152 tonnes)

DIMENSIONS: c. 70 ft x 14 ft x 5 ft (c. 21.3 m x 4.3 m x 1.5 m)

RIG: One to three masts, lateen or settee rig

ARMAMENT: Not usually armed but could mount one to six light cannons

CREW: 10–50

Dhow

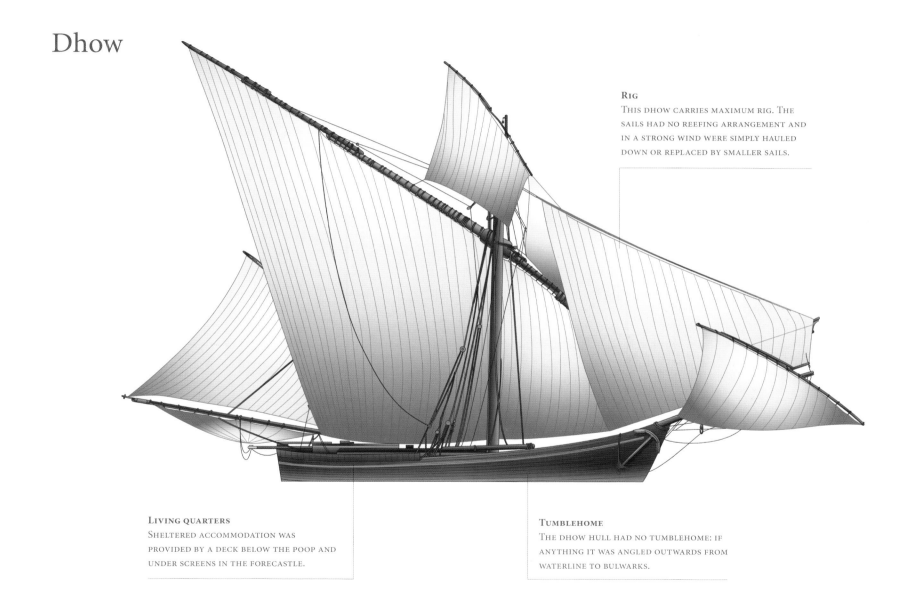

RIG
THIS DHOW CARRIES MAXIMUM RIG. THE
SAILS HAD NO REEFING ARRANGEMENT AND
IN A STRONG WIND WERE SIMPLY HAULED
DOWN OR REPLACED BY SMALLER SAILS.

LIVING QUARTERS
SHELTERED ACCOMMODATION WAS
PROVIDED BY A DECK BELOW THE POOP AND
UNDER SCREENS IN THE FORECASTLE.

TUMBLEHOME
THE DHOW HULL HAD NO TUMBLEHOME: IF
ANYTHING IT WAS ANGLED OUTWARDS FROM
WATERLINE TO BULWARKS.

Pirate Junk *(1800)*

THE JUNK, ITS NAME STEMMING FROM AN OLD CHINESE WORD FOR BOAT OR SHIP, HAS A VERY LONG HISTORY. THE NAME DOES NOT GIVE MORE THAN A GENERAL INDICATION OF THE TYPE OF VESSEL: OF TRADITIONAL APPEARANCE WITH A BUILT-OUT PLATFORM BOW, A CENTRAL WELL, AND A HIGH POOP, CARRYING FROM ONE TO THREE MASTS WITH SAILS DIVIDED HORIZONTALLY.

The longevity of the junk is explained by its success: although the upper hull design may look cumbrous, its underwater lines are fine and the sail arrangement makes it fast, easily controlled, and capable of sailing very close to the wind. The traditional hull is built of softwood planks, edge-on, with several separate internal compartments that improve buoyancy and preventing flooding. Shallow draft could be compensated for by leeboards or centerboards. Size varied from small single-masted vessels to oceangoing ships over 200 ft (60 m) long or more and with up to eight masts.

Pirate Attacks

Piracy in the seas off China was endemic, particularly at times of weak government. A large three-masted junk made a very effective pirate ship, and pirates often combined in fleets to attack merchant vessels sailing in convoy or to extort payment for freedom to proceed. It could carry a large number of armed pirates, and could also be armed with from eight to ten small cannons. By the end of the 18th century, as world trade routes were becoming firmly established and busier, the British government in particular sought to curb pirate activities.

The establishment of naval stations and the use of naval escorts brought a rapid diminution in pirate attacks by around 1810, although they continued past mid-century. On August 4, 1855 at Kowloon, Hong Kong, HMS *Rattler* and USS *Powhatan* fought a battle with 14 large pirate junks and 22 smaller ones, which had seized several merchant ships. The larger junks were armed with cannons. *Rattler* and *Powhatan* put out their boats, each armed with a howitzer or small cannon, to spread the attack. In total 14 junks were destroyed while others fled the scene, and it was estimated that 500 pirates were killed or wounded, and around 1,000 were taken prisoner, while nine American and British sailors were killed. The action, known as the Battle of Ty-ho Bay, reduced the level of piracy but did not kill off the pirate culture.

SPECIFICATIONS

DISPLACEMENT: 20 tons (20.3 tonnes) upwards

DIMENSIONS: c. 90 ft x 24 ft x 6 ft (c. 27.4 m x 7.3 m x 1.8 m)

RIG: Two or three masts, junk rig

ARMAMENT: Eight to ten small cannons

CREW: 20–60

Pirate Junk

SAILS
THE JUNK SAIL IS DIVIDED BY RIGID MEMBERS
OR BATTENS, WHICH EXTEND IT FORWARD OF
ITS MAST.

POOP DECK
THE HIGH POOP DECK MADE
FOR A BETTER FORWARD VIEW
AND FACILITATED BOARDING
OF MERCHANT SHIPS.

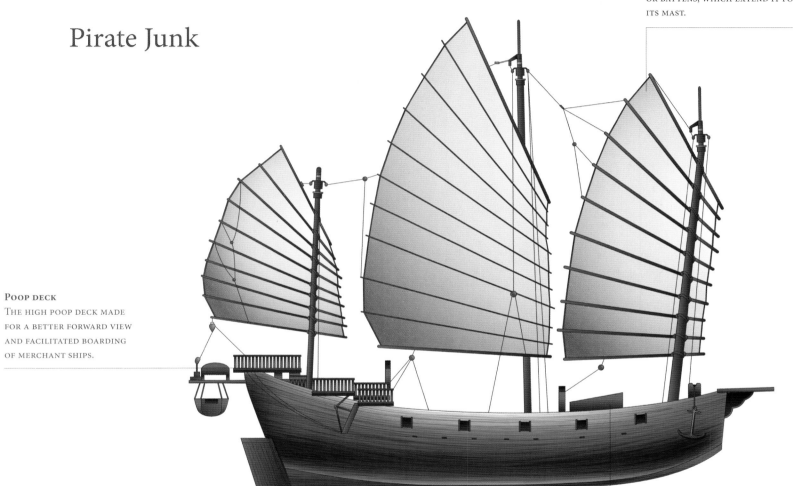

LODGING
BAMBOO DECKHOUSES COULD BE
RAPIDLY PUT UP FOR SHELTER.

Xebec *(1800)*

ALWAYS ASSOCIATED WITH THE "BARBARY PIRATES," THE XEBEC WAS DEVELOPED FROM THE LATE
17TH INTO THE 19TH CENTURY. POWERED BOTH BY WIND AND OARS, IT WAS A VERSATILE CRAFT IN
TERMS OF HANDLING, AND PROVED IDEAL FOR ONE PURPOSE—TO CHASE AND CAPTURE MERCHANT
CRAFT IN THE MEDITERRANEAN SHIPPING LANES.

The xebec began as a merchant vessel but in the 18th century was already being used as a naval craft by both Spain and France, and as a pirate ship by the corsairs of the North African coast. In these forms they carried guns and were comparable in force to a sloop or a light pre-1750 frigate. By 1800 the Spanish Navy had large xebec-frigates of 600 tons (609.6 tonnes), one of which, *El Gamo*, with 32 guns and over 300 men, was captured by the British sloop HMS *Speedy* of only 14 guns and with a crew of 54, on May 6, 1801.

The typical Barbary xebec was, however, considerably smaller than *El Gamo*: a ship of distinctive appearance, with a built-out stern platform, sometimes also at the bow, a forward-raked foremast, and a lateen rig. There was also a modified rig, the *polacca* or polacre, with square sails mounted on the foremast. The striped sails identified them from a distance. An important feature were the oars, nine on each side, which enabled the xebec to pull towards a victim that was becalmed or moving slowly in a light wind. The xebec had shallow draft, enabling it to run close inshore if pursued by a larger ship, and fine underwater lines which gave it a good turn of speed.

Ocean Raiders

The xebec was the standard vessel of the lawless pirate groups operating from Algiers, Tunis, and Tripoli under the protection of local governors. At times these Barbary corsairs would raid as far as southern England, although the Mediterranean was by far their main scene of activity. Slave trading was their main activity, although they routinely plundered any vessel they caught. By the 19th century they rarely attacked ships of the major European powers, but considered American vessels as safe game until the United States dispatched powerful frigate squadrons that bombarded their harbors and could deal at long range with the xebecs. By 1815 they were much less of a threat and by 1830 the French conquest of Algiers finally ended their depredations.

SPECIFICATIONS

DISPLACEMENT: c. 190 tons (c. 193 tonnes)

DIMENSIONS: 103 ft 9 in x 22 ft x 8 ft 2 in (31 m x 6.7 m x 2.5 m) (typical)

RIG: Three masts, lateen rig

PROPULSION: Sails and 18 oars

ARMAMENT: Fifteen to eighteen 12 pounder guns

CREW: 24 seamen

Xebec

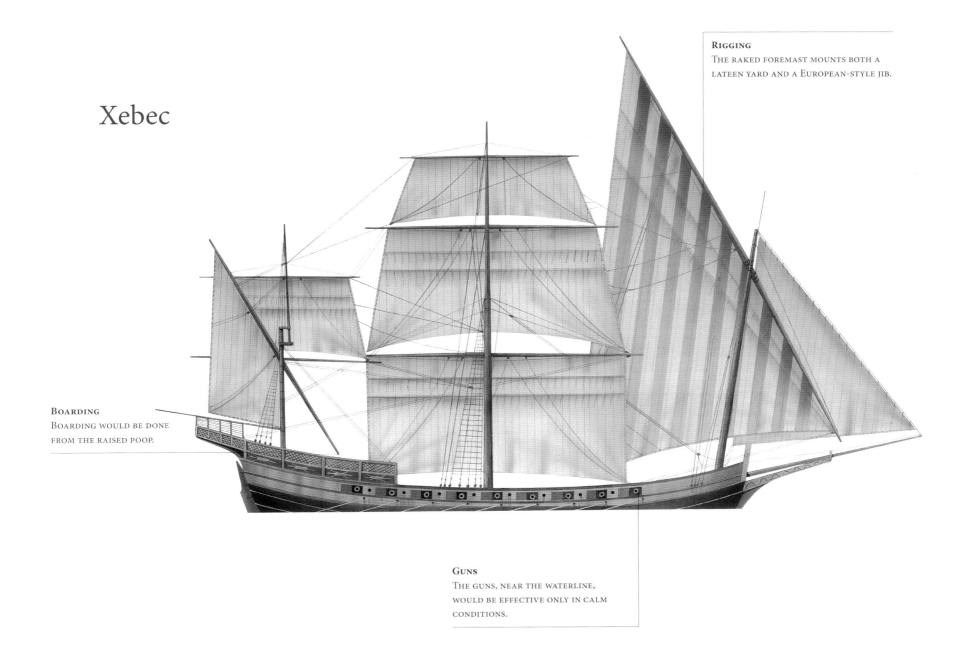

RIGGING
THE RAKED FOREMAST MOUNTS BOTH A
LATEEN YARD AND A EUROPEAN-STYLE JIB.

BOARDING
BOARDING WOULD BE DONE
FROM THE RAISED POOP.

GUNS
THE GUNS, NEAR THE WATERLINE,
WOULD BE EFFECTIVE ONLY IN CALM
CONDITIONS.

Bucentaure *(1803)*

THE FRENCH NAVY MADE FAR MORE USE OF THE 80-GUN TWO-DECKER THAN THE BRITISH, AND *BUCENTAURE* WAS THE FIRST OF A CLASS OF 16 LAUNCHED BETWEEN 1803 AND 1815, WITH A FURTHER FIVE UP TO 1824. ON OCTOBER 21, 1805, IT LED THE COMBINED FLEET OF FRANCE AND SPAIN FROM CADIZ AND PUT UP A GALLANT FIGHT IN THE BATTLE OF TRAFALGAR.

*B*ucentaure was laid down at Toulon in November 1802, launched on July 13, 1803, and commissioned in January 1804 under Captain Jean-Jacques Magendie. Its name commemorates the French conquest of Venice in May 1797—the state barge of the Doge of Venice was *Bucintoro*. Jacques-Noël Sané designed the class, which some experts consider to have been the finest ships of the line ever built. Longer than 74-gun three-deckers, as well as able to fire a heavier broadside, they were also faster and handled better to windward: always a weak point of the high-sided three-decker.

It was not the quality of its ships that put the French Navy at a disadvantage against the British, but the poor condition of the stores and material supplied, and the inadequate drilling of their crews. *Bucentaure's* first action was in the indecisive battle of Cape Finisterre

on July 22, 1805, when 20 French and Spanish ships under Admiral Villeneuve met 15 British ships of the line under Admiral Calder. Villeneuve's fleet lost two ships but made it to Cadiz safely; although he claimed a victory, Calder was court-martialed and severely reprimanded.

Battle of Trafalgar

Three months later Vice Admiral Nelson accomplished at Cape Trafalgar what Calder had failed to do, destroying the Combined Fleet. *Bucentaure* was central in the French-Spanish line and the British flagship HMS Victory cut across Villeneuve's just behind *Bucentaure*, firing a devastating broadside through the transom. In a few minutes *Bucentaure*, *Victory*, *Indomptable*, and HMS *Temeraire* were firing broadsides at close quarters.

With its decks piled with wreckage and all three masts fallen, *Bucentaure* surrendered to HMS *Conqueror* and

Villeneuve and Magendie were taken prisoner. *Conqueror* took the unsailable French flagship under tow, but the line parted and the French crew were able to overcome the British prize crew. In the storm that blew up, the dismasted ship was blown onto a reef in Cadiz Bay and sank, with only a handful of survivors.

SPECIFICATIONS

DISPLACEMENT: 1,455 tons (1,604 tonnes)

DIMENSIONS: 194 ft 6 in x 50 ft 3 in x 25 ft 6 in (59.3 m x 15.3 m x 7.8 m)

RIG: Three masts, full square rig

ARMAMENT: Thirty 36 pounders, thirty-two 24 pounders, eighteen 12 pounder guns; six 36 pounder howitzers

CREW: 866

Bucentaure

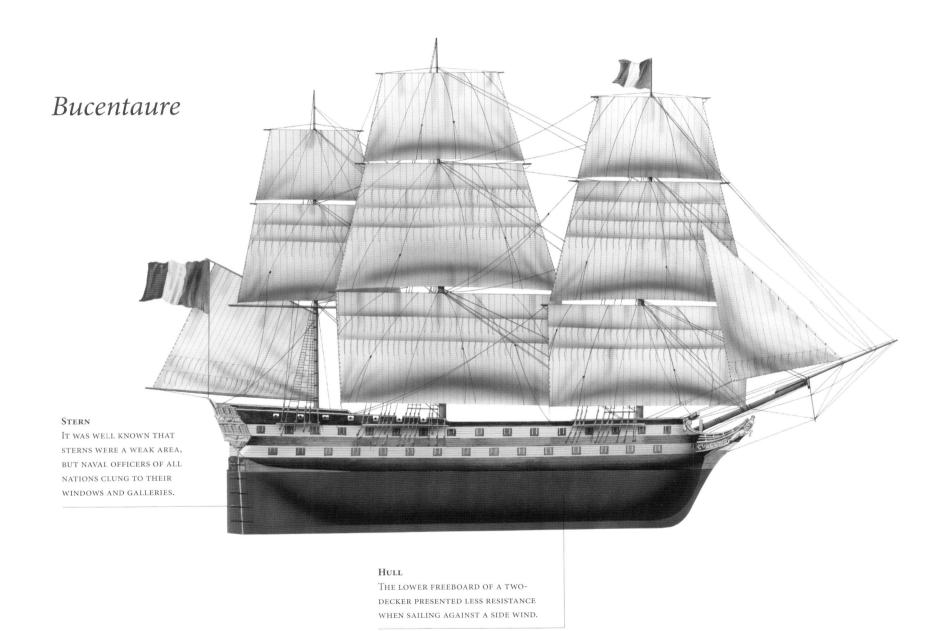

STERN
IT WAS WELL KNOWN THAT STERNS WERE A WEAK AREA, BUT NAVAL OFFICERS OF ALL NATIONS CLUNG TO THEIR WINDOWS AND GALLERIES.

HULL
THE LOWER FREEBOARD OF A TWO-DECKER PRESENTED LESS RESISTANCE WHEN SAILING AGAINST A SIDE WIND.

HMS *Euryalus* (1803)

ONE OF THE MOST FAMOUS OF THE BRITISH FRIGATES, WHICH AS A GROUP WERE DESCRIBED AS "THE EYES OF THE FLEET," *EURYALUS* WAS BRIEFLY THE FLAGSHIP AT TRAFALGAR WHEN ADMIRAL COLLINGWOOD SHIFTED HIS FLAG TO IT FROM THE HEAVILY DAMAGED *ROYAL SOVEREIGN*.

Launched at Buckler's Hard in 1803, its first captain was the Hon. Henry Blackwood, an able and ambitious officer. In 1805 *Euryalus* was part of the squadron off Cadiz, then returned to England, and escorted HMS *Victory* in early October back to the Spanish coast and to the rendezvous with Collingwood's blockading fleet. As the main fleet moved off towards Gibraltar, *Euryalus* remained on watch off Cadiz. Its lookouts saw the Combined Fleet emerging and Blackwood raced to pass on the news. At the Battle of Trafalgar it led a line of smaller ships to windward of Nelson's weather line, and after the fighting it took *Royal Sovereign* in tow.

Mediterranean Operations and the War of 1812

In July 1809 *Euryalus* was one of the ships sent to support the "Walcheren Expedition": an unsuccessful attempt to start a land campaign against Napoleon. It made numerous captures, including the *Etoile* (14 guns) off Cherbourg in November 1809. Deployed to the Mediterranean on April 26, 1810 it joined its former captain, now Commodore, Blackwood, off Toulon, and was in the Mediterranean through to 1814, hunting privateers and engaged in commerce raiding. In May 1813, it and HMS *Berwick* captured the French naval xebec *Fortune* (14 guns), destroyed nine and captured 14 of a French convoy of 23 coasting ships. Now commanded by Captain Charles Napier it sailed in June 1814 as one of the escorts of a Bermuda convoy, and then joined in operations off the coast of Maryland in the War of 1812–15. It sailed into the Potomac River in August–September of 1814, only 10 miles (16 km) or so below Washington, firing at shore installations, and attacked Baltimore. Napier issued a personal challenge to Captain Charles Gordon of the U.S. frigate *Constellation*, which was accepted, but the end of the war came before the duel could be arranged.

Its final service was as a prison hulk at Plymouth and then Gibraltar. A new *Euryalus* was launched in 1853 and the old ship was renamed *Africa*. It was sold for breaking in 1860.

SPECIFICATIONS

DISPLACEMENT: 946 tons (961 tonnes)

DIMENSIONS: 145 ft x 38 ft x 14 ft (44.2 m x 11.6 m x 4.27 m)

RIG: Three masts, square rig

ARMAMENT: Twenty-six 18 pounder guns, fourteen 32 pounder guns, two 9 pounder carronades

CREW: 264

HMS *Euryalus*

FORECASTLE GUNS
FOUR GUNS WERE MOUNTED IN THE
FORECASTLE: TWO 32 POUNDER
CARRONADES AND TWO LONG-
BARRELLED 9 POUNDERS.

HDMS *Christian VII* *(1803)*

FLAGSHIP OF THE DANISH NAVY, THIS BIG 90-GUN TWO-DECKER SHIP WAS THE MASTERPIECE OF THE DANISH DESIGNER, FRANTZ HOHLENBERG. BUT ITS DANISH SERVICE WAS BRIEF AND UNEVENTFUL BEFORE IT WAS CAPTURED BY THE BRITISH IN 1807, TO BECOME A HIGHLY EFFECTIVE UNIT OF THE BRITISH NAVY.

Built at the Nyholm Dockyard and launched in 1803, *Christian VII* appears to have gone straight into ordinary, despite a state of war with Great Britain. Under Admiral James Gambier, on board HMS *Prince of Wales*, a large British fleet appeared off Copenhagen on September 2, 1807, and bombarded the city until it surrendered.

The British then took over the naval dockyard. Every usable ship and piece of equipment was carried off: two 80-gun ships; twelve 74-gun, one 64-gun, two 38-gun, and two 36-gun frigates, and more than a dozen smaller craft. Virtually the whole Danish Navy was conscripted into the British fleet. Gambier had a great interest in ship design and ensured that the Danish ships were well studied.

Refit for the British Navy

In British service the ship was classed as a second-rate with guns reduced to 80, and a main armament of British 32 pounders rather than Danish 36 pounders. The broadside discharge was reduced from 1,236 lb (560 kg) to 1,029 lb (466 kg). But this certainly reduced strains on the hull which would have been exacerbated by the blockade duty and heavily armed patrolling required of Royal Navy ships.

Having completed refitting at Portsmouth, at a cost of £27,230 including new guns, *Christian VII* served in the North Sea where its modest draft (designed for the Baltic) helped, as well as the English Channel.

The sailing qualities of *Christian VII* were very much admired by British officers, and a new 80-gun design was ordered in 1810 based on the Danish ship, although omitting perhaps the most original feature: the stern design, which was intended to accommodate guns that could fire over a wide field against approaching gunboats or similar craft, by narrowing the transom and dispensing with the stern and quarter galleries. To British officers, this reduced their living space and was unacceptable.

Christian VII was the flagship of three admirals and had six captains from 1808 to 1813. Taken off active service in December 1813 it was refitted as a quarantine ship at Chatham Dockyard. Finally decommissioned in 1834, it was broken up at Chatham in March 1838.

SPECIFICATIONS

DISPLACEMENT: 2,128 tons (2,162 tonnes)

DIMENSIONS: 187 ft 2 in x 50 ft 10 in x 21 ft 7 in (57 m x 15 m x 6.58 m)

RIG: Three masts, full square rig

ARMAMENT: Thirty 32 pounders, thirty-two 18 pounder guns; twelve 32 pounders, two 18 pounders, four 12 pounder carronades (from 1810)

CREW: 670

HDMS *Christian VII*

STERN

THE STERN DESIGN ENABLED GUNS TO BEAR AFT BUT WAS NOT POPULAR WITH NAVAL OFFICERS. SOME CRITICIZED HOHLENBERG, THE DESIGNER, FOR HIS LACK OF SEA EXPERIENCE.

DRAFT

THE RELATIVELY SHALLOW DRAFT WAS TO ALLOW FOR OPERATIONS ALONG THE BALTIC COASTS, WITH THEIR MANY SANDBANKS AND LAGOONS.

BROADSIDE

WHEN RE-GUNNED BY THE BRITISH NAVY, THE SHIP'S BROADSIDE DISCHARGE WAS REDUCED FROM 1236 LB (560 KG) TO 1029 LB (466 KG).

HMS *Hibernia* (1804)

IN THE FIRST DECADE OF THE 19TH CENTURY ONLY TWO FIRST-RATES WERE ADDED TO THE BRITISH NAVY, *HIBERNIA* IN 1805 AND HMS *CALEDONIA* IN 1809, DESPITE THE FACT THAT FOR MOST OF THE DECADE A MAJOR WAR—OR INDEED, SEVERAL WARS—WAS GOING ON. IN 1804, WHEN *HIBERNIA* WAS LAUNCHED, THERE WERE SIX SHIPS OF 100 GUNS OR MORE IN ACTIVE SERVICE AND ONE UNDER REPAIRS.

Ordered on December 9, 1790, *Hibernia*, second Royal Navy ship of the name, was not laid down at Plymouth Naval Dockyard until November 1797, and launched seven years after that, on November 17, 1804. Even allowing for the slow assemblage of materials and the seasoning of timber, 14 years is a long time. But this was not unusual for such a large ship, and obsolescence was a much smaller problem around the turn of the 18th century than it would be 70 years later.

Blockade Duties

After the slow building it went straight into commission as the flagship of Admiral Lord Gardner, in the blockade of Brest, then in 1806–07 in the same duty under Admiral Jervis, now Lord St Vincent. A first-rate was an expensive and hazardous vessel to keep station off a stormy and rockbound coast and Admiral Howe had sent his home in winter, but St Vincent took a more robust view and was not proved wrong. In 1807 the fleet moved south to blockade the Tagus estuary when France invaded Portugal.

With a change of admiral to Sir Charles Cotton, *Hibernia* remained off the Tagus and helped in the expulsion of the French forces and obtained the surrender of a Russian squadron at Lisbon.

Long Service

Like other first-rates, *Hibernia* spent time laid up when not on active service, but in 1813 it was part of a fleet bombarding Cassis, on the south coast of France. On July 6, 1814, it was paid off, but in 1825 it was partially rebuilt and put back into commission.

Its last half-century was spent at Malta, first as flagship of the commander-in-chief of the Mediterranean Fleet, to 1855, then as flagship of the Admiral Superintendent of the Dockyard, in this role no longer seagoing but maintained as a depot ship. *Hibernia* was finally broken up in 1902 after 97 years of service.

SPECIFICATIONS

DISPLACEMENT: 2,530 tons (2,571 tonnes)

DIMENSIONS: 201 ft 2 in x 53 ft 1 in x 22 ft 4 in (61.3 m x 16.2 m x 6.8 m)

RIG: Three masts, full square rig

ARMAMENT: Thirty-two 32 pounders, thirty-two 24 pounders, thirty-four 18 pounder guns; sixteen 32 pounders, two 18 pounder carronades

CREW: 837

HMS *Hibernia*

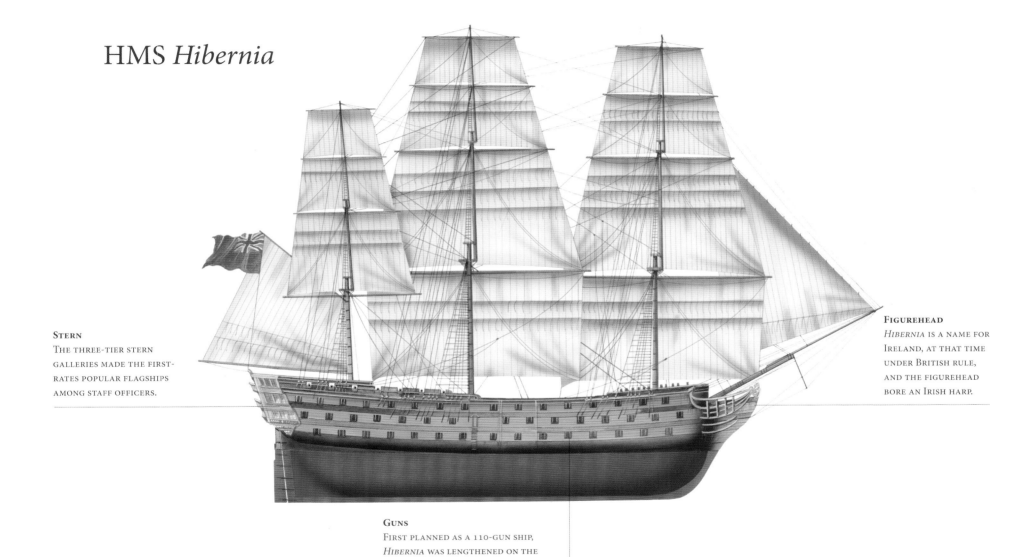

STERN
THE THREE-TIER STERN GALLERIES MADE THE FIRST-RATES POPULAR FLAGSHIPS AMONG STAFF OFFICERS.

FIGUREHEAD
HIBERNIA IS A NAME FOR IRELAND, AT THAT TIME UNDER BRITISH RULE, AND THE FIGUREHEAD BORE AN IRISH HARP.

GUNS
FIRST PLANNED AS A 110-GUN SHIP, *HIBERNIA* WAS LENGTHENED ON THE STOCKS TO CARRY 120.

HMS *Cheerful* (1806)

CUTTERS WERE THE SMALLEST CRUISING WARSHIPS IN THE BRITISH NAVY. THEY MIGHT OPERATE ALONE OR IN PAIRS, AGAINST OTHER SMALL CRAFT, BUT THEY ALSO CAME TO HAVE A FLEET ROLE AS DISPATCH CARRIERS AND RECONNAISSANCE SHIPS WHOSE SMALL SIZE COULD TAKE THEM INTO AREAS THAT WOULD HAVE BEEN HAZARDOUS FOR A LARGER VESSEL.

Although this was incidental, cutters and small schooners provided excellent training for able young lieutenants with aspirations to higher command. Cutters were given lively names, suggesting lightness and speed. HMS *Cheerful*, a 12-gun cutter built at Dover and launched in 1806, was a typical example. Single masted, with a pronounced V-section hull, vessels of this kind had been developed through the 18th century along the south-eastern coast of England.

Training and Dispatch Ships

The traditional basic rig was fore-and-aft, with a large gaff mainsail and two foresails, although by the early 19th century, a main course and topsails might be included. Their legal trade was carrying merchandise of all descriptions, but many were also used for smuggling. It was to suppress the smugglers' activities

that the Royal Navy began to use cutters, and at first they were not purpose-built but bought in or hired (provided with naval crews). However, the growing need for dispatch carriers ("advice boat" was the original term) bringing orders to distant stations or squadrons, and returning with reports, required vessels that were faster and could be better armed than merchant cutters.

The message was driven home by the capture of the 77-ton (78.2-tonne) *Swift*, carrying dispatches from Admiral Lord Nelson in April 1804, which fell victim to a privateer xebec, and the Royal Navy began to design its own cutters. While a displacement of 120–140 tons (122–142.25 tonnes) was most usual, some larger versions were built, like HMS *Busy*, launched in 1778, of 188 tons (191 tonnes) armed with two 12-pounder carronades and twelve 4-pounder long guns. At least 24 cutters were equipped to

fire Congreve rockets (see HMS *Shannon*) and used to attack the French at Boulogne on October 8–9, 1806. Essentially the cutter was a small craft, and in this respect differed from the schooner (often used for the same purposes) which could be enlarged and multiple-masted, while a two-masted cutter would have effectively been a brig.

Cheerful's tasks were Channel patrols, message carrying, and dealing with venturesome chasse-marées. It was sold in 1816.

SPECIFICATIONS

DISPLACEMENT: 111 tons (113 tonnes)

DIMENSIONS: 68 ft (20.7 m) x 20 ft (6 m) x 7 ft (2.13 m)

RIG: Single mast, hybrid rig of gaff with yards and topsails

ARMAMENT: Twelve 4 pounder guns

CREW: 50

HMS *Cheerful*

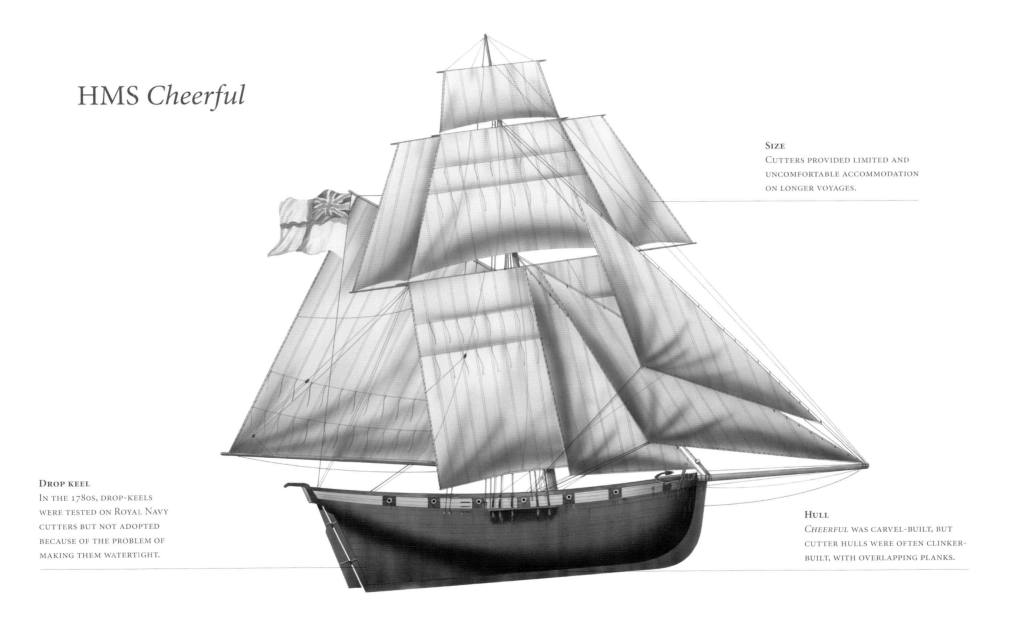

SIZE
CUTTERS PROVIDED LIMITED AND
UNCOMFORTABLE ACCOMMODATION
ON LONGER VOYAGES.

DROP KEEL
IN THE 1780S, DROP-KEELS
WERE TESTED ON ROYAL NAVY
CUTTERS BUT NOT ADOPTED
BECAUSE OF THE PROBLEM OF
MAKING THEM WATERTIGHT.

HULL
CHEERFUL WAS CARVEL-BUILT, BUT
CUTTER HULLS WERE OFTEN CLINKER-
BUILT, WITH OVERLAPPING PLANKS.

HMS *Shannon* (1806)

BY THE 1800S FRIGATES COULD BE QUITE LARGE SHIPS MOUNTING 38 GUNS, OR EVEN 44 IN THE CASE OF THE USS *CONSTITUTION* AND ITS SISTER SHIPS. A SINGLE GUN DECK WAS STILL A DEFINING FACTOR, AND SPEED AND MANEUVERABILITY THE MOST DESIRED CHARACTERISTICS. THE *SHANNON* WAS LAID DOWN AT BRINDLEY'S SHIPYARD AT FRINDSBURY, KENT, IN AUGUST 1804.

Launched on May 5, 1808, and completed at Chatham on August 3, 1806, the 38-gun *Shannon* was commanded for its first seven years by Captain Philip Broke.

At first with the Channel Fleet, on October 8, 1806 it joined a squadron under Commodore Edward Owen, firing Congreve rockets (an early form of explosive shell, propelled by a charge from a launching frame), at French ships in Boulogne harbor. Until September 28, 1807, it patrolled the northern North Sea, protecting whaling ships against privateers. Refitted in October–December of 1807, it was part of Admiral Hood's fleet for the capture of Madeira on December 26 before returning to the Channel Fleet. With other ships it shared the capture of the French *Comète* and *Espoir*, July 20 and August 21, 1808, and took the privateer *Pommereuil* (14 guns) on January 27, 1809.

Challenge off of Boston

Newly re-coppered and refitted, in August 1811 *Shannon* was deployed to Halifax, Nova Scotia, in anticipation of hostilities against the United States, and from July 5, 1812, it was engaged on blockade duty off New England. Broke, an eager, aggressive, and confident captain, focused on USS *Chesapeake* for a two-ship challenge "to try the fortune of our respective flags," and the American Captain James Lawrence was no less ready.

On June 1, 1813 the two ships met off Boston. They were evenly matched: although *Chesapeake* had a larger crew, they lacked the training and practice of *Shannon*'s men. The fight was short, but extremely active, with the ships only about 110 ft (33 m) apart. Very soon they ran together, still exchanging broadsides. Lawrence was already fatally wounded when the British sailors boarded *Chesapeake* for hand-to-hand fighting.

Less than 15 minutes after the start, *Chesapeake* surrendered. In that time 48 Americans and 30 Britons were killed, with 154 men wounded from both sides.

Shannon remained in service until 1830, when it became a receiving hulk at Sheerness. Renamed *St Lawrence* on March 1, 1844, it was broken up at Chatham by November 12, 1859.

SPECIFICATIONS

DISPLACEMENT: 1,065 tons (1,082 tonnes)

DIMENSIONS: 150 ft 2 ins (45.8 m) x 39 ft 11 in (12.17 m) x 12 ft 11 in (3.94 m)

RIG: Three masts, full square rig

ARMAMENT: Thirty 36 pounders, thirty-two 24 pounders, eighteen 12 pounder guns; six 36 pounder howitzers

CREW: 330

HMS *Shannon*

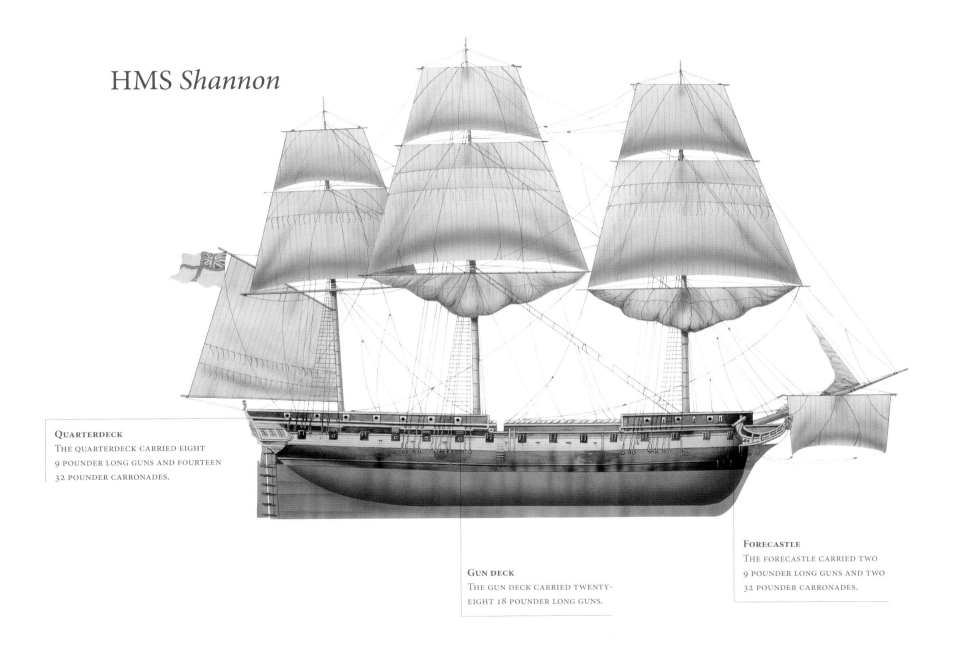

QUARTERDECK

THE QUARTERDECK CARRIED EIGHT
9 POUNDER LONG GUNS AND FOURTEEN
32 POUNDER CARRONADES.

GUN DECK

THE GUN DECK CARRIED TWENTY-
EIGHT 18 POUNDER LONG GUNS.

FORECASTLE

THE FORECASTLE CARRIED TWO
9 POUNDER LONG GUNS AND TWO
32 POUNDER CARRONADES.

HMS *Caledonia* (1808)

CONSTRUCTION OF A FIRST-RATE VESSEL TOOK A LONG TIME AND MODIFICATIONS TO THE GENERAL DESIGN MIGHT BE MADE YEARS BEFORE THEY COULD BE PUT INTO EFFECT. HMS CALEDONIA (120 GUNS) SHOWED THE FINAL DEVELOPMENT OF THE BRITISH FIRST-RATE AT THE TIME OF THE NAPOLEONIC WARS, AND WAS THE LAST OF THESE SHIPS TO SEE MUCH ACTIVE SERVICE.

The *Caledonia* was laid down at Plymouth Dockyard in January 1805 and launched on June 25, 1808. Among the features that made it stand apart from its predecessors were a main gun deck higher above the waterline, a strengthened bow design that dispensed with the traditional "beak," and a fully enclosed, more vertical stern. The design was an effective one and it was recorded that "she steers, works and stays remarkably well, is a weatherly ship, and lies-to very close."

Active Service

Assigned to the Channel Fleet, *Caledonia* was the flagship of Admiral Lord Gambier in the controversial Battle of the Basque Roads, the bay between Rochefort and La Rochelle. On April 11, 1809, 11 French ships of the line and four frigates moored there were successfully attacked by Admiral Cochrane with fireships, but Gambier, his senior officer, declined to follow up the advantage.

In 1813 *Caledonia* was flagship of Vice Admiral Sir Edward Pellew, blockading Toulon, and on November 5, 1813, engaged the French 130-gun *Wagram* in a skirmish off the French port, during an indecisive encounter between two squadrons, with little damage to either.

On February 12, 1814, with HMS *Boyne*, it almost succeeded in trapping the 74-gun French *Romulus* off the same coast. After the final defeat of Napoleon in 1815, *Caledonia* had a long if relatively uneventful career in fleet service, spent largely as a flagship of the Mediterranean Fleet under successive admirals, with periods back in Portsmouth or Plymouth for refits. It participated in the bombardment of Algiers, then a pirate port, in 1816.

In 1831 *Caledonia* was part of an experimental squadron under Admiral Codrington, in the English Channel, exploring different forms of propulsion. By 1856 it was converted to a hospital ship at the Dreadnought Naval Hospital, Greenwich, and used as such until 1870, then briefly again in 1871. It was broken up in 1875. This ship of the line should not be confused with a brig of 1813 of the same name, used by the British on Lake Erie and captured by U.S. forces on October 9, 1812.

SPECIFICATIONS

DISPLACEMENT: 2,616 tons (2,658 tonnes)

DIMENSIONS: 205 ft (62 m) x 53 ft 6 in (16.3 m) x 23 ft 2 in (7 m)

RIG: Three masts, full square rig

ARMAMENT: Thirty-two 32 pounders, thirty-four 24 pounders, thirty-four, 18 pounders, six 12 pounder guns; twelve 32 pounders, two 12 pounder carronades

CREW: 891

HMS *Caledonia*

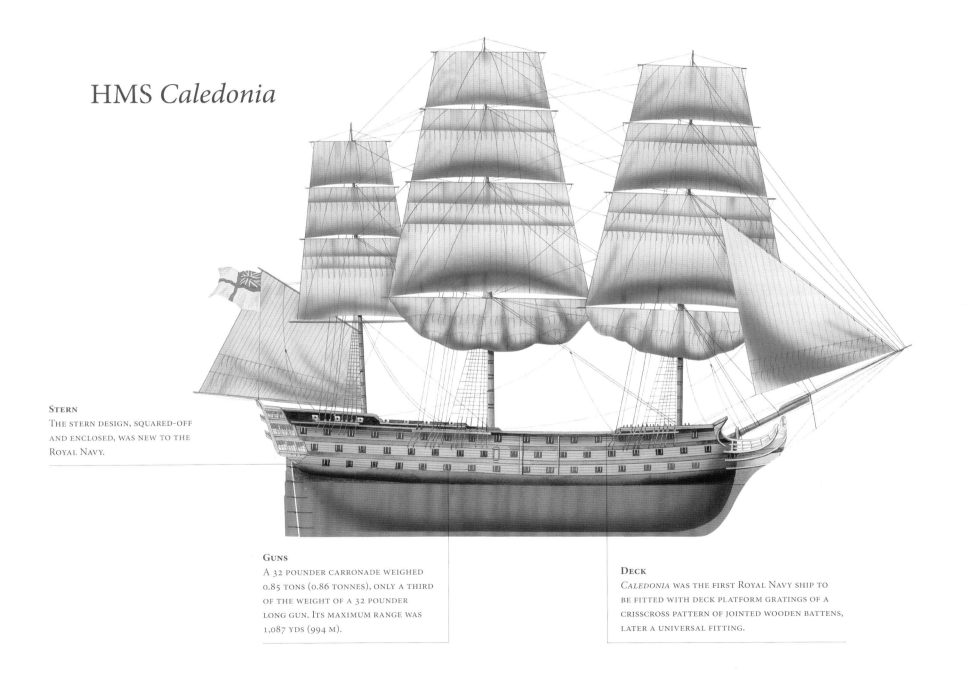

STERN
THE STERN DESIGN, SQUARED-OFF
AND ENCLOSED, WAS NEW TO THE
ROYAL NAVY.

GUNS
A 32 POUNDER CARRONADE WEIGHED
0.85 TONS (0.86 TONNES), ONLY A THIRD
OF THE WEIGHT OF A 32 POUNDER
LONG GUN. ITS MAXIMUM RANGE WAS
1,087 YDS (994 M).

DECK
CALEDONIA WAS THE FIRST ROYAL NAVY SHIP TO
BE FITTED WITH DECK PLATFORM GRATINGS OF A
CRISSCROSS PATTERN OF JOINTED WOODEN BATTENS,
LATER A UNIVERSAL FITTING.

USS *Oneida* (1809)

LAKE ONTARIO, FORMING PART OF THE BORDER BETWEEN THE INDEPENDENT UNITED STATES AND THE BRITISH COLONY OF CANADA, WAS AN INEVITABLE BATTLEGROUND IN THE EVENT OF A BRITISH–AMERICAN WAR. AS RELATIONS BECAME CRITICAL TOWARDS 1812, BOTH SIDES BUILT WARSHIPS SPECIFICALLY TO GAIN CONTROL OF THE LAKE. *ONEIDA* WAS THE FIRST OF A SQUADRON THAT CONFRONTED THE BRITISH MORE OFTEN THAN ANY OTHER U.S. SHIPS IN THE 1812 WAR.

*O*neida (named after a local Native American tribe) was laid down in 1808 at Oswego, on the southeast shore of Lake Ontario, and built by the shipwright Christian Bergh with the assistance of the New York shipbuilder Henry Eckford. It was launched on March 31, 1809. Completion and commissioning were not until late 1810, and the cost (with two small gunboats for Lake Champlain) was $23,772.86. It was classed as a brig of war, and based primarily at Sackets Harbor, at the east end of the lake, at first under the command of Lieutenant Melancthon T. Woolsey.

War of 1812

The British base at Kingston, not far away, was building a 20-gun corvette, HMS *Royal George*. Neither ship was specially designed for freshwater operations, being based on standard designs for the saltwater fleets. War was declared on June 18, 1812, and on August 31 Isaac Chauncey was appointed Commodore of a not-yet existent American squadron. Ice each winter put a halt to naval operations, but shipbuilding went on. Through 1813 and 1814 the two small fleets on Lake Ontario maneuvered and counter-maneuvered, their main contribution being in the transport and support of land forces.

On April 27, 1813, York, Ontario, was captured and a British warship burned on the stocks; this was a meticulously planned amphibious warfare operation, the first in U.S. military history. On May 29 the British attacked Sackets Harbor and destroyed stores assembled for the building of USS *General Pike*.

In February 1814 *Oneida* was careened at Sackets Harbor, but, never a good sailer, it had by now been supplanted by newer ships and played less and less of a role. The war ended in mid-February 1815 and *Oneida's* guns were transferred to gunboats. It was used as a transport until December 1816, being described as "rotten and unfit."

In 1823 it sank in harbor, was purchased with other redundant vessels, raised in May 1826, and refitted as the merchant ship *Adjutant Clitz*, carrying timber. It plied the lake for a few more years until it sank around 1840, probably at Clayton, New York.

SPECIFICATIONS

DISPLACEMENT: 243 tons (247 tonnes)

DIMENSIONS: 85 ft 6 in x 22 ft 6 in x 16 ft (26 m x 6.8 m x 4.8 m)

RIG: Two masts, square rig

ARMAMENT: Eighteen 24 pounder carronades

CREW: 117

USS *Oneida*

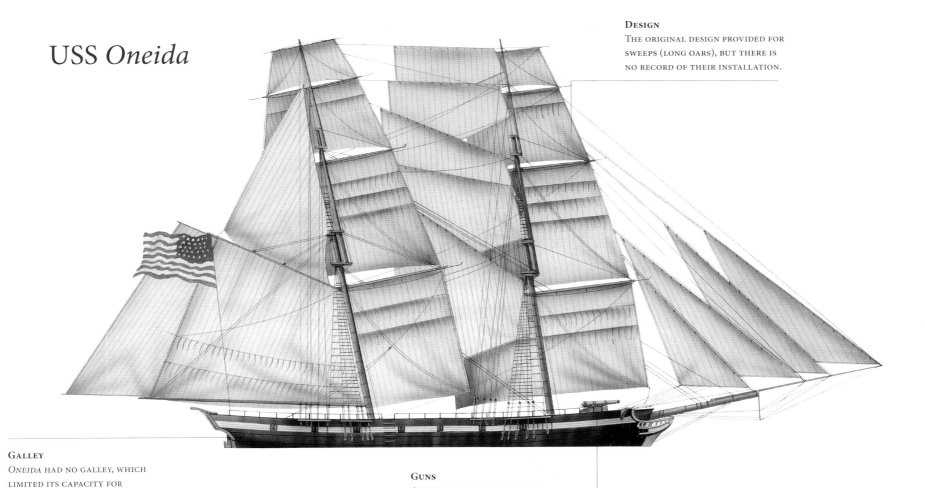

DESIGN
THE ORIGINAL DESIGN PROVIDED FOR
SWEEPS (LONG OARS), BUT THERE IS
NO RECORD OF THEIR INSTALLATION.

GALLEY
ONEIDA HAD NO GALLEY, WHICH
LIMITED ITS CAPACITY FOR
STAYING OUT ON THE LAKE.

GUNS
A PIVOT GUN IN THE BOWS WAS
PART OF THE ORIGINAL DESIGN,
BUT, IF INSTALLED, WAS REMOVED
AT AN EARLY DATE.

Montebello (1812)

LAUNCHED WHILE NAPOLEON BONAPARTE WAS STILL EMPEROR OF FRANCE, *MONTEBELLO'S* LONG CAREER OF 45 YEARS WAS NOT UNUSUAL FOR A FRENCH FIRST-RATE. IT SURVIVED LONG ENOUGH, AND ITS HULL REMAINED SUFFICIENTLY ROBUST, TO HAVE A STEAM ENGINE INSTALLED IN 1852.

Montebello was laid down in 1810 and launched in December 1812 at Toulon. At long intervals the same design was followed by *Souverain* (1819) and *Friedland* (1840), a tribute to the lasting impact of Jacques-Noël Sané's design.

However, many historians consider all 16 ships of the *Océan* type, *Montebello* included, as forming a single class, and certainly they all shared the same characteristics: clean and simple lines, minimal forecastle and very modest raised poop deck, tumblehome sides, stability as gun platforms, and good sailing qualities. Guns were carried on a spar deck connecting the forecastle and quarterdeck, a French feature not found on British first-rates.

Montebello served until 1821 before a major refit, effectively a rebuild, was considered necessary. After that it was in routine service for periods with the Mediterranean Fleet, punctuated by long spells laid up in ordinary at the Toulon naval base.

Crimean War Service

In 1852 an Indret 140 horsepower auxiliary engine and screw propeller were fitted, but the addition did nothing to improve speed and made the ship more difficult to handle.

It was deployed to the Black Sea in the Crimean War of 1855, when France and Great Britain were in alliance against Russia, as flagship of Admiral Bruat. It participated in shore bombardments at Sevastopol and Fort Kinburn, and in the landings at Kerch, but its crew was ravaged by cholera, with 150 dying in a matter of days.

On returning, Bruat died just before the ship reached Toulon. That was the last of *Montebello's* active service. In 1860 it was used as a training ship for gunners at Toulon, and finally it was converted to a floating barracks and used as such until it was broken up in 1889.

SPECIFICATIONS

DISPLACEMENT: 2,456 tons (2,495 tonnes)

DIMENSIONS: 207 ft 4 in x 57 ft 5 in x 82 ft (63.2 m x 17.5 m x 25 m)

RIG: Three masts, full square rig

ARMAMENT: Thirty-two 36 pounders, thirty-four 24 pounders, fifty-two 8 pounder guns; six 26 pounder carronades

CREW: 1,079

Montebello

MASTS
THE MAINMAST, IN THREE SECTIONS,
MEASURED 233 FT (71 M) FROM KEEL
TO TOP.

SAILS
MONTEBELLO CARRIED 24,380
SQUARE FT (2,265 SQ M) OF SAIL.

MASTS
THE DIAMETER OF
THE MASSIVE LOWER
MAINMAST WAS 3 FT
5 IN (1.05 M).

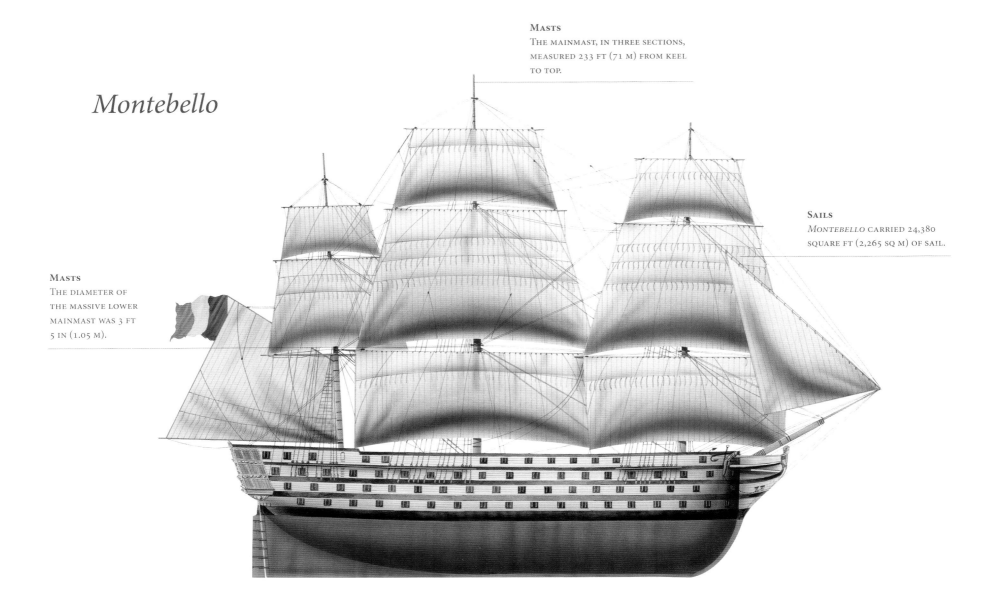

U.S. Gunboat *(1812)*

THE GUNBOAT PROBABLY BEGAN AS A VARIANT OF THE FLAT-BOTTOMED BOATS WIDELY USED FOR TROOP LANDINGS DURING COASTAL OPERATIONS BOTH IN EUROPE AND NORTH AFRICA IN THE CAMPAIGNS OF THE LATE 18TH AND EARLY 19TH CENTURIES. SUCH CRAFT WERE OFTEN USED IN THE AMERICAN WAR OF INDEPENDENCE, AND TO EMPLOY SIMILAR VESSELS FOR DEFENSE, WITH A SINGLE GUN, WAS THE NATURAL NEXT STEP.

The United States was the most prolific user of gunboats in the early 1800s. Political ideas took a hand here. The Continental Navy had been done away with in 1785, in the belief that a "fleet in being" was not necessary. Even though the need to defend American shipping on the high seas was recognized in 1794, there was a reluctance to build a large fleet of seagoing ships: President Jefferson called it "a ruinous folly," and the concept of locally-held gunboats was developed.

These were solidly built small vessels, at first still with a single cannon mounted on a slide or a pivot. They were numbered rather than named and variously rigged, with a crew of about 20. If the wind failed, or in close combat, they could be propelled by oars. Each carried two to three guns: 18- to 24-pound swivel-mounted guns or 32 pounders on traversing carriages. Larger variants might have more guns, including side-firing carronades. Bigger guns could weigh as much as 7,000 lb (2,778 kg), weighing down a shallow-draft gunboat and making handling difficult in heavy weather.

Policy Reversal

Jefferson's "gunboat navy" was not a success. In the decade before 1812, around 175 gunboats were built and many more had been ordered. But following the inauguration of James Madison in March 1809, the United States moved away from its gunboat policy, and by December 1811 most of the existing boats were in ordinary. Only 62 remained in service, and the frigate fleet was being enlarged. One hundred gunboats already authorized for construction were never built. When war was declared on June 15, 1812, the U.S. Navy had seven frigates, four schooners, four ketches, and 170 gunboats.

The gunboats' best service during the war was at the taking of Mobile and in resistance to the British advance on New Orleans at Lake Borgne. After 1815 most were sold off as trading ships, and by 1822 only No.158 remained in service.

SPECIFICATIONS

DISPLACEMENT: 50–120 tons (50.8–122 tonnes)

DIMENSIONS: typically 60 ft x 20 ft x 6 ft (18.3 m x 6 m x 1.83 m)

RIG: Two masts, schooner rig

ARMAMENT: One to two 24 pounder guns

CREW: 20–50

U.S. Gunboat

RIGGING
THE RIG WAS DESIGNED TO HELP HOLD
THE VESSEL'S HEAD INTO THE WIND.

STEERING
TILLER STEERING WAS
EMPLOYED. NOTE ALSO
THE ELBOWED SPAR
CONTROLLING MOVEMENT
OF THE SPANKER BOOM.

CANNON
ON THIS BOAT THE CANNON IS MOUNTED
CENTRALLY FOR STABILITY. THE SLIDE
MOUNT WAS TO HELP ABSORB RECOIL
FROM FIRING.

USS *General Pike* (1813)

U.S. GENERAL ZEBULON PIKE WAS KILLED IN THE SUCCESSFUL ATTACK ON YORK, ONTARIO, ON APRIL 27, 1813, BUT HIS NAME WAS COMMEMORATED IN THIS SHIP, THE SECOND AMERICAN WARSHIP BUILT ON THE SHORE OF LAKE ONTARIO, TO FIGHT FOR CONTROL OF THE LAKE AGAINST THE BRITISH SQUADRON BASED AT KINGSTON, ONTARIO.

Classed as a corvette, *General Pike* was laid down at Sackets Harbor by Henry Eckford on April 9, 1813. Set on fire on May 29 during a British attack, the unfinished ship was saved and launched on June 12 after only 63 days on the stocks, with Master Commandant Arthur Sinclair as the first captain. Ready to sail by July 21, it became Commodore Isaac Chauncey's flagship on the lake, and sailed to Niagara in a demonstration of American power, engaging British vessels under Commodore Yeo in an indecisive battle on August 10–11.

British Engagement

Back in Sackets Harbor on August 13, the ship was provisioned before returning to the head of the lake to search out British ships. A further short battle took place off the mouth of the Genesee River on September 11. On September 28 the two forces again met at York Bay, Ontario, and engaged in a fierce but still indecisive battle, with heavy exchange of gunfire between *General Pike* and the British flagship HMS *Royal George*. After returning to Sackets Harbor early in October, *General Pike* supported troop movements against the British at the lower end of Lake Ontario until mid-November, when it returned to the Niagara Peninsula to cover the transfer of American troops from Fort Niagara to Sackets Harbor. It remained at the iced-up Sackets Harbor during the winter months.

Throughout the remainder of the War of 1812, *General Pike* continued to operate with Chauncey's squadron. After the British withdrew their blockading ships from Sackets Harbor early in June 1814, it took part in an American blockade of Kingston, Ontario. The British were held inside Kingston harbor, and *General Pike* cruised Lake Ontario freely from the head of the St Lawrence River to Sackets Harbor. After the end of the war, in poor condition, it was laid up at Sackets Harbor and sold in 1825.

SPECIFICATIONS

DISPLACEMENT: 875 tons (889 tonnes)

DIMENSIONS: 174 ft x 37 ft x 15 ft (55 m x 11.3 m x 4.57 m)

RIG: Three masts, full square rig to skysails

ARMAMENT: Twenty-six 24 pounder guns; two 24 pounder carronades

CREW: 300 (at maximum)

USS *General Pike*

RIGGING
THE LONG JIBBOOM CARRIES
FORE TOPMAST STAYSAIL, JIB,
FLYING JIB, AND OUTER FLYING
JIB OR FORE ROYAL STAYSAIL.

SAILS
FULLY RIGGED, *GENERAL PIKE*
CARRIED SIX LEVELS OF SAILS,
WITH SKYSAILS AND STAYSAILS.

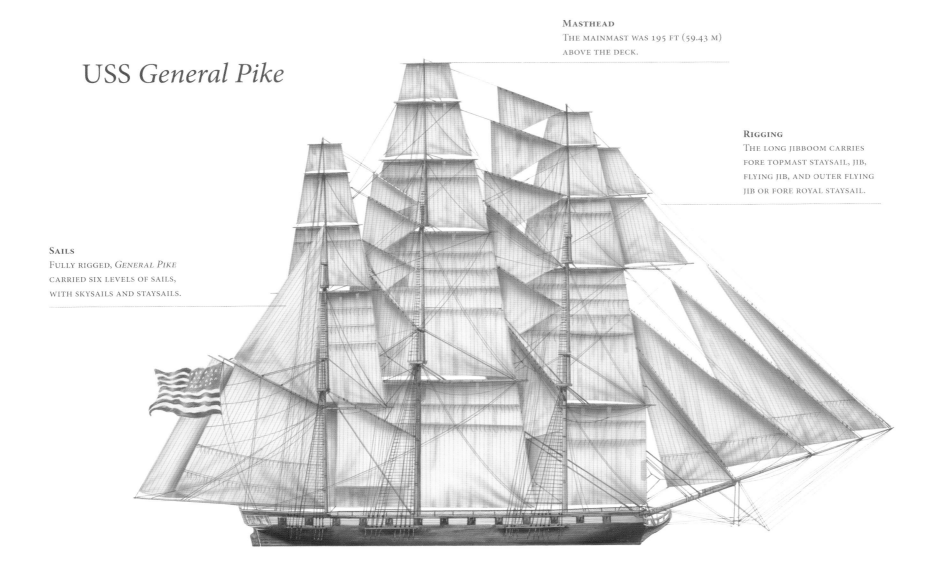

USS *Rattlesnake* (1813)

THE FIRST *RATTLESNAKE* WAS A 14-GUN AMERICAN PRIVATEER WITH A VERY SHORT
CAREER, COMMISSIONED IN JUNE 1781 AND CAPTURED BY THE BRITISH FRIGATE *ASSURANCE*
IN THE SAME MONTH. THE SECOND *RATTLESNAKE*, ALSO BUILT AS A PRIVATEER, BECAME AN
OFFICIAL U.S. NAVY SHIP AND HAD A SOMEWHAT MORE SUCCESSFUL EXISTENCE BEFORE
ALSO SUCCUMBING TO CAPTURE.

Built in Medford, Massachusetts, *Rattlesnake* was purchased by the US Navy at the yard in 1813. It is often referred to as a brig, and also as a schooner, and it is likely that the rig was altered at some point, as happened with its companion vessel USS *Enterprise*, which was converted from schooner rig to topsail schooner, and finally to brig in 1812. Most depictions, as here, show it as a three-masted ship with a square rig.

First Mission

Rattlesnake sailed from Portsmouth, New Hampshire, on January 10, 1814, under the command of Master Commandant John O. Creighton, and, along with *Enterprise*, headed for the Caribbean Sea. The two ships took three prizes but the Caribbean was heavily patrolled by the British Royal Navy, and on February 25 the appearance of a British frigate forced them to separate.

Rattlesnake returned to U.S. waters, putting into Wilmington, North Carolina, on March 9, but was soon back at sea under the command of Lt. James Renshaw. This time it tried its luck in northern waters, but its efforts were terminated on June 22 when the ship ran foul of a large British frigate, the newly built 50-gun HMS *Leander*.

A long chase followed, during which *Rattlesnake* jettisoned all but two of its guns in order to gain speed, but bad weather favored the bigger ship and Renshaw was finally forced to surrender off Cape Sable, Nova Scotia.

Mysterious End

The subsequent history of *Rattlesnake* is not wholly clear. It was sailed across the Atlantic by a prize crew from *Leander*, but there are no records of it being taken into the Royal Navy. According to some sources it was last heard of in the Mediterranean Sea.

SPECIFICATIONS

DISPLACEMENT: 278 tons (282 tonnes)

DIMENSIONS: Not known

RIG: Three masts, ship rig

ARMAMENT: 14 guns

CREW: Not known

USS *Rattlesnake*

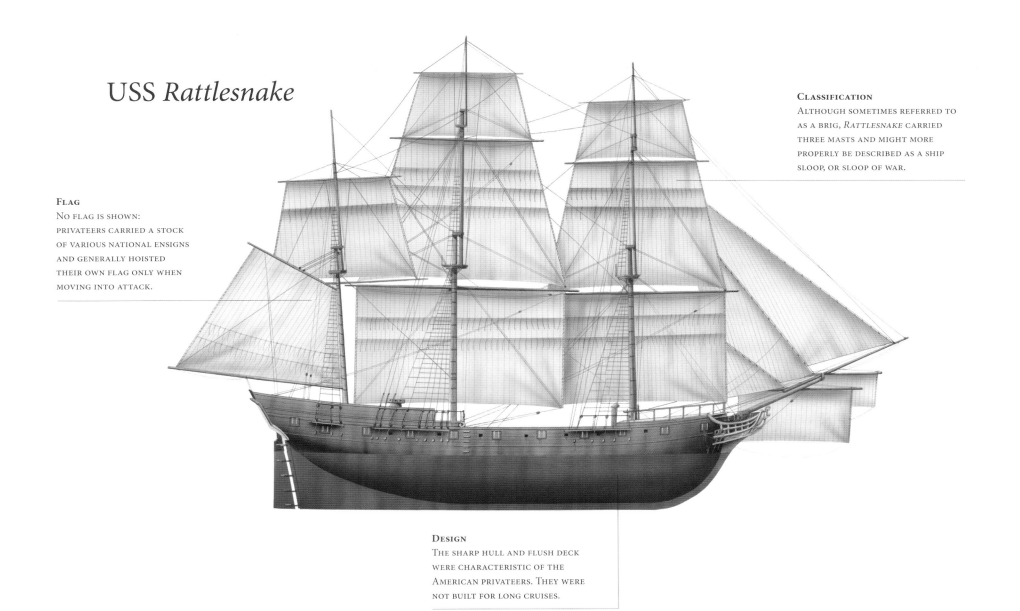

CLASSIFICATION
ALTHOUGH SOMETIMES REFERRED TO
AS A BRIG, *RATTLESNAKE* CARRIED
THREE MASTS AND MIGHT MORE
PROPERLY BE DESCRIBED AS A SHIP
SLOOP, OR SLOOP OF WAR.

FLAG
NO FLAG IS SHOWN:
PRIVATEERS CARRIED A STOCK
OF VARIOUS NATIONAL ENSIGNS
AND GENERALLY HOISTED
THEIR OWN FLAG ONLY WHEN
MOVING INTO ATTACK.

DESIGN
THE SHARP HULL AND FLUSH DECK
WERE CHARACTERISTIC OF THE
AMERICAN PRIVATEERS. THEY WERE
NOT BUILT FOR LONG CRUISES.

HMS *Newcastle* (1814)

IN 1813 THE ROYAL NAVY WAS STILL BUILDING 36-GUN FRIGATES ARMED WITH 18 POUNDER GUNS, BUT CONFRONTATION FROM 1812 WITH SPAR-DECKED AMERICAN FRIGATES OF THE *CONSTITUTION* TYPE, CARRYING 44 GUNS AND FIRING A BROADSIDE HALF AS HEAVY AGAIN, BROUGHT A CHANGE IN CONSTRUCTION POLICY, WITH TWO RAPIDLY BUILT "DOUBLE-BANKED" FRIGATES, *NEWCASTLE* AND HMS *LEANDER*.

Newcastle, fourth warship to bear the name, was launched from Wells, Wigram & Green's Yard, Blackwall, London, on February 10, 1814 and commissioned by May 7, when it was at Portsmouth. Traditionally British frigates were built of seasoned hardwood, although some were of softwood as early as 1757, when speedy construction was required. This was very much the case with *Newcastle* and *Leander*, which were both constructed of yellow pitch pine. Designed by different designers to the Admiralty's tight specifications, they were virtually identical except that *Leander*, unusually, had the upper deck gunports directly above the main-deck ports. Both followed the American practice of bridging the well between forecastle and quarterdeck with a spar deck on which guns could be mounted, and so were equipped with two tiers of artillery. *Newcastle* cost £39,243.

Vessel in Action

Dispatched as soon as possible for North American waters, *Newcastle* was stationed at Halifax, Nova Scotia, but its patrols ranged widely into the Atlantic, as far as Tenerife (February 1815). On August 9, 1814 it captured the U.S. privateer *Ida*. On December 19 its crew made a shore attack on the township of Orleans, Massachusetts, and on December 28 with *Leander* and the older 40-gun frigate HMS *Acasta* it captured the privateer *Prince de Neufchatel*.

On March 11, 1815, although the War of 1812 was over, *Newcastle*, *Acasta*, and *Leander* pursued USS *Constitution* off Porto Praya, in the Cape Verde Islands, but lost it through bad signaling, although they recaptured the British sloop HMS *Levant*.

The fir-built ships were very fast but not built for long life. *Newcastle* was part of the squadron escorting Napoleon Bonaparte to exile on St Helena, in September 1816. In 1819–21 it was back in the North Atlantic, based at Halifax. On April 30, 1823, it was put up for sale but no buyer appeared and it went into harbor service. From 1830 it was a quarantine ship at Liverpool, and was finally sold for scrapping in 1850.

HMS *Newcastle*

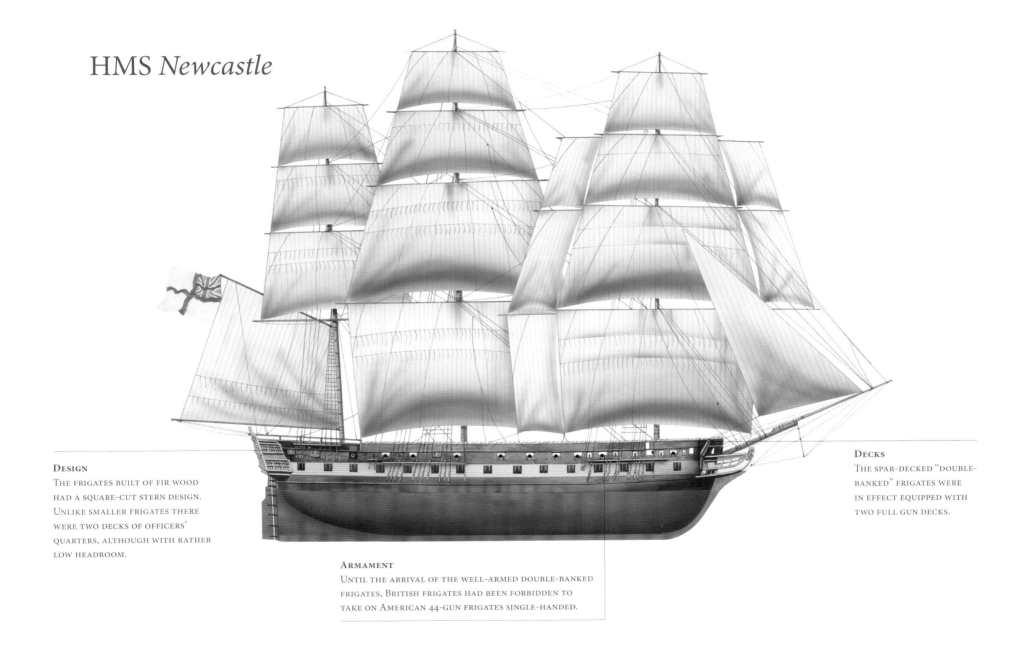

DESIGN
THE FRIGATES BUILT OF FIR WOOD
HAD A SQUARE-CUT STERN DESIGN.
UNLIKE SMALLER FRIGATES THERE
WERE TWO DECKS OF OFFICERS'
QUARTERS, ALTHOUGH WITH RATHER
LOW HEADROOM.

DECKS
THE SPAR-DECKED "DOUBLE-
BANKED" FRIGATES WERE
IN EFFECT EQUIPPED WITH
TWO FULL GUN DECKS.

ARMAMENT
UNTIL THE ARRIVAL OF THE WELL-ARMED DOUBLE-BANKED
FRIGATES, BRITISH FRIGATES HAD BEEN FORBIDDEN TO
TAKE ON AMERICAN 44-GUN FRIGATES SINGLE-HANDED.

USS *Prometheus* (1814)

PROBABLY DESTINED FOR A LIFE OF ROUTINE COASTAL SHIPPING, THIS SHIP WAS PURCHASED FOR THE U.S. NAVY AND NAMED FOR THE MYTHICAL GREEK HERO WHO WAS READY TO DO BATTLE WITH THE GODS. IT PLAYED A PART IN THE WAR OF 1812 AND LATER SERVED THE GOVERNMENT ON A DIPLOMATIC MISSION.

It was built by William Seguin at Philadelphia for the shipowners Savage & Dryan, as the brig *Escape*, a name that strongly hints it was intended to operate as a privateer rather than as a conventional merchant vessel. It was purchased for the Navy in 1814 at a time when rapid expansion of the fleet was vitally necessary, with a maritime war going on against Great Britain. Renamed *Prometheus*, it was fitted out as a 9-gun warship and captained by Master Commandant Joseph J. Nicholson.

Nothing is known about its movements in the course of the war. Soon after hostilities had ended, it made a cruise to the West Indies in March–May 1815. In August of the same year it carried a special messenger from the U.S. government to the Tsar of Russia, crossing the Atlantic and sailing up the Baltic Sea to Saint Petersburg, and was back at New York in November.

From 1817 it was used as a coastal survey ship, first on the northeast coast, then in 1818 on the southern coast. Found to be unseaworthy in October 1818, it was decommissioned that month and dismantled and sold at auction in New Orleans in 1819.

Built for Speed

Prometheus has been described as a hermaphrodite schooner, a term employed in the USA for a vessel whose foremast is identical to that of a brig or brigantine but whose mainmast is that of a schooner; the mainmast is made in two spars and carries no yards. A sail plan of the ship survives showing the standard two-masted brig arrangement, with noticeably long bowsprit and spanker boom, and a sharp rake to the mainmast compared to the almost vertical foremast. The mainmast carried yards for topsail and topgallant, which is not normal in a hermaphrodite schooner, leaving no doubt that this ship was built and rigged for speed.

SPECIFICATIONS

DISPLACEMENT: 290 tons (294 tonnes)

DIMENSIONS: 82 ft x 27 ft x 11 ft 4 in (25 m x 8.23 m x 3.45 m)

RIG: Two masts, brig rig

ARMAMENT: One 32 pounder, four 18 pounders, four 9 pounder guns

CREW: Not known

USS *Prometheus*

RIGGING

THE RIG OF AMERICAN BRIGS VARIED CONSIDERABLY AND WAS OFTEN ALTERED ON INDIVIDUAL SHIPS AS THE CAPTAINS SOUGHT TO FIND THE OPTIMUM FORM FOR THEIR VESSEL. THIS ILLUSTRATION SHOWS *PROMETHEUS* IN WARTIME MODE.

SAILS

A BRIG WAS GENERALLY A FAST SHIP, AND IT CAN BE SEEN THAT *PROMETHEUS* CARRIED A LARGE EXTENT OF SAIL IN RELATION TO ITS MODEST SIZE.

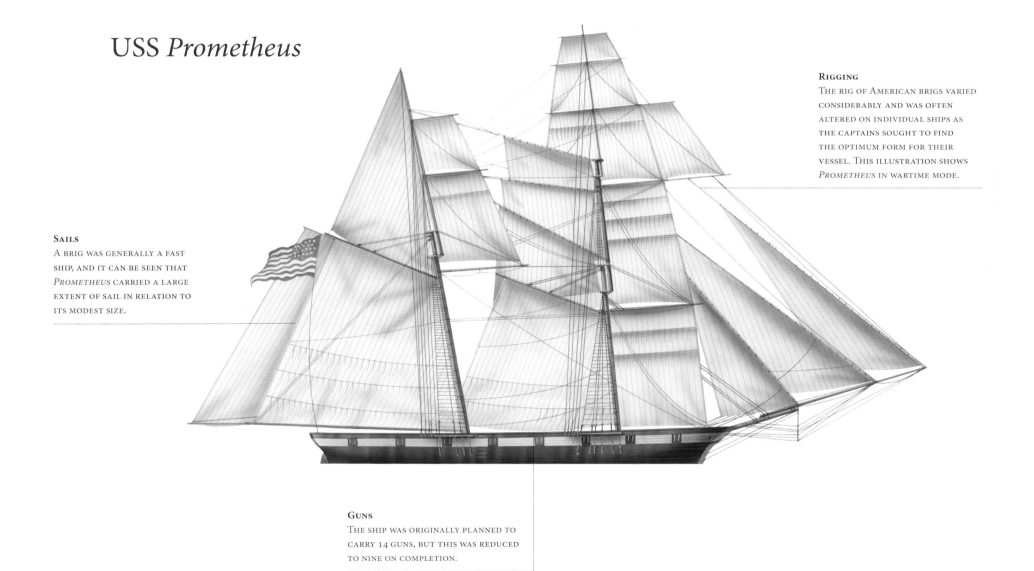

GUNS

THE SHIP WAS ORIGINALLY PLANNED TO CARRY 14 GUNS, BUT THIS WAS REDUCED TO NINE ON COMPLETION.

USS *Java* *(1815)*

JAVA WAS A PRIZE-NAME IN THE U.S. NAVY, COMMEMORATING THE CAPTURE AND DESTRUCTION OF HMS *JAVA* BY USS CONSTITUTION OFF BRAZIL IN 1812. THIS SHIP WAS A LARGE 50-GUN SPAR-DECKED FRIGATE WHOSE ACTIVE SERVICE WAS MOSTLY IN THE MEDITERRANEAN SEA.

At the time of its ordering, the naval shipyards could not cope with the increased demand for new ships and orders were placed with civilian yards. Laid down in 1814 at Flannigan & Parsons' Yard, Baltimore, *Java* was built with a spar deck over the central well, but guns were not mounted on it, as their placement here had been found to restrict the large frigates' performance under sail.

Commander Perry

Classed as a first-class frigate, it was launched and ready for sea by August 5, 1815. In July 1814 its command was offered to Commodore Oliver Hazard Perry, a national hero following his naval exploits on Lake Erie, and he supervised the outfitting of the vessel. *Java* was finished too late for the War of 1812–15, but was deployed to the Mediterranean from January 22, 1816.

Crossing the Atlantic, a mast snapped in a storm, killing five men who were on a yardarm. With USS *Constellation*, *Ontario*, and *Erie*, the aim of the cruise was to demonstrate American naval strength to the Barbary pirate fleets of North Africa in what was known as the Second Barbary War.

In April Perry met the Dey of Algiers under a flag of truce and prevailed on him to honor the treaty of non-aggression against U.S. shipping, signed in 1815, which he had been ignoring. A show of force was also made at Tripoli. During this cruise, Perry slapped a Marine officer, John Heath, and both men were censured.

From January 25 to March 2, 1817 *Java* crossed from Gibraltar back to Boston, and was then laid up at Newport, Rhode Island. Recommissioned in 1827, it returned to the Mediterranean for two years, latterly as flagship of Commodore

James Biddle. In 1831 it returned to Norfolk, Virginia, and was converted into a receiving ship. In 1842 it was broken up.

SPECIFICATIONS

DISPLACEMENT: 1,511 tons (1,535 tonnes)

DIMENSIONS: 175 ft x 44 ft 6 in x 13 ft 8 in (53.3 m x 13.5 m x 4.16 m)

RIG: Three masts, full square rig

ARMAMENT: Thirty-three 32 pounder guns; twenty 42 pounder carronades

CREW: 400

USS *Java*

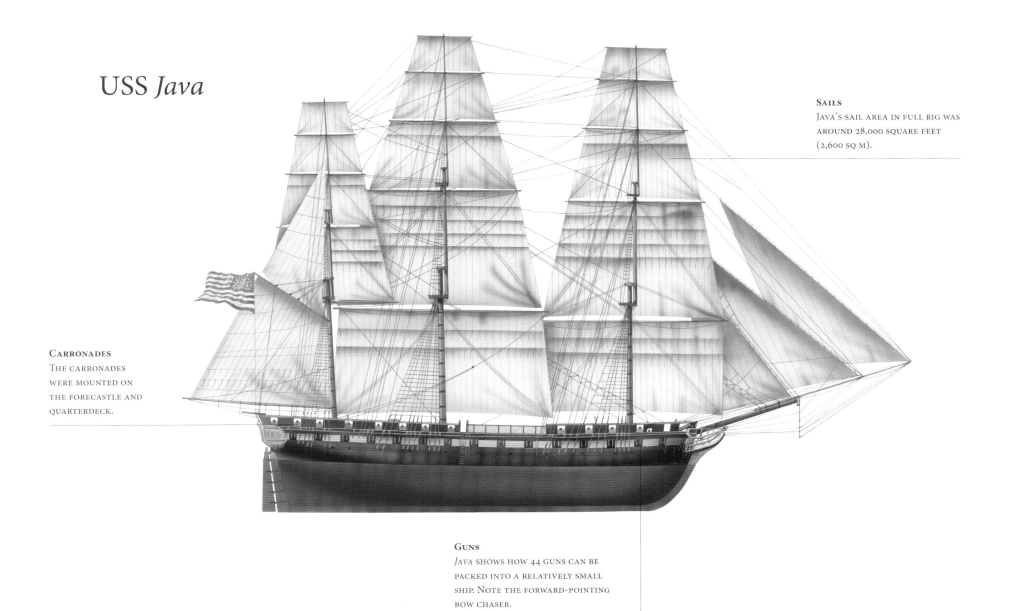

SAILS
JAVA'S SAIL AREA IN FULL RIG WAS
AROUND 28,000 SQUARE FEET
(2,600 SQ M).

CARRONADES
THE CARRONADES
WERE MOUNTED ON
THE FORECASTLE AND
QUARTERDECK.

GUNS
JAVA SHOWS HOW 44 GUNS CAN BE
PACKED INTO A RELATIVELY SMALL
SHIP. NOTE THE FORWARD-POINTING
BOW CHASER.

USS *Delaware* (1820)

BY 1813 THE U.S. CONGRESS HAD DECIDED THAT THE NAVY NEEDED LARGER SHIPS AS WELL AS FRIGATES IN ORDER TO MAINTAIN NATIONAL DEFENSE AND PRESTIGE, AND AN ACT OF JANUARY 2 PROVIDED FOR FOUR SHIPS OF THE LINE. A FURTHER NINE "TO RATE NOT LESS THAN 74 GUNS EACH" WERE AUTHORIZED ON APRIL 29, 1816. *DELAWARE*, THIRD U.S. NAVY SHIP OF THE NAME, WAS LAID DOWN AT THE NORFOLK NAVY YARD IN AUGUST 1817 AND LAUNCHED ON OCTOBER 21, 1820. EXPENSIVE TO MAINTAIN, IT SPENT 18 YEARS LAID UP BEFORE ITS FINAL DECOMMISSIONING.

The country's largest warship was not immediately put in service, but was roofed over and kept in ordinary at the yard until March 27, 1827, when it was ordered to be fitted for sea. It finally made its first cruise on February 10, 1828, under the command of Captain J. Downs, to become the flagship of Commodore W. I. M. Crane in the Mediterranean. Arriving at Algeciras Bay, Spain, on March 23, it served in the interests of American commerce and diplomacy in that area until returning to Norfolk on January 2, 1830.

Mediterranean and South American Operations

Delaware was decommissioned on February 10, 1830, and lay in ordinary at Norfolk until 1833. It was the first ship to enter the Navy Yard's new dry dock on June 17, 1833; recommissioned on July 15, it was inspected by President Jackson on the 29th, firing a 24-gun salute at both his arrival and departure. The following day it left for the Mediterranean to serve as flagship for Commodore D. T. Patterson until returning to Hampton Roads on February 16, 1836. It was placed in ordinary from March 10, 1836, until it was recommissioned on May 7, 1841, for local operations from Norfolk.

On November 1, 1841, the ship made a tour of duty on the Brazil Station as flagship of Commodore C. Morris, patrolling the coasts of Brazil, Uruguay, and Argentina to represent United States interests during a period of unrest as these countries fought for independence from Portugal and Spain.

On February 19, 1843, *Delaware* sailed from Rio de Janeiro for another cruise in the Mediterranean, returning to Hampton Roads March 4, 1844, and was decommissioned at Norfolk Navy Yard on the 22nd. Still held in ordinary there in 1861, it was burned to the waterline on April 20, along with other ships and the yard facilities, to prevent their falling into Confederate hands.

SPECIFICATIONS

DISPLACEMENT: 2,633 tons (2,675 tonnes)

DIMENSIONS: 196 ft 2 in x 53 ft x 26 ft 2 in (59.8 m x 16.15 m x 7.9 m)

RIG: Three masts, full square rig

ARMAMENT: Seventy-four 32 pounder carronades

CREW: 820

USS *Delaware*

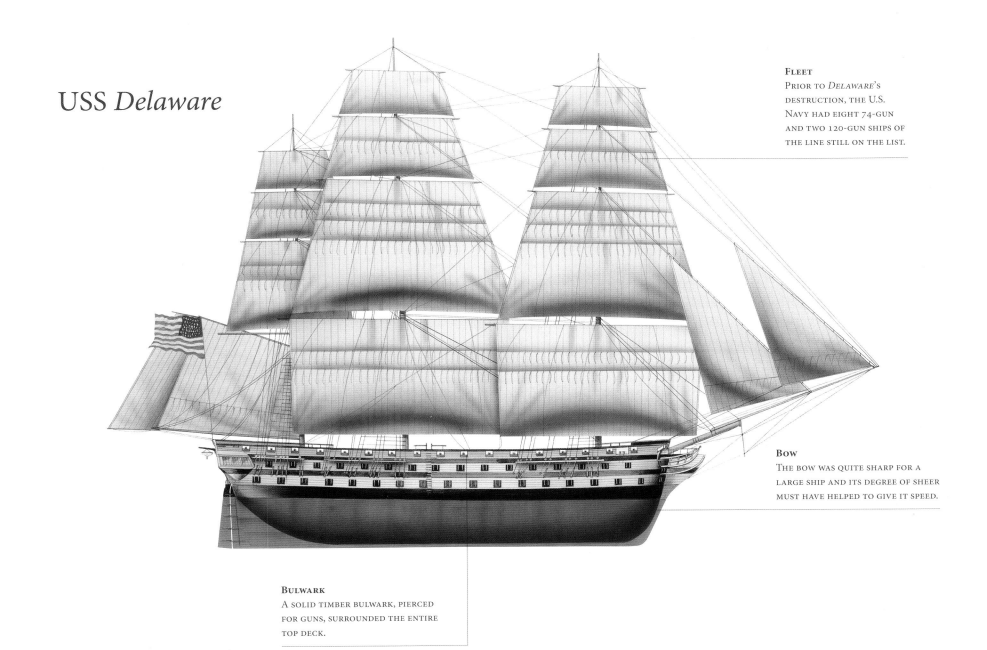

FLEET
PRIOR TO *DELAWARE*'S
DESTRUCTION, THE U.S.
NAVY HAD EIGHT 74-GUN
AND TWO 120-GUN SHIPS OF
THE LINE STILL ON THE LIST.

BOW
THE BOW WAS QUITE SHARP FOR A
LARGE SHIP AND ITS DEGREE OF SHEER
MUST HAVE HELPED TO GIVE IT SPEED.

BULWARK
A SOLID TIMBER BULWARK, PIERCED
FOR GUNS, SURROUNDED THE ENTIRE
TOP DECK.

USRC *Morris* (1831)

WITH THE TRADITION OF SMALL, HANDY, WELL-ARMED VESSELS WELL ESTABLISHED FROM THE TIME OF THE WAR OF INDEPENDENCE, THE SPHERE OF ACTION MOVED FROM PATRIOTIC DEFENSE TO ILLEGAL SMUGGLING. IN RESPONSE THE U.S. REVENUE SERVICE BUILT FAST CUTTERS, WHICH COULD INTERCEPT OR CHASE CONTRABAND RUNNERS. SOME, INCLUDING *MORRIS*, WERE PROVIDED WITH ADDITIONAL GUNPORTS TO SERVE, IF REQUIRED, WITH THE U.S. NAVY.

The United States Revenue Cutter *Morris*, named after a signatory of the Declaration of Independence, was one of 13 ships of the Morris-Taney class to be launched, all named after Secretaries of the Treasury. Samuel Humphreys, Chief Constructor for the Navy between 1826 and 1846, designed them for roles that might include fighting pirates and privateers, combating smugglers, and operating with naval forces. His design was based on a naval schooner concept, and they were given Baltimore Clipper lines: sharply shaped hulls, with a V-shaped section below the waterline, and a very pronounced rake to the masts, stem, and sternpost.

Coastguard vessels built by Webb and Allen, New York, designed by Isaac Webb, resembled Humphreys' but had one less gunport. These cutters were the backbone of the Service for more than a decade. In normal service they mounted six 9 pounder guns but could carry up to 14, making them a match, or more than a match, for the typical smugglers' boat of similar size but less gunpower.

Naval Career

The *Morris* began its career on a cruise from Maine to Sabine, Texas. On October 20, 1831, it arrived for duty at Portland, Maine. In May 1846 it sailed to Key West to participate in the Mexican War. On October 11, 1846, a hurricane drove *Morris* ashore three miles northwest of Key West. The following month the Key West Collector of Customs received instructions to sell the vessel, and it was formally stricken in January 1847.

The ships were known as the Morris-Taney class, although the first to be launched were *Dexter*, *Crawford*, *Hamilton*, and *Gallatin*, all in 1830. Of the 13 that made up the class, seven were eventually sold: one, *Gallatin*, was transferred to the Coast Survey; two, *Rush* and *Wolcott*, to the Lighthouse Service; *Ingham* was sold to the Republic of Texas; and two were wrecked.

SPECIFICATIONS

DISPLACEMENT: 112 tons (113 tonnes)

DIMENSIONS: 73 ft 4 in x 20 ft 6 in x 9 ft 7 in (22.4 m x 6.3 m x 3 m)

RIG: Two masts, topsail schooner

ARMAMENT: Six 9 pounder guns (extendable to 14)

CREW: 24

USRC *Morris*

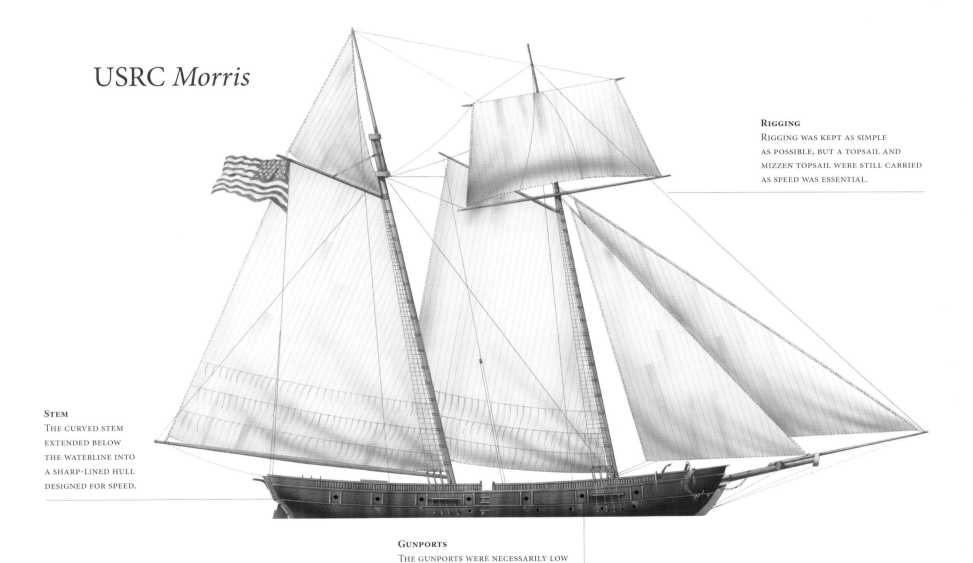

RIGGING
RIGGING WAS KEPT AS SIMPLE AS POSSIBLE, BUT A TOPSAIL AND MIZZEN TOPSAIL WERE STILL CARRIED AS SPEED WAS ESSENTIAL.

STEM
THE CURVED STEM EXTENDED BELOW THE WATERLINE INTO A SHARP-LINED HULL DESIGNED FOR SPEED.

GUNPORTS
THE GUNPORTS WERE NECESSARILY LOW DOWN, BUT WERE NOT INTENDED FOR LONG-RANGE FIRING.

USS *Pennsylvania* (1837)

PENNSYLVANIA WAS THE LARGEST SAILING SHIP BUILT FOR THE U.S. NAVY. AUTHORIZED BY CONGRESS ON APRIL 29, 1816, ITS CONSTRUCTION WAS SLOW AND SPORADIC. BY THE TIME OF ITS LAUNCH IN 1837, MODERNIZATION OF WARSHIP DESIGN WAS BEGINNING TO TAKE OFF, MAKING IT A DISTINCTLY OLD-FASHIONED SHIP EVEN THOUGH IT WAS ULTIMATELY PROVIDED WITH SHELL-FIRING GUNS.

Designed and built by Samuel Humphreys, Chief Constructor to the Navy from 1826 to 1846, *Pennsylvania* was laid down at Philadelphia Navy Yard in 1821 and would occupy its slipway for 16 years before being launched on July 18, 1837.

Fitting Out

Commissioned late in 1837, it was moved to Chester, Pennsylvania, on November 29, although fitting-out work was not complete.

Despite protests from the city of Philadelphia that the work should be done in the ship's "native state," in December it sailed for Gosport Navy Yard, across the bay from Norfolk, Virginia, where it was dry-docked in January 1838 for the hull to be coppered. There were four complete gun decks, three of them covered, and the hull was pierced for 136 guns.

That short voyage from Delaware Bay to Chesapeake Bay showed it as a fine-looking ship but it also turned out to be *Pennsylvania's* only trip out of harbor. It remained in ordinary at Norfolk until 1842, when it was converted into a receiving ship.

The high cost of maintaining such a huge ship, the lack of any particular need for a vessel of such size and potential gunpower, and its increasing obsolescence all ensured that *Pennsylvania* would not see blue water service. Its existence was a political football between those who saw it as "the pride of our Navy and the honour of our Union" and those who considered it as a hugely unjustifiable expense on the taxpayers.

Burned to the Waterline

It was still at Norfolk on the outbreak of the Civil War in April 1861 when it was burned to the waterline along with other ships and equipment to prevent use by the Confederacy. After the war the wreck was raised for salvage.

SPECIFICATIONS

DISPLACEMENT: 3,241 tons (3,293 tonnes)

DIMENSIONS: 210 ft x 56 ft 9 in x 24 ft 4 in (64 m x 17.3 m x 7.42 m)

RIG: Three masts, full square rig

ARMAMENT: Ninety 32 pounders, two 9 pounder guns; twelve 8-in-chambered cannons (1846)

CREW: 1,100

USS *Pennsylvania*

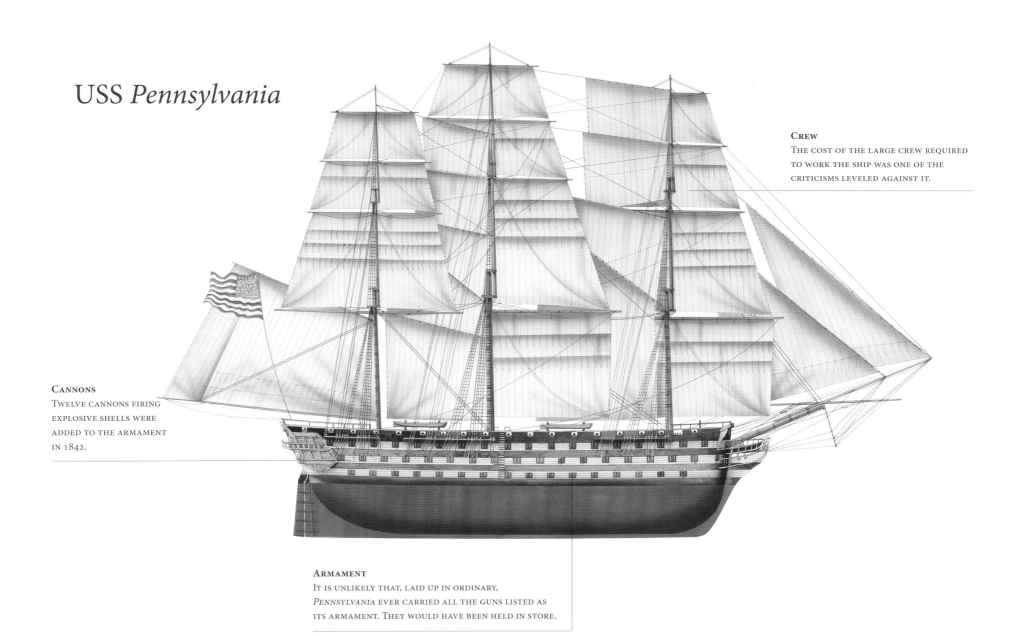

CREW
THE COST OF THE LARGE CREW REQUIRED
TO WORK THE SHIP WAS ONE OF THE
CRITICISMS LEVELED AGAINST IT.

CANNONS
TWELVE CANNONS FIRING
EXPLOSIVE SHELLS WERE
ADDED TO THE ARMAMENT
IN 1842.

ARMAMENT
IT IS UNLIKELY THAT, LAID UP IN ORDINARY,
PENNSYLVANIA EVER CARRIED ALL THE GUNS LISTED AS
ITS ARMAMENT. THEY WOULD HAVE BEEN HELD IN STORE.

USS *Mississippi* *(1842)*

Mississippi, a ship-rigged side-wheel steamer, was laid down at the Philadelphia Navy Yard in 1839, built under the supervision of Commodore Matthew C. Perry, and commissioned on December 22, 1841, with Captain W. D. Salter in command. It was launched in January 1842.

After several years of service in the Home Squadron, employed mainly in tests to do with development of a steam-powered Navy, *Mississippi* joined the West Indian Squadron in 1845 as Perry's flagship during the Mexican War. It returned to Norfolk for repairs on January 1, 1847, then arrived at Vera Cruz on March 21 and was immediately engaged in amphibious operations against the city and Mexico's east coast, taking part in the capture of Tabasco in June.

Mississippi cruised the Mediterranean during 1849–51, then returned to the United States to prepare for service as flagship in Perry's momentous first voyage to Japan. The squadron cleared Hampton Roads on November 24, 1852, and entered Tokyo Bay on July 8, 1853. Perry proceeded, in one of the most significant naval/diplomatic missions ever recorded, to negotiate a trade treaty with the Japanese. After further cruising in the Far East, the squadron returned to Japan on February 12, 1854, and on March 31 the Treaty of Kanagawa was signed.

Return to the U.S. and Civil War Engagement

Mississippi returned to New York on April 23, 1855. Again deployed to the Far East from August 19, 1857, it was based at Shanghai and was present during the British and French attack on the Chinese forts at Taku in June 1859. Two months later it landed a force at Shanghai.

Returned to ordinary service at Boston in 1860, it was reactivated to institute the blockade of Key West on June 8, 1861, and was with Farragut's squadron for the assault on New Orleans.

On April 7, 1862, with USS *Pensacola,* it crossed the bar at Southwest Pass, the heaviest ships yet to enter the river. During the fight with Forts Jackson and St Philip on April 24, *Mississippi* ran the Confederate ram CSS *Manassas* ashore, wrecking it with two broadsides. Ordered upriver with six other ships for operations against Port Hudson, on March 14, 1863, it grounded. Efforts to refloat it by Capt. Melancthon Smith and his executive officer, later Admiral George Dewey, failed, and they fired the ship to prevent its capture, with 64 killed and the escorting ships saving 223 of her crew.

SPECIFICATIONS

DISPLACEMENT: 3,220 tons (3,271 tonnes)

DIMENSIONS: 229 ft x 40 ft x 19 ft (70 m x 12 m x 5.8 m)

RIG: Three masts, barque rig

PROPULSION: Sails, side paddles

ARMAMENT: Two 10 in, eight 8 in guns (1841)

SPEED: 8 knots (9.2 mph; 14.8 km/h)

CREW: 257

USS *Mississippi*

DESIGN
MISSISSIPPI WAS A SHIP OF
ELEGANT LINES DESPITE THE
PADDLE WHEELS, HELPED BY
A SLIGHT RAKE TO THE MASTS.

BULWARKS
THE FORWARD BULWARKS, BETWEEN
THE BOWSPRIT SOCKET AND THE
FOREMAST, COULD BE DROPPED TO
ENABLE GUNS TO BEAR.

USS *Powhatan* (1850)

PAINTED BLACK WITH A BROAD WHITE STRIPE, *POWHATAN* WAS THE FLAGSHIP OF COMMODORE MATTHEW PERRY'S SQUADRON OF "BLACK SHIPS" ON HIS SECOND JAPANESE MISSION IN 1854. IT WAS THE LAST AND ONE OF THE LARGEST OF THE U.S. NAVY'S PADDLE FRIGATES, RIGGED AS A BARQUE AND LATER AS A BRIGANTINE.

Built at the Gosport Navy Yard, Virginia, launched on February 14, 1850, and commissioned at Norfolk Navy Yard on September 2, 1852, *Powhatan* cost $785,000. It served first as flagship of the Home Squadron under Commodore John T. Newton, and carried the new U.S. Minister to Vera Cruz, Mexico, in October 1852; then from June 15, 1863, it was assigned to the Far East Squadron under Commodore Perry. The commercial Treaty of Kanagawa was signed on its deck in Edo (Tokyo) harbor on March 31, 1854.

On the return voyage it co-operated with the British screw frigate HMS *Rattler* in the Battle of Ty-Ho Bay against a Chinese pirate fleet off the port of Kulan (Kowloon), rescuing several captured merchant vessels. In February 1856 it was back in home waters and served with the West Indies Squadron. In February 1860

Powhatan carried the first Ambassador of Japan to the USA across the Pacific (through a typhoon) to Panama.

Civil War Operations and Beyond

In the course of the Civil War *Powhatan* assisted in the relief of Fort Pickens, Florida, in April 1861, and subsequently participated in blockading the port of Mobile and the Mississippi Delta. From October 1862 to August 1863 it was blockading Charleston, and from November 1863 to September 1864 it was Rear Admiral James L. Lardner's flagship in the West Indies.

Back off the U.S. coast, *Powhatan* joined in the capture of Fort Fisher, North Carolina, in December 1864–January 1865. From October 1865 it was deployed to the Pacific, via Cape Horn, escorting the monitor USS *Monadnock*, reaching San Francisco on June 22, 1866, and assuming the role of flagship to the South

Pacific Squadron. Returned to the East Coast in 1869, it was flagship of the Home Squadron from September 15, 1869, to December 30, 1870, and again from July 4, 1877, to December 10, 1879.

Powhatan's final service was in commerce protection off Cuba in early 1886. On June 2 of that year the ship was decommissioned; it was sold on July 30 for breaking up at Meriden, Connecticut.

SPECIFICATIONS

DISPLACEMENT: 3,765 tons (3,825 tonnes)

DIMENSIONS: 253 ft 8 in x 45 ft x 18 ft 6 in (77.3 m x 14 m x 5.64 m)

RIG: Three masts, brigantine rig

PROPULSION: Sails and side paddles, steam engine, 1,500 ihp (1,119 kW)

ARMAMENT: One 11 in (280 mm), ten 9 in (230 mm) SB guns; five 12 pounder guns

SPEED: 11 knots (12.6 mph; 20.3 km/h)

CREW: 289

USS *Powhatan*

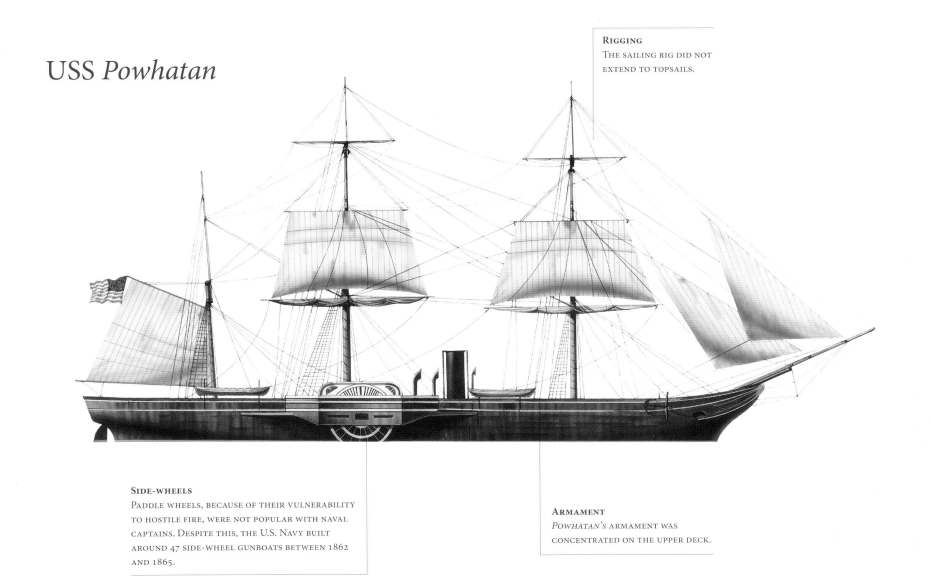

RIGGING
THE SAILING RIG DID NOT
EXTEND TO TOPSAILS.

SIDE-WHEELS
PADDLE WHEELS, BECAUSE OF THEIR VULNERABILITY
TO HOSTILE FIRE, WERE NOT POPULAR WITH NAVAL
CAPTAINS. DESPITE THIS, THE U.S. NAVY BUILT
AROUND 47 SIDE-WHEEL GUNBOATS BETWEEN 1862
AND 1865.

ARMAMENT
POWHATAN'S ARMAMENT WAS
CONCENTRATED ON THE UPPER DECK.

USS *San Jacinto* (1851)

THE EXPLOITS OF *SAN JACINTO* SHOW CLEARLY THE USE OF THE WARSHIP AS AN INSTRUMENT OF GOVERNMENT POLICY IN DIPLOMATIC AND SOCIAL MATTERS. ONE OF THE SQUADRON THAT VISITED JAPAN IN 1856, IT PATROLLED AGAINST SLAVE SHIPS AND WAS INVOLVED IN THE INTERNATIONAL CRISIS OF THE TRENT AFFAIR IN 1861.

One of the first U.S. warships to be powered by combined sail and screw, *San Jacinto* was laid down at the New York Navy Yard in August 1847 and was launched on April 16, 1850. Classed as a screw frigate and commissioned in November 1851, it was used in trials to assess the effectiveness of the new machinery. This was not high, and after a cruise to Europe new engines were installed between July 5, 1853 and August 6, 1854.

Another European visit was followed by brief service in the Home and West Indies squadrons, then a spell in ordinary between June 21 and October 4, 1855. After that *San Jacinto* was deployed to the Far East on a visit to Japan to set up a U.S. consulate and bolster trade relations, and to protect American citizens and commercial interests in China during the Second Opium War, until 1858. Engine trouble was still a problem.

Decommissioned between August 4, 1858 and July 6, 1859, *San Jacinto* then went on Atlantic patrols against slave ships, capturing the slaver *Storm King* with 616 Africans on board, on August 8, 1860, and landing them at Monrovia, Liberia.

The *Trent* Affair

A diplomatic crisis was caused on November 8, 1861 when *San Jacinto*, commanded by Charles Wilkes, arrested the British ship *Trent*, carrying two Confederate agents, on the high seas.

It saw much other action in the Civil War, as flagship of the East Gulf Blockading Squadron, then with the North Atlantic Squadron, on the watch for Confederate commerce raiders and blockade runners. It captured four merchant ships between August 1863 and March 1864 but failed in its hunt for such ships as CSS *Alabama* and *Tallahassee*. From December 3, 1864, it was flagship

at Key West, but on January 1, 1865, it struck a reef off Great Abaco Island and filled with water. The guns and some other items were salvaged, but the hull was unrecoverable and finally sold at Nassau on May 17, 1871.

SPECIFICATIONS

DISPLACEMENT: 1,567 tons (1,592 tonnes)

DIMENSIONS: 234 ft x 37 ft 9 in x 23 ft 3 in (71 m x 11.5 m x 7 m)

RIG: Three masts, full square rig

PROPULSION: Sails and screw propeller

ARMAMENT: Two 8 in, four 32 pounder guns

SPEED: 8 knots (9.2 mph; 14.8 km/h)

CREW: 278

USS *San Jacinto*

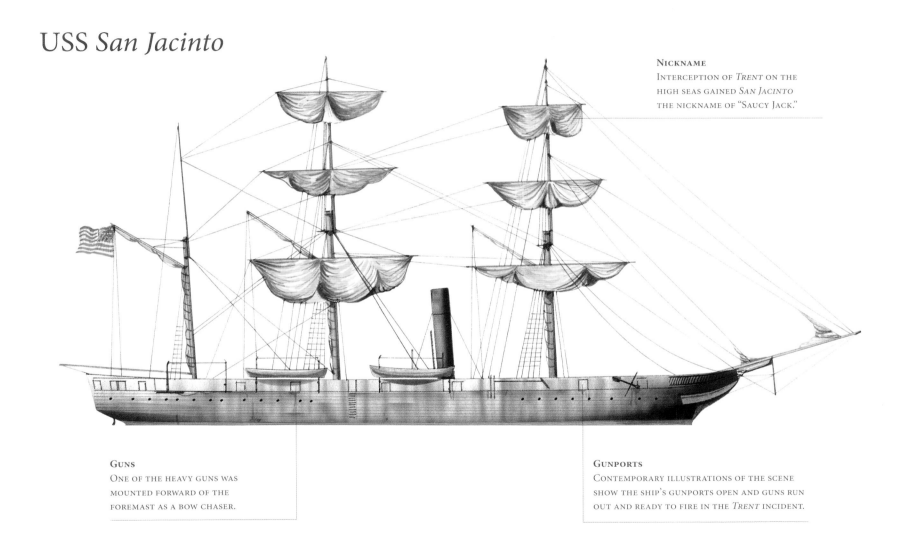

NICKNAME
INTERCEPTION OF *TRENT* ON THE
HIGH SEAS GAINED *SAN JACINTO*
THE NICKNAME OF "SAUCY JACK."

GUNS
ONE OF THE HEAVY GUNS WAS
MOUNTED FORWARD OF THE
FOREMAST AS A BOW CHASER.

GUNPORTS
CONTEMPORARY ILLUSTRATIONS OF THE SCENE
SHOW THE SHIP'S GUNPORTS OPEN AND GUNS RUN
OUT AND READY TO FIRE IN THE *TRENT* INCIDENT.

USS *Brooklyn* (1858)

IN A 30-YEAR CAREER, THIS WOODEN-HULLED SCREW SLOOP FIRST SERVED IN THE CARIBBEAN, WAS VERY ACTIVE IN THE CIVIL WAR—MOST NOTABLY IN THE FIERCE FIGHTING AROUND MOBILE— AND AFTERWARDS SERVED WIDELY IN CRUISES TO THE WEST INDIES, EUROPE, THE EAST AFRICAN COAST, PATAGONIA, AND THE FAR EAST.

One of five screw sloops authorized by the U.S. Congress on March 3, 1857, *Brooklyn* was laid down at the New York yard of Jacob A. Westervelt and Son that year, launched in 1858, and commissioned on January 26, 1859. Its first captain was David C. Farragut, the future Admiral, and in February 1859 its first cruise was to Haiti and Panama. From April 1859 to July 1860 it assisted the U.S. mission to President Benito Juarez's government in Mexico. On October 20, 1860, Captain William S. Walker took over command.

Civil War Action and Postwar Service

Brooklyn served with the West Gulf Blockading Squadron from 1861 to 1864, effecting the relief of Fort Pickens, Florida, and with other ships pursuing the elusive CSS *Fort Sumter*. Between July and December 1861 it underwent repairs and

refit at Philadelphia Navy Yard and on December 19 it sailed to rejoin Farragut's squadron, soon to take part in the heavy fighting on the lower Mississippi, assisting in the capture of New Orleans on April 25 and joining in the battle around Vicksburg.

After repairs at New York from August 1863 it was recommissioned on April 14, 1864, and returned to the South, leading Farragut's fleet into Mobile Bay on August 5. In the Battle of Mobile Bay it was hit 40 times, with 11 crew killed and 43 wounded. From October 1864 *Brooklyn* joined the North Atlantic Blockading Squadron until January 1865, and was then laid up for repairs.

Brooklyn's postwar career was the usual combination of cruises interspersed with periods in ordinary, but the ship ranged exceptionally widely in the South Atlantic, Pacific, and Indian Oceans. Between April 4, 1887, and April 24, 1889, it made

a full circumnavigation of the Earth as a termination of a distinguished career. Decommissioned at the New York Navy Yard on May 14, 1889, it was stricken from the Navy List on January 6, 1890, and sold for scrapping on March 25, 1891.

SPECIFICATIONS

DISPLACEMENT: 2,532 tons (2,572 tonnes)

DIMENSIONS: 233 ft x 43 ft x 16 ft 3 in (71 m x 13 m x 4.95 m)

RIG: Three masts, square rig

PROPULSION: Sails and screw propeller

ARMAMENT: One 10 in (254 mm), twenty 9 in (228 mm) guns

SPEED: 11.5 knots (13.2 mph; 21.2 km/h)

CREW: 335

FUNNEL
THE FUNNEL COULD BE RETRACTED
WHEN THE SHIP WAS UNDER FULL SAIL.

USS *Brooklyn*

GUNS
BROOKLYN'S GUNS WERE ALL SMOOTH
BORE, MUZZLE LOADING TYPE.

DAMAGE
DURING THE ATTACK ON FORTS ST. PHILIP AND JACKSON,
ON APRIL 24, 1862, THE CONFEDERATE RAM *MANASSAS*
RAMMED *BROOKLYN*, PUNCHING A 24-FT (7.3-M) HOLE IN
THE STARBOARD SIDE.

USS *Hartford* (1858)

ITS NAME ALWAYS ASSOCIATED WITH THE DASHING COMMODORE DAVID FARRAGUT, *HARTFORD* WAS HEAVILY INVOLVED IN CIVIL WAR NAVAL BATTLES BUT SURVIVED TO GIVE LONG SERVICE ON FOREIGN STATIONS AND AS A TRAINING VESSEL. IT REMAINED AFLOAT UNTIL IT FOUNDERED IN 1956.

Built by Harrison Loring of Boston, Massachusetts, *Hartford* was launched on November 22, 1858, and commissioned as a screw sloop on May 27, 1859, under Captain Charles Lowndes. Immediately after shaking down it was deployed as flagship of the East India Squadron, but ordered home when the Civil War began, arriving in Philadelphia on December 2, 1861.

Quickly refitted, it became flagship of the West Gulf Blockading Squadron under Farragut. During April 1862 the squadron crossed the mud bar into the Mississippi and fought its way upriver against intense resistance.

On April 25 New Orleans was taken, but the challenge of seizing control of the highly strategic Mississippi waterway remained, and there was more hard fighting on the river against sailing ships, ironclads, and fire barges, as well as shore forts, before the Vicksburg fort was taken

on July 4, 1863. A year later on August 5, 1864, Confederate and Union squadrons fought a fierce battle in Mobile Bay, with *Hartford* still as Farragut's flagship, ending in a Union victory despite the heroic stand of the ironclad CSS *Tennessee*.

After the War

In the postbellum years *Hartford*, once repaired, spent two tours of duty as flagship of the East India Squadron in 1865–68 and 1872–75. After a long spell in ordinary it was made a sail training ship based at Mare Island, California, from 1887–90.

Another spell laid up was ended in 1899 when, after a substantial rebuild, it was recommissioned as a training ship on the Atlantic coast until 1912; then was a station ship at Charleston, South Carolina. In 1938 it was moved to Washington D.C., by now in a venerable but leaky state, then transferred to Norfolk Navy

Yard in October 1945. Although classed as a relic, little was done to preserve it and the old ship sank at its moorings on November 20, 1956, and was subsequently broken up.

SPECIFICATIONS

DISPLACEMENT: 2,900 tons (2,947 tonnes)

DIMENSIONS: 225 ft x 44 ft x 17 ft 2 in (69 m x 13 m x 5.2 m)

RIG: Three masts, full square rig

PROPULSION: Sails, screw propeller, horizontal double piston engine

ARMAMENT: Twenty 9 in SB, twenty 20 pounder RB, two 12 pounder guns

SPEED: 13.5 knots (15.5 mph; 25 km/h)

CREW: 302

USS *Hartford*

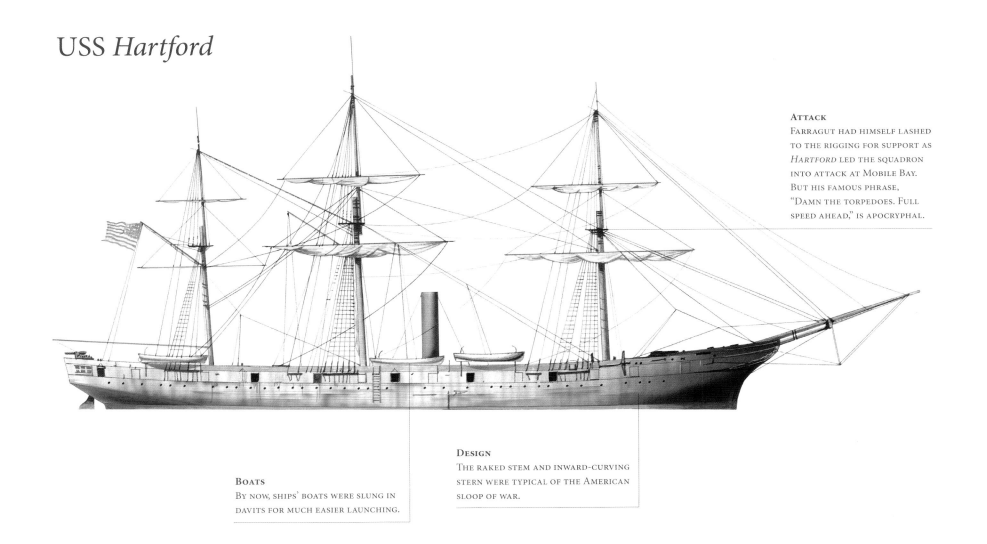

ATTACK
FARRAGUT HAD HIMSELF LASHED
TO THE RIGGING FOR SUPPORT AS
HARTFORD LED THE SQUADRON
INTO ATTACK AT MOBILE BAY.
BUT HIS FAMOUS PHRASE,
"DAMN THE TORPEDOES. FULL
SPEED AHEAD," IS APOCRYPHAL.

DESIGN
THE RAKED STEM AND INWARD-CURVING
STERN WERE TYPICAL OF THE AMERICAN
SLOOP OF WAR.

BOATS
BY NOW, SHIPS' BOATS WERE SLUNG IN
DAVITS FOR MUCH EASIER LAUNCHING.

HMS *Victoria* (1859)

THE LARGEST WOODEN-HULLED WARSHIP EVER TO ENTER SERVICE, AND THE LAST OF THE THREE-DECKERS, *VICTORIA* WAS A HUGELY IMPOSING VESSEL WHOSE IMPRESSIVE APPEARANCE BELIED THE FACT THAT IT WAS ESSENTIALLY AN OBSOLETE DESIGN. *VICTORIA* WAS LAID DOWN AT PORTSMOUTH ON APRIL 1, 1856, AND LAUNCHED ON NOVEMBER 12, 1859.

V*ictoria* was planned from the start as a sail-assisted steamship. In the British Admiralty's typical knee-jerk response to French developments, it was intended to rival the 130-gun French three-decker *Bretagne*, which had been laid down as a sailing ship but was converted to steam propulsion while building, and launched in February 1855.

Size and Firepower

The total cost of building *Victoria* was £150,578. The hull was heavily strapped on the inner side with diagonal iron riders, 5 in (127 mm) wide and 1 in (25 mm) thick, to hold the planking together against the vibrations from machinery and screw. Even so, the seams tended to separate and it was a leaky ship.

Victoria has been described as "the acme of the three-decker," at twice the tonnage of HMS *Victory* and with a far

higher destructive capacity. Fire could be directed on more than one target at a time, and the 30-pounder guns fired explosive shells that penetrated wood planking and then burst. As a result of this, the giant three-deckers were acknowledged as obsolescent, and by the end of the 1860s they were largely out of use.

From February 28, 1854, the Royal Navy's steam-powered ships were equipped with furnaces and handling gear for firing red-hot shot. Of course this required very careful handling, and only 32-pounder guns of the most robust construction were considered really safe to fire them.

From 1860 to 1864, *Victoria* was held in reserve at Portsmouth; then from 1864, with the number of guns reduced to 102, it was flagship of the Mediterranean Fleet. The last time the great wooden-hulled ships went on parade was at the Spithead

Naval Review of July 1867, before Queen Victoria and the Ottoman Emperor. In August 1867 *Victoria* was paid off and technically placed on reserve, but in fact the old wooden vessels were either converted to other uses or left to rot away. The hull was sold for scrap in May 1893.

SPECIFICATIONS

DISPLACEMENT: 6,959 tons (7,070 tonnes)

DIMENSIONS: 260 ft x 60 ft x 25 ft 9 in (79.2 m x 18.3 m x 7.8 m)

RIG: Three masts, full square rig

PROPULSION: Sails, screw propeller, Maudslay 4,403 ihp (3,283 kW) engine

ARMAMENT: Sixty-two 8 in (200 mm), thirty-two 30 pounders, thirty-six 32 pounders, one 68 pounder gun

SPEED: 11.8 knots (13.5 mph; 21.8 km/h)

CREW: 1,000

HMS *Victoria*

MASTS
MAST HEIGHTS WERE: FOREMAST,
61 FT (18.6 M); MAIN, 67 FT (20.4 M);
MIZZEN, 51 FT 6 IN (15.7 M).

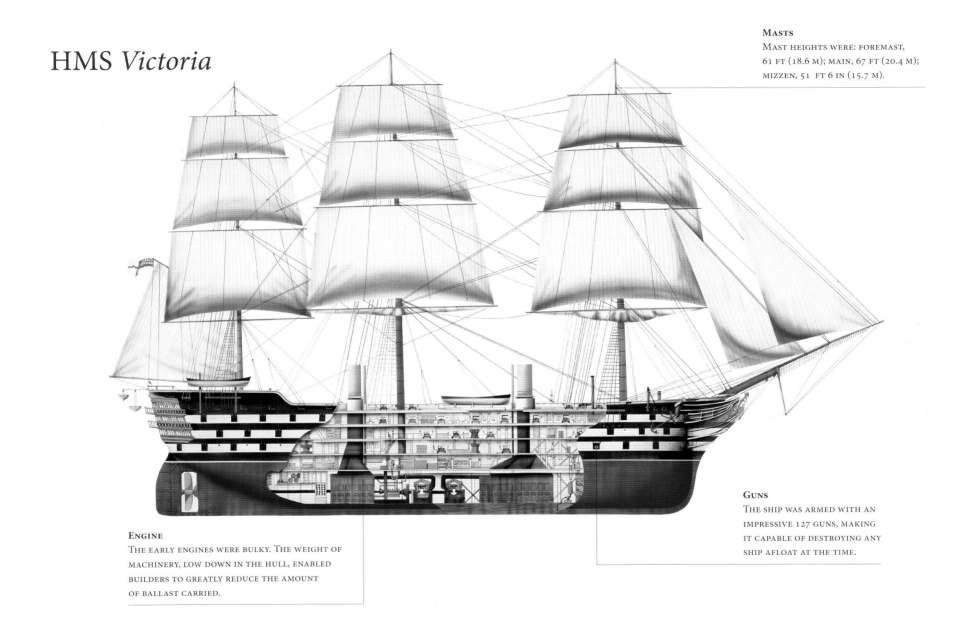

ENGINE
THE EARLY ENGINES WERE BULKY. THE WEIGHT OF
MACHINERY, LOW DOWN IN THE HULL, ENABLED
BUILDERS TO GREATLY REDUCE THE AMOUNT
OF BALLAST CARRIED.

GUNS
THE SHIP WAS ARMED WITH AN
IMPRESSIVE 127 GUNS, MAKING
IT CAPABLE OF DESTROYING ANY
SHIP AFLOAT AT THE TIME.

Gloire (1859)

CLASSED AS A *FRÉGATE CUIRASSÉE*, OR ARMORED FRIGATE, *GLOIRE* WAS BUILT TO A DESIGN BY THE CELEBRATED NAVAL ARCHITECT DUPUY DE LÔME, AND AS THE FIRST OCEANGOING "IRONCLAD," REPRESENTED A NEW MILESTONE IN WARSHIP DEVELOPMENT. DESPITE ITS LARGE MACHINERY, *GLOIRE* CARRIED A FULL SET OF SAILS, WITH THE RIG VARYING AT DIFFERENT TIMES.

Gloire ("Glory"), eighth French warship of the name, owed its "frigate" designation to its single gun deck; in armament, protection, and speed it outclassed any other warship at the time of its commissioning. Laid down at Toulon in April 1858, launched on November 24, 1859, and commissioned in August 1860, its building was rapid for a large ship but the general design was on conventional lines.

By the late 1850s, the use of rifled guns and highly explosive shells had made most ships' hulls far more vulnerable than before. Dupuy de Lôme devised a strengthening scheme of heavy iron plates applied to a wooden hull structure. The plates, made by the engineer Eugène de la Charrière at the Allevard Ironworks, were 4.7 in (12 cm) thick, and had been tested against heavy guns at only 65 ft (20 m) range without breaking. The armor, in an upper belt of 4 in (10 cm) and a lower belt of 4.7 in (12 cm) weighed 810 tons (823 tonnes), and to compensate for this a second gun deck, otherwise normal in a ship of this size, was dispensed with.

As with all technical innovations, the first ironclad initiated an era in which gunmakers and ship designers (and metallurgists) would vie with each other to outdo the latest advance made by the other side.

Although provided with one of the most powerful engines yet fitted to a ship, *Gloire* carried a full suit of sails, being changed from the original barquentine rig to full square rig, with 27,000 sq ft (2,508 sq m) of sail surface. This was in part because the engine did not provide the specified speed of 13 knots (14.9 mph; 24 km/h).

A Symbolic Vessel

Gloire did not have an eventful career, stationed mostly at Cherbourg as if to remind the Royal Navy, just across the Channel, that the Marine Nationale was a force to contend with. In 1886 its 36 muzzle-loader guns were replaced by 14 more up-to-date and higher-caliber breech-loaders. Its very existence stimulated urgent changes in warship design by other countries, especially Great Britain, which built the iron-hulled HMS *Warrior* (1861) as a direct response. *Gloire* was decommissioned in 1879 and scrapped in 1883.

SPECIFICATIONS

DISPLACEMENT: 5,675 tons (5,766 tonnes)

DIMENSIONS: 254 ft 5 in x 53 ft x 25 ft 7 in (77.25 m x 16.16 m x 7.8 m)

RIG: Three masts, barquentine, later full square rig

PROPULSION: Sails, screw propeller, 2-cycle trunk engine, 2,500 ihp (1,864 kW).

ARMAMENT: Thirty-six MLR guns

SPEED: 13.5 knots (15.5 mph; 25 km/h)

CREW: 550

Gloire

DECK
ON THE DECK AN OVAL
REDOUBT 4 IN (10 CM)
THICK SURROUNDED THE
HELM AND COMMAND POST.

GUNS
ITS NEW MLR GUNS OF 1866 COULD
PIERCE 4.7-IN (12-CM) IRON PLATES AT
880 YARDS (805 M) BUT WERE REPLACED
BY BL GUNS IN 1886.

BOW
THE BOW DESIGN, ALTHOUGH BLUNT
AND INELEGANT, PROVED EFFECTIVE.

HMS *Warrior* (1860)

THE SAIL-STEAM IRONCLAD *WARRIOR* WAS PLANNED AS A DIRECT RESPONSE TO FRANCE'S *GLOIRE*. ITS IRON HULL MARKED A CLEAR BREAK WITH THE WOODEN-HULLED TRADITION. BUT THE DESIGN SHOWED COMPROMISES BETWEEN THE NEW AND THE OLD: *WARRIOR* WAS ONE OF THE LAST THREE ROYAL NAVY SHIPS TO BE GIVEN A CARVED FIGUREHEAD.

Laid down at Ditchburn & Mare's yard at Blackwall on the Thames on May 25, 1859, launched on December 29, 1860, commissioned at Portsmouth in August 1861, and completed on October 24 that year, it cost £377,292. The heavy "knee bow" design weighed the vessel down at the bow end until a shelter deck was erected at the poop. Another traditional feature, not necessary on an ironclad, was the solid timber bulwarks surrounding the upper deck. Teak-backed armor plating was applied to the midship section only— 213 ft (64.9 m) long and 27 ft (8.23 m) vertically, with 6 ft (1.83 m) below the waterline. The Penn horizontal trunk engine was the most powerful yet installed on a warship.

The 4.5-in (114-mm) steel plating was impenetrable by any naval gun of the time (but by 1863 guns would be introduced to pierce such armor).

Warrior's 340-ft (103.6-m) length was notable: great length was identified with the ability to go fast, and care had been taken in designing the underwater lines—even under canvas alone, *Warrior* recorded 13 knots (14.9 mph; 24 km/h) under plain sail and stunsails, and under combined power on November 15, 1861, it made 16.3 knots (18.7 mph; 30.1 km/h). But its length made it difficult to handle in close maneuvers.

Service History

From 1861 to 1864 *Warrior* served with the Channel Fleet, and was out of commission while re-arming, 1864–67, then it rejoined the Channel Fleet. With HMS *Black Prince* it towed a floating dock across the Atlantic from Madeira to Bermuda in 1869. Another refit in 1872–75 saw it provided with the poop deck and steam capstan. It was a coastguard ship at Portland, then in 1881

was reclassified as an armored cruiser, and served until 1884 as a training ship for reservists on the River Clyde.

In 1904 it was adapted for service with the HMS *Vernon* torpedo school, and the cut-down hull was finally transferred to Pembroke to provide a pier for an oil pipeline. Restored in the 1980s, *Warrior* is preserved at Portsmouth naval base, England.

SPECIFICATIONS

DISPLACEMENT: 9,137 tons (9,283 tonnes)

DIMENSIONS: 420 ft x 58 ft 4 in x 26 ft (128 m x 17.78 m x 7.9 m)

RIG: Three masts, full square rig including stunsails

PROPULSION: Sails, screw propeller, Penn horizontal trunk engine, 5,267 ihp (3,874 kW)

ARMAMENT: Four 8 in, twenty-eight 7 in ML guns

SPEED: 16.3 knots (18.7 mph; 30.1 km/h)

CREW: 707

HMS *Warrior*

SAILS
WARRIOR'S SAIL AREA WAS
48,400 SQUARE FT (4,459 SQ M).

LENGTH
AT 420 FT (128 M)
WARRIOR WAS 166 FT
(50 M) LONGER THAN
ITS FRENCH RIVAL
GLOIRE.

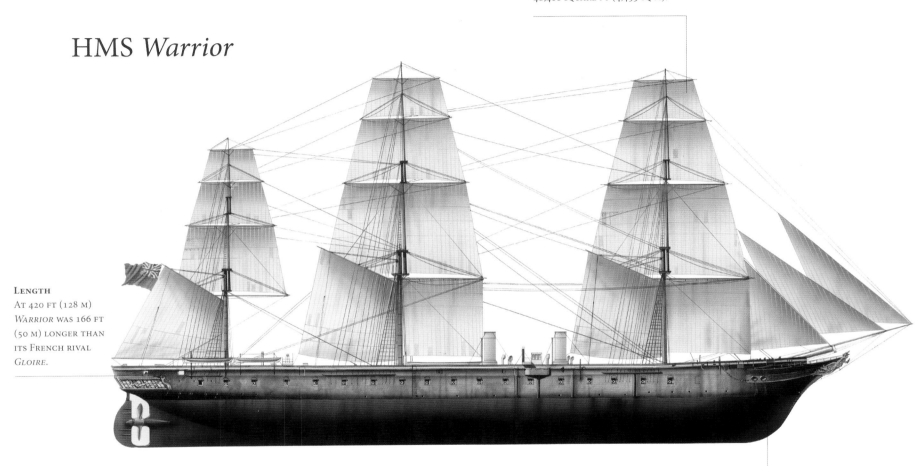

ANCHORS
THE SHIP CARRIED TWO BOWER AND TWO SHEET ADMIRALTY-PATTERN
WOODEN-STOCKED ANCHORS, EACH OF 4.75 TONS (4.83 TONNES), ONE
28 CWT (1.42 TONNES) IRON-STOCKED STREAM ANCHOR, AND TWO
IRON-STOCKED 19 CWT (965 KG) KEDGE ANCHORS.

USS *Kearsarge* (1861)

Kearsarge became famous as a result of its duel with CSS *Alabama* off Cherbourg, France, in June 1864. But it had a useful and varied career for some 30 years after that until it hit a reef in the Caribbean Sea in 1894. Ordered under the emergency war program of 1861, launched on September 11, 1861, at Portsmouth Navy Yard, New Hampshire, *Kearsarge* was commissioned as a screw sloop under Captain Charles Pickering on January 24, 1862.

With scant time for shaking down, *Kearsarge* was dispatched across the Atlantic to Gibraltar in pursuit of the highly elusive Confederate raider CSS *Sumter*, and it remained as part of the European Squadron, patrolling the western Atlantic sea lanes.

In June 1864, captained now by John A. Winslow, it was at Flushing, Holland, when reports came of CSS *Alabama* at Cherbourg, and *Kearsarge* immediately sailed to confront it. On June 19 the two ships met outside French territorial waters. *Kearsarge*, with the additional protection of chain cable triced in tiers along its most vulnerable middle section, was in better condition than *Alabama*, which sank after an hour's battle, with *Kearsarge* rescuing most of its crew.

Decommissioned at Boston for repairs between November 26, 1864, and April 1, 1865, *Kearsarge* made a failed attempt to

intercept CSS *Stonewall* before hostilities ended, and at the end of a tour that took it to the Mediterranean and Liberia, was laid up from August 14, 1866, to January 16, 1868.

On February 12 *Kearsarge* left for Valparaiso, and served on the Pacific coast and in ocean cruises until March 14, 1874, when it transferred to the Asia Station at Yokohama.

Scientific Mission

From September–December it took a scientific party to Vladivostok, Russia, to observe the transit of Venus. On December 30, 1877 it was back at Boston, via the Suez Canal, and laid up until May 15, 1879, when it had a further seven years of sea service with the Atlantic and Mediterranean squadrons. Again out of service between December 1, 1886, and November 2, 1888, it was then deployed to the Caribbean.

On February 2, 1894, *Kearsarge* was wrecked on the Roncador Reef, off the east coast of Nicaragua. Although Congress voted to provide $45,000 for salvaging it, this proved impossible and it was stricken from the Navy List.

SPECIFICATIONS

DISPLACEMENT: 1,550 tons (1,575 tonnes)

DIMENSIONS: 198 ft 5 in x 33 ft 8 in x 15 ft 8 in (60.5 m x 10.3 m x 4.8 m)

RIG: Three masts, barque rig

PROPULSION: Sails, screw propeller, horizontal back-acting engine, 842 ihp (628 kW)

ARMAMENT: Two 11 in, four 32 pounder guns

SPEED: 12 knots (13.8 mph; 22.2 km/h)

CREW: 212 (maximum)

USS *Kearsarge*

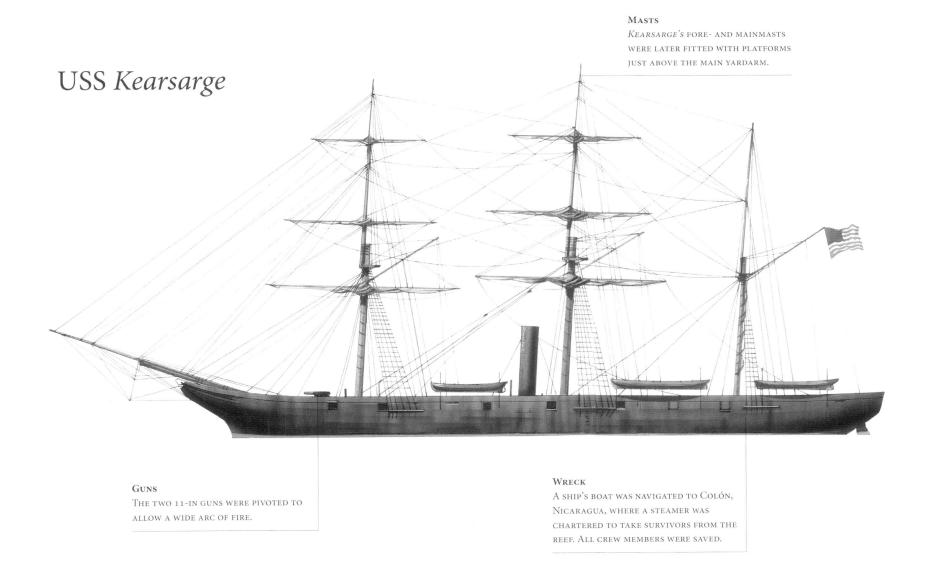

GUNS
THE TWO 11-IN GUNS WERE PIVOTED TO
ALLOW A WIDE ARC OF FIRE.

WRECK
A SHIP'S BOAT WAS NAVIGATED TO COLÓN,
NICARAGUA, WHERE A STEAMER WAS
CHARTERED TO TAKE SURVIVORS FROM THE
REEF. ALL CREW MEMBERS WERE SAVED.

USS *Housatonic* (1861)

FOUR WOODEN-HULLED SCREW SLOOPS OF THE OSSIPEE CLASS WERE ORDERED FOR THE UNION NAVY IN 1861, AND *HOUSATONIC* WAS LAID DOWN IN THAT YEAR. ITS CAREER WAS SHORT AND THE SHIP HAS THE MELANCHOLY DISTINCTION OF BEING THE FIRST TO BE SUNK BY A SUBMARINE, MARKING A TURNING POINT IN NAVAL WARFARE.

Built at the Boston Navy Yard, *Housatonic* was launched on November 20, 1861 and commissioned on August 29, 1862. In September it was deployed to the Charleston Blockading Squadron, and engaged the Confederate ironclad rams CSS *Chicora* and *Palmetto State* on January 31, 1863, fighting off their attempt to break the blockade, just after the blockade runner USS *Princess Royal*, with a valuable cargo of machinery and war material, had been captured on the 29th.

First Submarine Attack

As the largest Union vessel on the scene, *Housatonic* was singled out for an attack by the pioneer submarine *H.L. Hunley*, manned by eight men and armed with a spar torpedo. On the evening of February 17, 1864, the officer of the watch saw something moving in the water, and ordered the anchor to be

slipped and the engine started and put into reverse. There was no time to effect either of those actions. Similarly there was no time to load and train the guns, or else it was impossible to depress the barrels sufficiently to hit the *Hunley* as it closed in. The torpedo was lodged against the starboard hull, just forward of the mizzenmast, and successfully detached from its spar. The explosion blew a hole beneath the waterline and *Housatonic* rapidly filled with water and sank in the shallow water, its mastheads still above the surface. Five men were lost, and the survivors were picked up by other ships of the squadron.

The *Hunley* and its crew did not survive their unique exploit. Small arms fire was directed on it from the *Housatonic*, and it has been suggested that a rifle shot pierced one of *Hunley's* viewing ports. But it is equally possible that the submarine was damaged by the shock of the explosion

even though it was already moving away from the *Housatonic*. The Confederate Navy maintained its torpedo attacks with surface boats (*see New Ironsides*).

SPECIFICATIONS

DISPLACEMENT: 1,934 tons (1,965 tonnes)

DIMENSIONS: 205 ft x 38 ft x 16 ft 6 in (62.48 m x 11.58 m x 5.02 m)

RIG: Three masts, barque rig

PROPULSION: Sails, screw propeller, 2 Martin boilers, 700 ihp (522 kW)

ARMAMENT: One 6.4 in, three 4.2 in rifled ML guns; one 11 in, two 32 pounder SB; fourteen 11 in, one 12 pounder SB guns

SPEED: 10 knots (11.5 mph; 18.5 km/h)

CREW: 214

USS *Housatonic*

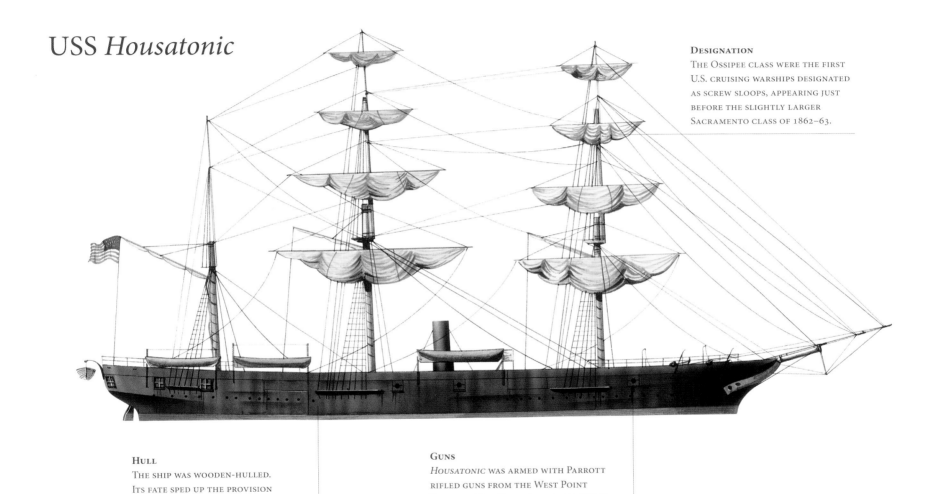

DESIGNATION

THE OSSIPEE CLASS WERE THE FIRST
U.S. CRUISING WARSHIPS DESIGNATED
AS SCREW SLOOPS, APPEARING JUST
BEFORE THE SLIGHTLY LARGER
SACRAMENTO CLASS OF 1862–63.

HULL

THE SHIP WAS WOODEN-HULLED.
ITS FATE SPED UP THE PROVISION
OF ARMORED WATERLINE PROTECTION
FOR WARSHIPS.

GUNS

HOUSATONIC WAS ARMED WITH PARROTT
RIFLED GUNS FROM THE WEST POINT
FOUNDRY, NEW YORK. ALTHOUGH GIVING
ACCURATE FIRE WITH SOLID SHOT, THEY HAD
A POOR REPUTATION FOR SAFETY.

CSS *Alabama* (1862)

ALABAMA WAS A HIGHLY SUCCESSFUL COMMERCE RAIDER, PERHAPS THE MOST SUCCESSFUL EVER, WITH A TOTAL OF 55 SHIPS CAPTURED AND DESTROYED, AND A FURTHER TEN BOARDED AND SEIZED, WITH THEIR VALUE ESTIMATED AT AROUND $6 MILLION. THIS WAS ACCOMPLISHED DURING A CAREER OF ONLY TWO YEARS BEFORE IT WAS SUNK IN A FAMOUS TWO-SHIP DUEL.

Built at Birkenhead, England, ostensibly as the merchant vessel *Enrica*, it left port on July 29, 1862, and in a rendezvous at the Azores was armed and equipped as a warship. It was commissioned by Captain Raphael Semmes on August 24 as *Alabama*.

Over a wide sweep of the Atlantic it sank 27 ships before the end of the year. In the course of 1863 it sailed into the Indian Ocean, reaching Singapore before returning to European waters. By this time the ship was badly in need of a refit, which Semmes hoped to have done at Cherbourg, but a change in French policy towards the Confederacy meant he could only take on coal and provisions.

Fight with *Kearsarge*

On June 14 USS *Kearsarge* entered the port but was requested to leave for violation of French neutrality. It waited outside the territorial limit, and on June 19 *Alabama*

sailed out, noted by an observer to have a strong list to starboard. Semmes's plan was to board, but *Kearsarge's* superior speed made this impossible. The two vessels circled each other at a range of about half a mile (800 m), exchanging fire, but the 11-in shells of *Kearsarge's* muzzle-loading Dahlgren guns did severe damage, with one hit piercing the hull at the waterline and disabling the engine.

After about an hour, Semmes struck his flag. *Kearsarge* lowered boats to take survivors, but *Deerhound*—a large three-masted British steam yacht, privately owned, which had come out to watch the battle—picked up Semmes, his first officer, Kell, and 40 others. This was allegedly at the request of Captain Winslow of *Kearsarge*, but—as a neutral ship was entitled to do—*Deerhound* did not hand them over.

Considering him a pirate, the Union government dearly wanted to get hold

of Semmes, who lay flat in the bottom of *Deerhound's* boat as *Kearsarge's* launch passed close by. He survived to become both an admiral in the Confederate forces. *Alabama's* wreck was located in November 1984, six miles off Cherbourg.

SPECIFICATIONS

DISPLACEMENT: 1,050 tons (1,067 tonnes)

DIMENSIONS: 220 ft x 31 ft 9 in x 14 ft (67.1 m x 9.7 m x 4.3 m)

RIG: Three masts, barque rig

PROPULSION: Sails and screw, direct acting 600 ihp (447 kW) engine

ARMAMENT: Six 32 pounders, one 110 pounder, one 68 pounder guns

SPEED: 13 knots (14.9 mph; 24 km/h)

CREW: 148

CSS *Alabama*

RIGGING
THE RIG DID NOT EXTEND BEYOND THE
TOPSAILS. *ALABAMA* DID MUCH OF ITS
VOYAGING UNDER SAIL ALONE.

HULL
DESCRIBED AS AN "AUXILIARY BARK,"
ALABAMA'S HULL WAS DESIGNED ON
SLOOP LINES.

INSURANCE
THE SUCCESS OF *ALABAMA* AND OTHER
SHIPS SUCH AS CSS *FLORIDA* AND
SHENANDOAH CAUSED INSURANCE RATES
FOR U.S.-REGISTERED VESSELS TO RISE BY
900 PER CENT.

Magenta *(1862)*

MAGENTA AND ITS SISTER SHIP *SOLFÉRINO* WERE DISTINGUISHED AS THE ONLY BROADSIDE IRONCLADS TO HAVE TWO DECKS OF GUNS, AND THE FIRST TO HAVE SPUR RAMS. DESPITE THEIR HEAVY ARMAMENT, AS WOODEN-HULLED SHIPS—ONLY PARTIALLY ARMORED—THEY WERE VULNERABLE TO EXPLOSIVE SHELLS.

Built to a design drawn up by Stanislas Dupuy de Lôme, *Magenta* (named after the French victory over Austria in June 1859) was laid down at Brest Naval Dockyard on June 22, 1859, launched on June 22, 1861, and completed on January 2, 1862. A complete belt of wrought-iron armor, 4.7 in (119 mm) thick, protected the waterline, but the battery deck's armor did not extend to the ends of the ship.

Numerous changes to the ship's armament were made in the course of *Magenta's* career, and in 1867–68 the lower-deck guns, 6 ft 3 in (1.9 m) above the waterline, were replaced by ten 9.4 in (339 mm) muzzle-loading guns. *Solférino's* lower-deck guns were removed entirely in 1868–69.

Transatlantic Operations

Originally rigged as a barquentine, *Magenta* carried 18,400 sq ft (1,709.4 sq m) of sail, but in 1864 the arrangement was changed to a barque rig and the sail area increased to 21,000 sq ft (1,951 sq m). With its high freeboard it was considered a good sea boat. After fitting-out at Brest, from 1863 to 1867 *Magenta* was flagship of the Cherbourg squadron, engaging in cruises and exercises in the English Channel and making a transatlantic voyage to Vera Cruz, Mexico, and back from January 3 to May 8, 1867.

In January 1869 *Magenta* was careened at Toulon and the wood backing of its waterline armor was reinforced. It remained in the Mediterranean as flagship of the Mediterranean fleet, based at Toulon. In the summer of 1875 it picked up a collection of archaeological relics from diggings near Tunis and still had them on board at Toulon on October 31, 1875 when an accidental fire started in the wardroom galley and spread rapidly. It proved impossible to flood the aft magazines and eventually they blew up, destroying the ship, already evacuated by its crew.

SPECIFICATIONS

DISPLACEMENT: 6,715 tons (6,822 tonnes)

DIMENSIONS: 282 ft 1 in x 56 ft 8 in x 27 ft 8 in (91.9 m x 17.3 m x 8.44 m)

RIG: Three masts, barquentine then barque rig

PROPULSION: Sails, screw propeller, horizontal return rod engine, 3,540 ihp (2,604 kW)

ARMAMENT: Ten 240 mm, four 190 mm, fifty 30 pounder MLR guns

SPEED: 12 knots (13.8 mph; 22.2 km/h)

CREW: 681

Magenta

RAM
THE SPUR RAM PROJECTED 6 FT 5 IN
(2 M) FORWARD AND WAS COVERED WITH
A 14-TON (14.2-TONNE) STEEL CONE.

GUNS
THE DOUBLE DECK OF GUNS WAS INTENDED
TO RIVAL THE NEW BRITISH IRON SHIPS HMS
WARRIOR AND *BLACK PRINCE*, IN A SHIP OF
MUCH SHORTER LENGTH.

BRIDGE
AN ARMORED COMMAND BRIDGE WITH A SMALL
WHEELHOUSE WAS SET JUST ABAFT THE FUNNEL.

USS *New Ironsides* (1862)

Named in honor of USS *Constitution*, this was a literally iron-sided ship, with a belt of armor and an armored deck, although the hull was of wood. Its career was nowhere near as long as its namesake's—after active service in the Civil War, *New Ironsides* was laid up in 1865 and destroyed by fire on December 16, 1866.

New Ironsides was contracted with Merrick & Sons of Philadelphia, who built the engine, the hull construction being subcontracted to William Cramp & Son's yard in Philadelphia on a contract dated October 15, 1861. The ship was launched on May 10, 1862, and commissioned on August 21.

In wartime haste, it was immediately assigned to the South Atlantic Blockading Squadron as flagship of Rear Admiral Samuel Du Pont, and stationed off Charleston, South Carolina. In April the shore forts were bombarded and returned fire, with the ship taking 55 noted hits without serious damage being done. In the bombardment of Morris Island, under Rear Admiral John A. Dahlgren, 214 hits were recorded, again doing little damage.

The iron armor once again proved its worth when on October 5, 1863, the ship was attacked by the torpedo boat CSS *David*, which detonated a 70-pound spar torpedo off the starboard quarter, again without serious effect. *New Ironsides* remained on the station until May 1864 when it went to Philadelphia for repairs and refit.

In October it was assigned to the North Atlantic Blockading Squadron, assisting with the capture of Fort Fisher, North Carolina, between December 24, 1864, and January 15, 1865, in the campaign to capture Wilmington. Until the end of hostilities it acted as a guard ship at Hampton Roads.

Design Flaws

New Ironsides was not regarded as a particularly satisfactory ship, which explains its early laying-up. Flat-bottomed and of relatively shallow draft (although this was not unusual with American warships, which often had to operate in shallow water, as at Charleston), it had a tendency to roll, and the masts were reduced in height. Its horizontal direct-action engine failed to deliver the specified speed of 9.5 knots (10.9 mph; 17.5 km/h). But the iron armor was undoubtedly effective, and the lesson was not lost on U.S. warship designers. Laid up at League Island Navy Yard, Philadelphia, after the Civil War, *New Ironsides* was destroyed in an accidental fire, started by a night watchman's stove, on December 16, 1866.

SPECIFICATIONS

DISPLACEMENT: 4,120 tons (4,186 tonnes)

DIMENSIONS: 232 ft x 57 ft 6 in x 15 ft (70.7 m x 17.53 m x 4.57 m)

RIG: Barque rig, without royals

PROPULSION: Sails, screw propeller, 4 Martin boilers, 700 ihp (522 kW)

ARMAMENT: Two 8 in, two 5.1 in, one 3.4 in rifled ML guns

SPEED: 7 knots (8 mph; 12.9 km/h)

CREW: 449

USS *New Ironsides*

DECK
AN ARMORED DECK OF 1-IN (25-MM)
IRON RAN THE LENGTH OF THE SHIP.

TOWER
AN ARMORED LOW CONNING TOWER
WAS FITTED BETWEEN THE MAIN- AND
MIZZENMASTS, LATER REPLACED BY A
CYLINDRICAL "PILLBOX" TOWER.

HULL
THE SIDE ARMOR WITHSTOOD A
CONFEDERATE TORPEDO, ALTHOUGH
SOME 45 FT (13.7 M) OF THE WOODEN
HULL WAS SPRUNG.

SMS *Kaiser Max* (1863)

LEAD SHIP OF A CLASS OF THREE BROADSIDE IRONCLADS, *KAISER MAX* WAS AN ENLARGED VERSION OF THE PRECEDING DRACHE CLASS OF 1861. ALL WERE ENGAGED IN THE BATTLE OF LISSA, BETWEEN AUSTRIA-HUNGARY AND ITALY, THE FIRST NAVAL BATTLE FOUGHT BETWEEN FLEETS OF IRONCLAD WARSHIPS.

Named for the 15th-century Emperor Maximilian I, *Kaiser Max* incorporated engine parts and other elements of its predecessor of the same name, a wooden-hulled frigate of 1873. It was laid down at the Stabilimento Tecnico Triestino (STT) Yard in October 1861, launched on March 14, 1862, and completed in early 1863, designated as a second-class armored frigate. Two sister ships, *Prinz Eugen* and *Juan de Austria*, were built simultaneously to the same design: the Austro-Hungarian Empire was in a hurry to have a war fleet to match that of newly independent Italy.

By 1866 the Empire was at war with Italy and Prussia, and on July 20 that year the Austrian fleet, totaling 27 vessels with 532 guns, under Admiral Tegetthoff, and an Italian fleet of 37 vessels with 645 guns, under Admiral Persano, met off the island of Lissa (Vis), in the Adriatic Sea, for the first major battle on the high seas since

Trafalgar in 1805. Better handled, the Austrian fleet won a convincing victory in a close-range fight often obscured by smoke from guns and funnels, although achieved more by ramming Italian ships than by artillery fire. *Kaiser Max*, in the first division of Tegetthoff's fleet, cut across the Italian line, sustaining severe damage through gunfire. One result of Lissa was that battleships would be fitted with armored ram prows for the next 30 years, although improved gunnery very soon made the ram redundant.

Rebuild

The class was not considered very effective, with poor seakeeping ability. A partial rebuild was effected in 1867 when the open bow section was plated to prevent seawater washing in. In 1873 *Kaiser Max* was returned to STT at Trieste for a drastic rebuilding, and emerged as a center-battery ship, with its rig reduced

in 1880 from 17,579 sq ft (1,633.15 sq m) to 12,471 sq ft (1,158.6 sq m) and finally removed altogether. It was stricken from the Navy List on December 30, 1905, and used as an accommodation ship at Cattaro Bay. In 1920 it was ceded to Yugoslavia and renamed *Tivat*.

SPECIFICATIONS

DISPLACEMENT: 3,548 tons (3,605 tonnes)

DIMENSIONS: 232 ft 2 in x 45 ft 11 in x 20 ft 9 in (70.8 m x 14 m x 6.3 m)

RIG: Three masts, barquentine rig

PROPULSION: Sails, screw propeller, 2-cylinder horizontal engine, 1,926 ihp (1,436 kW)

ARMAMENT: Fifteen 24 pounders, sixteen 48 pounders, one 12 pounder, one 6 pounder guns (1866)

SPEED: 11.4 knots (13.1 mph; 21.1 km/h)

CREW: 386

SMS *Kaiser Max*

MASTS
PLACING OF THE MASTS WAS DISTINCTIVE, WITH THE MAINMAST SET WELL AFT OF THE CENTER.

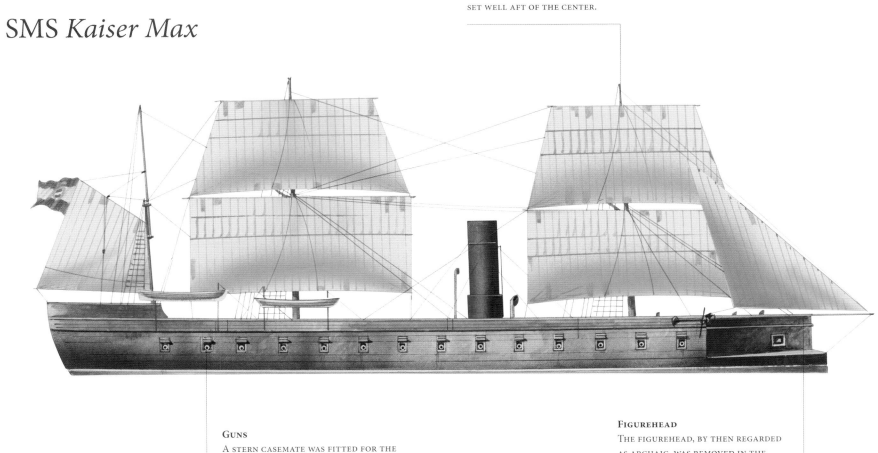

GUNS
A STERN CASEMATE WAS FITTED FOR THE INSTALLATION OF A STERN-CHASER GUN.

FIGUREHEAD
THE FIGUREHEAD, BY THEN REGARDED AS ARCHAIC, WAS REMOVED IN THE REBUILD OF 1867.

Numancia (1863)

CLASSED AS A "FRAGATA BLINDADA" OR ARMORED FRIGATE, *NUMANCIA* WAS THE FIRST IRONCLAD WARSHIP TO COMPLETE A CIRCUMNAVIGATION OF THE GLOBE. ITS MAIN ACTION WAS IN THE PERUVIAN/ CHILEAN WAR AGAINST SPAIN IN 1865. *NUMANCIA* WAS BUILT IN FRANCE, AT THE LA SEYNE SHIPYARD, TOULON, AND LAUNCHED ON NOVEMBER 19, 1863.

Numancia was iron-hulled, but a traditional broadside vessel armed with forty 68 pounder smooth-bore guns on a single gun deck.

In the mid-1860s the long struggle of Spain's South American colonies for independence was reaching its final phase, and *Numancia* was sent in late 1864 as flagship of a squadron to counter the forces mustered by the alliance of Chile and Peru. The efforts of the squadron were unsuccessful, and its first commander, Vice Admiral José Manuel Pareja, committed suicide.

He was followed by Vice Admiral Casto Méndez Núñez. On March 31, 1865, the Spanish ships shelled the undefended town and port of Valparaiso and destroyed the Chilean merchant fleet. Thirty-three vessels were burned or sunk, leaving virtually nothing of Chile's merchant fleet. The Spanish then moved on Callao, a fortified harbor, and the Battle of Callao took place on May 2. Both sides claimed victory, but the Spanish, who withdrew while the Chilean cannons were still firing, had nothing to show for their efforts. The Spanish squadron returned to Spain via the Philippines, completing a circumnavigation of the Earth.

Revolution and Refit

On its return, *Numancia* was based at Cartagena, and brought the new Spanish King Amedeo I from Genoa on December 30, 1870. In 1873, the year of the first Spanish Republic, it was seized by its crew in July and participated in the "Cantonal Revolution," accidentally ramming and sinking the steamer *Ferdinand* which was carrying many of the cantonal leaders on October 20.

On January 17, 1874, it was recommissioned in the royal Spanish Navy. In 1897–98 the ship returned to La Seyne where it was completely rebuilt and re-engined, and armed with new-type quick-firing guns, four 6.4 in (163 mm), six 5.5 in (140 mm), and three 4.7 in (119 mm), plus 12 machine guns and two torpedo tubes. The sailing rig was removed. The refit kept it out of the Spanish–American War. In December 1909 it was flagship of the Second Division of the Moroccan Squadron; then in 1912 it was converted to a depot ship at Tangier.

Eventually sold for breaking up, *Numancia* was on tow to Spain when it broke away and grounded at Sesimbra, Portugal, on December 17, 1916, and was broken up on the beach there.

SPECIFICATIONS

DISPLACEMENT: 7,189 tons (7,304 tonnes)

DIMENSIONS: 315 ft x 57 ft x 27 ft (96 m x 17.4 m x 8.23 m)

RIG: Three masts, square rig

PROPULSION: Sails, screw propeller, 3,700 ihp (2,759 kW)

ARMAMENT: Forty 68 pounder guns (1863)

SPEED: 10 knots (11.5 mph; 18.5 km/h)

CREW: 500

Numancia

SPEED
DE-RIGGED AND RE-ENGINED IN
1897–98, THE SHIP COULD THEN MAKE
13 KNOTS (14.9 MPH; 24 KM/H).

ARMOR
FOR LATERAL PROTECTION *NUMANCIA*
HAD A 5.5-IN (140-MM) WATERLINE BELT
AND A 4.75-IN (121-MM) BATTERY BELT.

ARMAMENT
NUMANCIA WAS SUBSTANTIALLY LARGER
AND MORE HEAVILY ARMED THAN THE
CHILEAN AND PERUVIAN WARSHIPS OF
THE 1860S.

HMS *Research* (1864)

DESPITE THE NAME, *RESEARCH* WAS NOT ONE OF THE ROYAL NAVY'S SURVEY OR EXPLORATION VESSELS, BUT A SMALL IRONCLAD SLOOP WITH A CENTRAL BATTERY, HEAVILY ARMED FOR ITS SIZE, AND THE FIRST SHIP OF ITS KIND TO BE BUILT FOR THE BRITISH FLEET. THE *RESEARCH* WAS LAID DOWN AT PEMBROKE DOCKYARD ON SEPTEMBER 3, 1861 AND COMPLETED IN APRIL 1864.

Originally intended as a 17-gun wooden screw sloop to be named HMS *Trent*, a change in Admiralty policy in 1862 ordered its conversion to an ironclad, lengthened by 10 ft (3 m), widened by 5 ft 6 in (1.6 m), and with the standard sloop bow and stern converted into a ram and rounded stern.

The design was by Sir Edward Reed, appointed Chief Constructor to the Royal Navy in 1863, and responsible for introducing the concept of the central "box" battery instead of the traditional broadside arrangement. Displacement was increased by 500 tons (508 tonnes), of which 352 tons (358 tonnes) was armor plating. A full-length waterline belt 10 ft (3 m) high and 4.5 in (11 cm) thick was added, with a central battery contained inside an armored area 34 ft (10.36 m) long and set between the top of the waterline belt and the tops of the wooden bulwarks. Teak backing 19.5 in (50 cm) thick went between the armor plate and the hull. Gunports in the armored bulkheads allowed for fore and aft as well as lateral fire.

Engine and Rigging

Research was fitted with a two-cylinder Boulton and Watt horizontal single-expansion direct-acting steam engine. Steam was provided by two tubular boilers, and the screw, which was 12 ft (4 m) in diameter, could be hoisted clear of the water for better performance under sail, as was frequent with British warships of the time. The rig was barque-style with a sail area of 18,250 sq ft (1,695.5 sq m). Under sail alone it made around 6 knots (6.9 mph; 11.1 km/h): combined power gave around 10 knots (11.5 mph; 18.5 km/h).

Research had a reputation as a heavy roller and a poor sea boat in rough conditions, and was normally laid up in the winter months. In a refit in 1869–70 its 100-pounder SB guns were replaced by four 7 in MLR guns, a spar deck was installed between forecastle and quarterdeck, and the funnel was moved forward out of the armored box holding the guns. In 1878 it was placed on reserve, and sold for breaking up in 1884.

SPECIFICATIONS

DISPLACEMENT: 1,743 tons (1,771 tonnes)

DIMENSIONS: 195 ft x 38 ft 7 in x 14 ft 6 in (59.4 m x 11.76 m x 4.4 m)

RIG: Three masts, barque rig

PROPULSION: Sails, screw propeller, Watt 2-cylinder horizontal engine, 1,040 ihp (775.5 kW)

ARMAMENT: Four 100 pounder SB guns

SPEED: 10.3 knots (11.8 mph; 19 km/h)

CREW: 150

HMS *Research*

RIGGING
THE MIZZEN TOPSAIL IS OF UNUSUAL
DESIGN WITH ITS SHORT FORE-AND-
AFT GAFF.

BOAT
THE SHIP'S BOAT SLUNG
FROM DAVITS, BEYOND
THE SIDES, WAS A TYPICAL
PRACTICE AT THIS TIME.

ANCHOR
NOTE THE DAVIT, MOUNTED FORWARD,
TO LOWER AND HOIST THE ANCHOR.

CSS *Shenandoah* (1864)

ONE OF THE CONFEDERATE NAVY'S MOST SUCCESSFUL OCEAN RAIDERS, THE CRUISES OF THE BRITISH-BUILT *SHENANDOAH* TOOK IT AS FAR AS AUSTRALIA AND IT CLAIMED 38 PRIZE SHIPS. UNAWARE OF OR IGNORING THE CIVIL WAR'S EFFECTIVE END, ITS CREW KEPT UP HOSTILITIES INTO AUGUST 1865.

Ordered by the British government as *Sea King*, for transporting troops to India, and built at Stephens' shipyard, Glasgow, Scotland, this ship was purchased on the stocks and sold to the Confederacy in 1864. Built as a sail/screw steamer with full rig, it had an iron frame and teak planking, but was not constructed as a ship of war. As a troop carrier it had space for a larger than usual crew and for storing goods taken from captured ships, as well as ample provision room.

The sale of ships to one side in a civil war by a supposedly neutral state was a very delicate diplomatic issue, and the deal was done in conditions of secrecy. On October 8, 1864, *Shenandoah* sailed from London, ostensibly bound for Bombay (Mumbai), but at Funchal, Madeira, it had a pre-arranged meeting with the steamship *Laurel*, carrying guns, ammunition, and other military stores.

Here on October 19 it was commissioned as *Shenandoah*, under Lt. J. Waddell, and began its war service.

Confederate Operations

Heading for the South Atlantic, it remained there for some time before passing into the Indian Ocean. On such long distances, its full square-sail rig was vital, and *Shenandoah* must have covered considerable distances under sail alone.

On January 25, 1865, it was recorded at Melbourne, Australia, where it took on provisions. From here it sailed northeastwards, but does not appear to have put in at an American port or gathered any news on its travels. In the sub-Arctic waters of the Bering Sea it continued to seize prize ships, mostly whaling craft. In fact two-thirds of its 38 prizes were taken after the cessation of hostilities (although the war did not formally end until August 20).

On August 2 Waddell discovered the news and took *Shenandoah* to Liverpool, England, with its guns dismantled. Arriving on November 6, he handed the ship over to the British authorities who in turn passed it to the U.S. government. The ship had been at sea for 12 months and 17 days, and had covered some 58,000 miles (93,340 km).

SPECIFICATIONS

DISPLACEMENT: 1,160 tons (1,178 tonnes)

DIMENSIONS: 230 ft x 32 ft x 20 ft 6 in (70.1 m x 9.75 m x 6.25 m)

RIG: Three masts, square rig

PROPULSION: Sails, screw propeller

ARMAMENT: Four 8 in SB, two 32 pounders, two 12 pounder MLR guns

SPEED: 9 knots (10.3 mph; 16.6 km/h)

CREW: 109

CSS *Shenandoah*

FITTINGS
THE SHIP AND FITTINGS WERE SOLD
BY THE U.S. CONSUL IN LIVERPOOL
FOR AROUND £17,000 IN APRIL 1866.

SPEED
IT WAS A FASTER SHIP UNDER SAIL
THAN UNDER STEAM: AS A SAILING
VESSEL IT WAS KNOWN TO BE CAPABLE
OF 16 KNOTS (18 MPH; 29 KM/H).

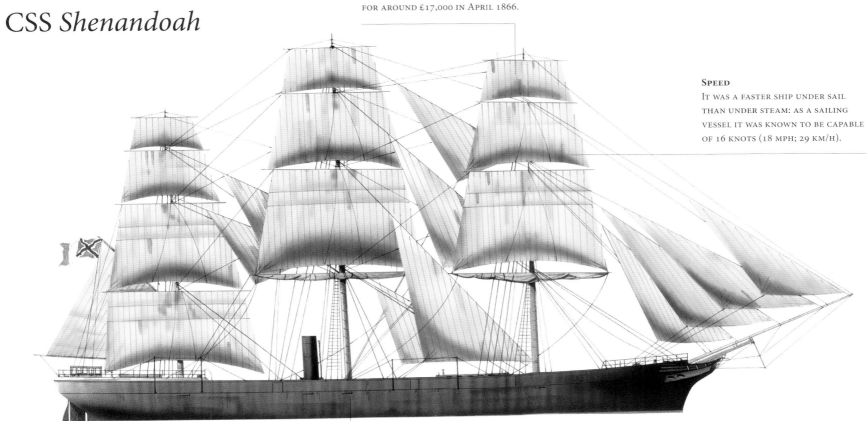

LEGACY
SHENANDOAH WAS CELEBRATED AS THE LAST
CONFEDERATE SHIP TO STRIKE ITS COLORS,
AND THE ONLY ONE TO SAIL AROUND THE EARTH.

HMS *Achilles* (1864)

ACHILLES WAS AN IMPROVED VERSION OF HMS WARRIOR, LAID DOWN BEFORE THE PREVIOUS SHIP
WAS COMPLETED, AND WHICH REMEDIED SEVERAL OF ITS DEFICIENCIES. BOTH SHIPS WERE ONE-OFFS,
BUILT WHILE THE BRITISH ADMIRALTY WAS STILL ASSESSING THE QUALITIES OF ALL-IRON ARMORED
WARSHIPS. ACHILLES WAS ALSO TO BE ONE OF THE MOST-RENAMED SHIPS IN THE ROYAL NAVY.

The ship was the first to be built in the dry dock at Chatham Naval Dockyard. Floated out on December 23, 1863, it was completed on November 26, 1864.

New thinking had been applied to the hull design and to the armor protection. A simplified blunt bow, capable of ramming, was provided, with a new rounded stern that enabled the steering gear to be protected. A waterline armor belt 13 ft (3.9 m) high ran along the entire hull, 4.5 in (110 mm) thick with 18-in (457-mm) wood backing; and the battery was protected by a 4.5-in (114-mm) lateral belt and by transverse bulkheads of the same thickness, at each end. The hull was divided into 106 watertight compartments and had a double bottom. Gun design was a major and controversial issue at this time, and its original guns were replaced in 1868, again in 1874, and followed by further alterations in 1889.

By then improved breech-loading guns had replaced the old muzzle-loaders and two 6 in (152 mm) BL guns were added, with eight quick-firing lighter guns (3-pounder) and 16 machine guns.

Redesign of the Rig

With a very long hull, *Achilles* carried four masts, the first British warship to do so since the bonaventure masts of the 16th century, but all fully rigged (the Minotaur class of 1867–68 would have five masts). There were problems with the rig, and in 1865 the bow mast and bowsprit were removed, with the headsails rigged to the stem. In 1866 the bowsprit was restored and the foremast moved 25 ft (7.6 m) forward. The 1867 arrangement allowed for a sail area of 30,133 sq ft (2,799.4 sq m). In 1877 the rig was reduced to barque rig.

Great length in relation to beam did not make for easy steering, but *Achilles*

was a more handy sea boat than *Warrior*. It was on the active list until 1885 and then laid up. In 1902 it was stationed at Malta as a base ship, named *Hibernia*, and renamed *Egmont* in 1904. In 1914 it returned to Chatham as a depot ship, named *Egremont* in 1918 and *Pembroke* in 1919. It was sold for breaking in 1925.

SPECIFICATIONS

DISPLACEMENT: 9,829 tons (9,986 tonnes)

DIMENSIONS: 380 ft x 58 ft 3 in x 27 ft 3 in (120 m x 17.75 m x 8.3 m)

RIG: Four masts, full square rig

PROPULSION: Sails, screw propeller, Penn trunk engine, 5,720 ihp (4,265.4 kW)

ARMAMENT: Four 110 pounders, sixteen 100 pounder guns

SPEED: 14.3 knots (16.4 mph; 26.4 km/h)

CREW: 709

HMS *Achilles*

SAILS
AS A FOUR-MASTER IT CARRIED
44,000 SQ FT (4,100 SQ M) OF SAIL,
CLAIMED TO BE THE MOST EVER
CARRIED ON A WARSHIP.

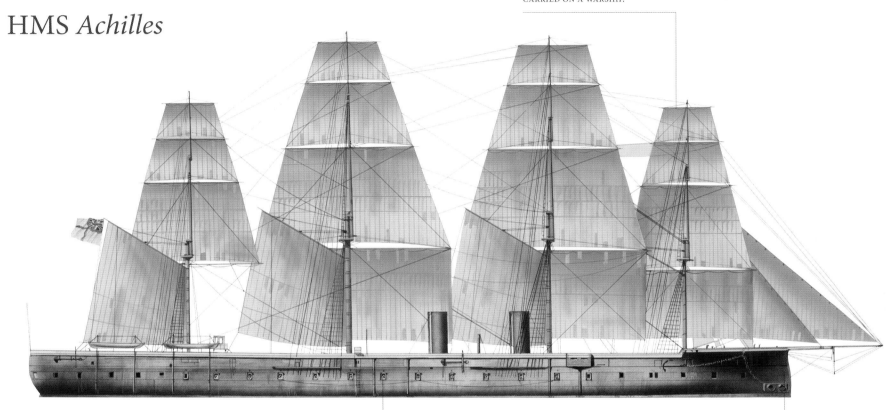

CANNONS
THE ORIGINAL GUNS WERE "SOMERSET"
CANNONS MADE BY ARMSTRONG'S,
SMOOTH-BORED AND MUZZLE-LOADING.
NOT A SUCCESSFUL DESIGN, THEY WERE
SOON WITHDRAWN FROM SERVICE.

STEM
THE FORM OF THE STEM WAS A BLUNT
RAM, WITHOUT A PROJECTING SPUR.

CSS *Stonewall* (1865)

STONEWALL WAS CLASSED AS AN "IRONCLAD RAM," POWERED BOTH BY SAIL AND STEAM. ORDERED BY THE CONFEDERATE STATES, BUILT IN FRANCE WHOLLY AS A SHIP OF WAR, BY THE TIME IT REACHED THE WESTERN ATLANTIC, HOSTILITIES HAD ENDED. IT SAW VIRTUALLY NO SERVICE WITH THE CONFEDERATE NAVY, BUT PLAYED AN IMPORTANT PART IN JAPANESE NAVAL HISTORY.

Contracted for on July 16, 1863, with the builders L. Arman, of Bordeaux, *Stonewall* was launched on June 21, 1864, and commissioned in January 1865.

Built ostensibly as *Sphinx* for the Egyptian Navy, its construction was composite, with iron frames and wooden planking. An armored belt extended 5 ft (1.5 m) below the waterline. The hull was copper-sheathed and a massive plough ram was fitted, with a bad effect on the ship's handling.

The guns were mounted on pivots in round-faced, armored gunhouses giving a wide range of fire. The single 10 in (254 mm) gun was set forward and could fire ahead and on either beam. The aft gunhouse, oval in shape, held two 6.4 in (163 mm) guns, one on each side; with only a vestigial poop and folding bulwarks they could be trained to fire over a wide arc.

The French government refused to hand the ship over to the Confederacy and as *Sphinx* it was sold to Denmark for use in war against Prussia, but arriving too late to participate it was finally sold via a middleman to the Confederacy and assumed the name *Stonewall* in December 1864. Until it was on the open seas it used further false names, *Staerkoder* and *Olinde*.

Confederate and Japanese Service

On March 24, 1865, it encountered the Union sloops USS *Niagara* and *Sacramento* off Ferrol, Spain, but they evaded a battle with the impregnable-looking *Stonewall*. When it reached Havana, Cuba, on May 25, hostilities had ended, and it was handed over to the authorities for cash to pay off the crew. Passed to the U.S. government in July, it was sold to the imperial Japanese government in 1867.

Immediately on arrival, the ship was renamed *Kotetsu*. Domestic war was going on and it was sent to fight the insurgent *Bakufu* forces. Off Hokkaido, *Kotetsu* repulsed a boarding attack at Miyako, assisted by newly fitted Gatling guns, and led the fleet to victory at the Battle of Hakodate in June 1869. Renamed *Azuma* in 1871, it remained active until 1888 when it was decommissioned and converted to harbor duties. It was scrapped around 1900.

SPECIFICATIONS

DISPLACEMENT: 1,400 tons (1,422 tonnes)

DIMENSIONS: 187 ft x 32 ft 8 in x 14 ft 4 in (57 m x 9.9 m x 4.36 m)

RIG: Two masts, brig rig

PROPULSION: Sails, two screw propellers, return connecting rod engine, 1,200 ihp (895 kW)

ARMAMENT: One 10 in (254 mm) RML, two 6.4 in (163 mm) RML guns

SPEED: 10 knots (11.5 mph; 18.5 km/h)

CREW: 130

CSS *Stonewall*

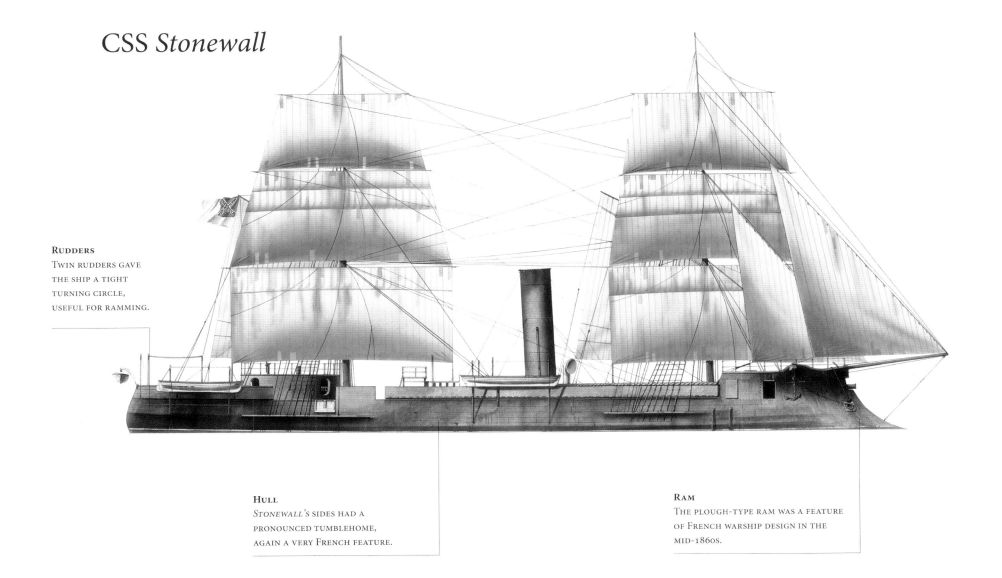

RUDDERS
TWIN RUDDERS GAVE
THE SHIP A TIGHT
TURNING CIRCLE,
USEFUL FOR RAMMING.

HULL
STONEWALL'S SIDES HAD A
PRONOUNCED TUMBLEHOME,
AGAIN A VERY FRENCH FEATURE.

RAM
THE PLOUGH-TYPE RAM WAS A FEATURE
OF FRENCH WARSHIP DESIGN IN THE
MID-1860S.

Huáscar (1865)

NAMED FOR THE LAST INCA RULER OF CUZCO, *HUÁSCAR* WAS ORDERED BY THE PERUVIAN NAVY AT A TIME OF WAR WITH SPAIN. ONE OF THE FIRST TURRET SHIPS, IT WAS LATER ENGAGED IN THE WAR OF THE PACIFIC AGAINST CHILE AND ENDED UP AS A CHILEAN PRIZE. IT IS NOW ONE OF THE FEW 19TH-CENTURY IRON WARSHIPS TO BE PRESERVED AFLOAT.

The concept of the turret ship was developed by the British naval captain Cowper Coles from 1855, and based on the possession of a small number of large-caliber guns with a wide range of fire. Built at Laird's shipyard, Birkenhead, England, it was launched on October 6, 1865. The hull was iron, supplemented by an armored belt 4.5 in (114 mm) thick at its widest point, tapering to 2.5 in (64 mm). The single centrally mounted turret was protected by armor 8–5.5 in (203–140 mm) thick, and the control tower by 3 in (75 mm). It mounted two 10 in (254 mm) and two 40 pounder guns. By the time the completed ship was delivered the War of Independence was over.

War of the Pacific

In 1877 *Huáscar* was seized by a rebel group and engaged in raids off the coast, but was regained by the Navy on May 30 after interception by the British cruiser HMS *Shah* and the corvette *Amethyst*. In April 1879, Peru and Bolivia went to war against Chile, and on May 21 *Huáscar* rammed and sank the Chilean screw corvette *Esmeralda*. On October 8 it encountered the *Blanco Encalada* and *Cochrane*, British-built central battery ships, and after taking around 70 direct hits, with 64 men killed including Captain Miguel Grau (Peru's most celebrated naval officer), *Huáscar* was captured. Accounts of this battle between modern warships were studied with great interest by all naval commands.

Rebuilt and re-armed with two 8 in (203 mm) Armstrong BLR in the turret, two 4.7 in (119 mm) 40 pounders, two 6 pounders, and three small revolving guns, and commissioned in the Chilean fleet, *Huáscar* was engaged on blockading the Peruvian coast until the war ended. It remained on the active list until 1901, latterly as a gunnery training ship, then, after a boiler explosion, it was laid up until 1917, from when it was used as a submarine tender until 1930. In 1952 it was restored as a museum ship at the Talcahuano naval base, where it remains, having survived the earthquake of 2010.

SPECIFICATIONS

DISPLACEMENT: 2,030 tons (2,062 tonnes)

DIMENSIONS: 190 ft x 35 ft x 18 ft 3 in (57.9 m x 10.7 m x 5.5 m)

RIG: Two masts, brig rig

PROPULSION: Sails, screw propeller, 1,650 ihp (1,230.4 kW) engine

ARMAMENT: Two 10 in (254 mm), two 40 pounder guns (to 1879)

SPEED: 12.3 knots (14.1 mph; 22.7 km/h

CREW: 170

Huáscar

MASTS
THE RIG WAS REMOVED, PROBABLY WHEN THE SHIP WAS
TAKEN OVER BY CHILE, AND THE RESTORED *HUÁSCAR*
SPORTS PLAIN MILITARY MASTS.

MASTS
THE RIG WAS REMOVED, PROBABLY WHEN THE SHIP WAS
TAKEN OVER BY CHILE, AND THE RESTORED *HUÁSCAR*
SPORTS PLAIN MILITARY MASTS.

FORECASTLE
HUÁSCAR HAD A HIGH FORECASTLE,
NECESSARY TO SUPPORT THE RAM PROW,
BUT PREVENTING FORWARD FIRE FROM
THE TURRET.

HMS *Bellerophon* (1866)

AN IRONCLAD WITH CENTRALLY MOUNTED BATTERY, THIS SHIP HAD MANY FEATURES THAT MADE IT AMONG THE MOST ADVANCED OF ITS TIME IN TERMS OF SHIP DESIGN, POWER, AND ARMAMENT. OUT OF ACTIVE SERVICE IN 1904, IT WAS FINALLY DISCARDED BY THE ROYAL NAVY IN 1922.

The Royal Navy's third *Bellerophon* was laid down at Chatham Dockyard on December 23, 1863, launched on May 26, 1865, and completed on April 11, 1866, at a cost of £356,493. Sir Edward Reed was the designer, and it proved very successful. The hull was of iron, with around 200–300 tons (203–305 tonnes) of steel incorporated to help in reducing its weight.

Constructed on the "bracket frame" system, it was the first Royal Navy ship with a complete double bottom. Wrought-iron armor protection was substantial, with a full belt from the main deck to 6 ft (1.8 m) below the waterline, 6 in (152 mm) amidships. The box battery, on the main deck, had 6-in (152-mm) armor on the sides and 5-in (127-mm) on the fore and aft bulkheads.

The machinery was powerful, intended to give speed of 14 knots (16.1 mph; 25.9 km/h) without sail assistance.

Bellerophon carried 23,800 sq ft (2,200 sq m) of sail, but was not a fast sailer, its best recorded speed under sail being 10 knots (11.5 mph; 18.5 km/h). It was converted to barque rig during its 1881–84 refit.

Armament and Service

Apart from the battery-mounted guns, there were two 7 in (178 mm) muzzle loader chase guns at both the forward and aft ends of the main deck, and a further 7 in MLR at the aft end of the upper deck.

Initial service was with the Channel Fleet until 1871, then with the Mediterranean Fleet until 1872. During a refit in 1872 a poop deck was added, and *Bellerophon* took over as flagship on the North America station, remaining until 1881 when a further major refit was carried out, until 1884, with new boilers and a complete rearmament. It was the only British ironclad to have only breech-loading guns: ten 8 in (203 mm) BLs in the main battery and four 6 in (152 mm) as chase guns, the forward ones being set in new embrasures on the forecastle.

Bellerophon then returned to the North America station at Halifax, Nova Scotia, serving until 1892. Paid off that year at Plymouth, it then served as guard ship at Pembroke until 1903, before being converted as a stokers' training ship in 1904, renamed *Indus III*. On December 12, 1922, it was sold for scrap, and broken up at Bo'ness in 1923.

SPECIFICATIONS

DISPLACEMENT: 7,551 tons (7,672 tonnes)

DIMENSIONS: 300 ft x 56 ft 1 in x 24 ft 8 in (91.4 m x 17 m x 7.52 m)

RIG: Three masts, square rig to 1884, then barque rig

PROPULSION: Sails, screw propeller, Penn 2-cylinder horizontal engine, 6,521 ihp (4,862.7 kW)

ARMAMENT: Ten 9 in (229 mm) MLR, five 7 in (178 mm) MLR guns

SPEED: 14.17 knots (16.3 mph; 26.2 km/h)

CREW: 650

HMS *Bellerophon*

RUDDER
BELLEROPHON WAS THE
FIRST ROYAL NAVY SHIP TO
HAVE A BALANCED RUDDER,
MAKING STEERING MUCH
EASIER.

TORPEDOES
AFTER 1884 TWO LAUNCHING
CARRIAGES FOR 16-IN (406-MM)
WHITEHEAD TORPEDOES WERE
MOUNTED ON THE MAIN DECK.

BOW
ORIGINALLY A BACK-SLOPING RAM
BOW WAS FITTED; THIS WAS LATER
ALTERED TO A CLIPPER FORM, WITHOUT
REMOVING THE RAM.

USS *Idaho* (1866)

Launched at a time when steam power in ships was still regarded by most people as an auxiliary, *Idaho* seemed to prove the skeptics and traditionalists right. Its steam engine was so ineffective that it was finally removed and the ship became a sailing frigate.

Intended as a sail/screw frigate, and part of a Civil War program designed to make a rapid addition to the fleet, *Idaho* was laid down at the George Steers yard, at Greenpoint, Long Island, NY. It was launched on October 8, 1864, and commissioned on May 15, 1866.

Its hull was of wood and unarmored. In addition to its three masts the *Idaho* had two propellers, driven by a 645 ihp (481 kW) Dickerson engine of a new and unproved design.

Trials established a modest steam-powered speed of no more than 8.27 knots (9.5 mph; 15.3 km/h), compared to the 15 knots (17.2 mph; 27.7 km/h) for a full 24 hours specified in the contract. The machinery was underpowered and unreliable, and only the engine builder's political influence got the ship accepted by the Navy. But the engine, the two funnels and screws

were soon removed and the ship was recommissioned as a sailing frigate on October 3, 1867, with Lt. Edward Hooker as captain.

Fast Under Sail

As a sailing ship, *Idaho* turned out to be very fast, making a maximum logged speed in excess of 18 knots (20.7 mph; 33.3 km/h). On November 1,1867, it sailed for the Far East, via Rio de Janeiro and Cape Horn, reaching the U.S. Navy base at Nagasaki on May 18, 1868. Here it joined the Asiatic Squadron as a stores and hospital ship, serving until mid-August 1869.

On September 20 that year *Idaho* left under orders for San Francisco, and almost immediately was caught in an extremely violent typhoon. All three masts were broken and the upper sections had to be cut away, but the crew managed to put up a jury rig and got

the ship back to Yokohama. It was not remasted, however, and remained as a hulk at Yokohama until it was stricken from the Navy List on December 31, 1873. In 1874 it was sold to the East Indies Trading Company.

SPECIFICATIONS

DISPLACEMENT: 3,241 tons (3,293 tonnes)

DIMENSIONS: 298 ft x 44 ft 6 in x 17 ft 1 in (90.8 m x 13.5 m x 5.2 m)

RIG: Three masts, full square rig

PROPULSION: Sail only from October 1867

ARMAMENT: 8 guns

SPEED: 18 knots (20.7 mph; 33.3 km/h)

CREW: Not known

USS *Idaho*

SPEED
ON DECEMBER 8, 1867, UNDER SAIL, *IDAHO* WAS LOGGED AS COVERING 130 MILES (209 KM) IN EIGHT HOURS.

MASTS
ONLY THE LOWER MASTS SURVIVED THE TYPHOON, AND WERE RETAINED IN ITS LATER FORM AS A ROOFED-OVER STORE SHIP.

HULL
IDAHO'S HULL WAS AN ELEGANT, SPARE DESIGN. THE LENGTH-TO-BEAM RATIO OF 6.72:1 WAS UNUSUALLY LONG.

HMS *Agincourt* (1867)

ORIGINALLY TO BE CALLED HMS *CAPTAIN*, *AGINCOURT*'S MOST DRAMATIC EPISODE WAS
RUNNING AGROUND OFF GIBRALTAR IN 1871. ALMOST ALWAYS A FLAGSHIP, SERVING WITH
BOTH THE MEDITERRANEAN AND CHANNEL FLEETS, IT ENDED ITS CAREER AS A COAL HULK,
WORKING UNTIL IT WAS SCRAPPED IN 1960.

The three ships of the Minotaur class (HMS *Northumberland* was the third) were the Royal Navy's only five-masted ships. In general design they were similar to HMS *Achilles* but larger in all respects. *Agincourt* was built in dry dock at Birkenhead, laid down on October 30, 1861, floated out on March 27, 1865, and commissioned on June 1, 1867.

Classed as an armored frigate, it had armor measuring 5.5 in (140 mm) along the waterline belt and the battery, tapering to 4.5 in (114 mm), with a forward bulkhead 5.5 in thick, which extended to the height of the bulwarks. After tests on *Minotaur*, yards were not fitted on *Agincourt*'s fourth mast and a gaff was fitted to all masts except the second. Total sail area was 32,377 sq ft (3,008 sq m). Despite the rig, it was not a good sailer, making around 9–10 knots (10.3–11.5 mph; 16.6–18.5 km/h) under sail.

Wreck and Recovery

With *Northumberland*, *Agincourt* towed a floating dock from England to Madeira in June 1868 before joining the Channel Fleet. While passing through the Straits of Gibraltar in very light winds on July 1, 1871, it was allowed to drift from the channel and grounded. It lay there for four days while everything of weight was removed, including the guns, and was then towed off by HMS *Hercules*—an embarrassing episode for the flagship of the Fleet's second-in-command. At the time *Agincourt* had a poor reputation as a badly run ship, but this was rectified by a new captain.

From 1873 to 1875 *Agincourt* was flagship of the Channel Fleet. Paid off in 1875, it was partly re-gunned with breech-loaders. In 1877 it was part of a special squadron under Admiral Geoffrey Hornby, sent to cruise off Constantinople when a Russian attack was feared; then it returned to the Channel Fleet until 1889. Held in reserve at Portsmouth until 1893, it was then moved to Portland as a training ship for 12 years. Transferred to Harwich, it was renamed *Boscawen III* in 1904, and *Ganges II* in 1906. Finally from 1909 it was coal hulk C109 at Sheerness, and was not scrapped until 1960.

SPECIFICATIONS

DISPLACEMENT: 10,600 tons (10,770 tonnes)

DIMENSIONS: 407 ft x 59 ft 6 in x 27 ft 9 in (124 m x 18.14 m x 8.46 m)

RIG: Five masts, modified square rig

PROPULSION: Sails, screw propeller, Maudslay return connecting rod engine, 6,545 ihp (4,880.6 kW)

ARMAMENT: Four 9 in (229 mm), twenty-four 7 in (178 mm) MLR, eight 24 pounder SB guns

SPEED: 14.13 knots (16.2 mph; 26.1 km/h)

CREW: 800

HMS *Agincourt*

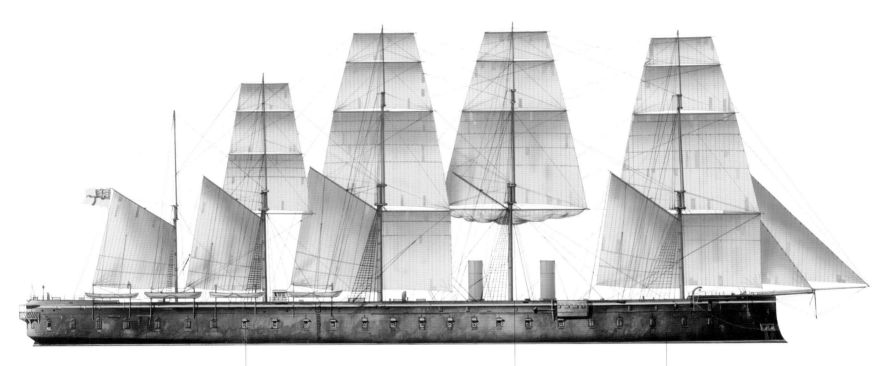

GUNS
BY THE EARLY 1880S, TWO OF THE 9-IN (229-MM) MLR GUNS HAD BEEN REPLACED BY 6-IN (152-MM) BL GUNS. IN 1890–91 FURTHER BL AND QF GUNS WERE ADDED, ALONG WITH TWO TORPEDO TUBES.

SEARCHLIGHTS
AGINCOURT'S 1875–77 REFIT INCLUDED THE INSTALLATION OF SEARCHLIGHTS.

LENGTH
THE MINOTAUR CLASS REPLACED HMS *ACHILLES* AS THE LONGEST WARSHIPS OF THEIR TIME.

Surveillante *(1867)*

THE PROVENCE CLASS OF ARMORED BROADSIDE FRIGATES WAS THE MOST NUMEROUS CLASS
OF FRENCH BATTLESHIPS, WITH 10 COMMISSIONED BETWEEN MAY 1865 AND OCTOBER 1867.
THEY WERE IMPROVED VERSIONS OF *GLOIRE* (1860), SHIP-RIGGED, AND SERVED AT ONE TIME
OR ANOTHER AT EVERY FRENCH NAVAL STATION.

Surveillante, third French warship of the name, was laid down at Lorient on January 28, 1861, launched on August 18, 1864, and completed October 21, 1867. Such a lengthy building period was not unusual in the French Navy yards at that time.

Described by a British observer as "a wood ship of the orthodox French pattern," it was wooden-hulled but completely iron-plated. *Gloire*, although an epoch-making warship, had various shortcomings, which the design of these later ships sought to improve.

The armoring was more comprehensive, with 6 in (152 mm) on the waterline and 4.3 in (109 mm) above, and better protection was given to the command tower, including an armored roof. The guns, changed at various times, were also of updated design. On *Surveillante*—one of the lighter ships of the class—displacement varied from 5,700 to 6,122 tons (5,791 to 6,220 tonnes); the gunports were 7 ft 3 in (2.21 m) above the waterline.

A Short Career

When war broke out between France and Prussia in 1870, *Surveillante*, captained by the future Rear Admiral Louis-Antoine Grivel, was flagship of a squadron of seven armored ships sent to blockade the Prussian coast of the Baltic Sea, a mission that achieved no success. Leaving Cherbourg on July 24, 1870, under Admiral Bouët-Villaumez, it returned on September 29.

After that the ship saw little active duty. Its last noted service was a voyage to Tabarka, Tunisia (then under French rule), in 1881. In 1882 it was recorded as awaiting repairs at Toulon.

In 1883 *Surveillante* was placed on reserve at Brest, then moved in the following year to Cherbourg, and was decommissioned there in 1885. In 1888 it was designated for breaking up, which was completed by 1890.

SPECIFICATIONS

DISPLACEMENT: 5,704 tons (5,795 tonnes)

DIMENSIONS: 262 ft 5 in x 55 ft 9 in x 28 ft (80 m x 17 m x 8.5 m)

RIG: Three masts, barque rig

PROPULSION: Sails, screw propeller, compound engine, 3,600 ihp (2,684.5 kW)

ARMAMENT: Four 9.4 in (238 mm), ten 7.6 in (193 mm) ML guns (1867)

SPEED: 14 knots (16.1 mph; 25.9 km/h)

CREW: 580

Surveillante

SAILS
SAIL AREA ON THE PROVENCE CLASS
WAS APPROXIMATELY 21,000 SQ FT
(1,951 SQ M).

SIZE
THE DIMENSIONS AND
DISPLACEMENT WERE
SLIGHTLY LESS THAN THE
BRITISH HECTOR CLASS
BROADSIDE FRIGATES OF
THE SAME PERIOD.

BOW
THE BOW DESIGN IS BASED ON *GLOIRE*'S
BUT MORE BUILT-UP, AND WITH
REINFORCED ARMOR AT THE WATERLINE.

HMS *Hercules* (1868)

COMPARISON WITH *BELLEROPHON* SHOWS HOW BATTLESHIP DESIGN WAS PROGRESSING. *HERCULES* CARRIED MORE ARMOR AND HEAVIER GUNS, WITH HULL EMBRASURES FORE AND AFT OF THE BATTERY TO ALLOW WIDER ARCS OF FIRE. PROGRESSIVE IMPROVEMENTS WERE MADE THROUGH THE SHIP'S ACTIVE LIFETIME.

Laid down at Chatham Naval Dockyard on February 1, 1866, and launched on February 10, 1868, *Hercules* was the sixth Royal Navy ship to carry the name, and was commissioned on November 21, 1868. Designed by Sir Edward Reed, it had a pointed ram bow and 73 ft 9 in (22.4 m) of waterline armor, 9 in (229 mm) thick and tapering fore and aft to 6 in (152 mm).

As a central battery ship, its main guns were enclosed in an armored "box" with protection from 8 in (203 mm) to 6 in (152 mm). It was the first ship to carry the latest guns of the time, 10-in (250-mm) muzzle-loaders—although they would soon be obsolete, they could fire 400-lb (181-kg) explosive shells. A 9-in (230-mm) gun was placed at the bow and stern to supplement the foremost and aftermost guns of the battery, which could be trained for almost end-on fire.

Hercules was ship-rigged, with a sail area of 49,400 sq ft (4,589 sq m), including stunsails, but—like other central battery ships—did not make a great speed under sail, 11 knots (12.6 mph; 20.3 km/h) being its best performance. In 1874–75 steam-powered steering was installed (prior to that it could take from eight to 12 men to effect a full turn), two 14 in (356 mm) torpedo tubes were mounted in 1878, and a net defense system in 1886, reflecting the new peril of the submarine. A reconstruction in 1892–93 gave *Hercules* a new engine and the rig was reduced to a pair of military masts, without sails.

Royal Navy Service

Hercules served with the Channel Fleet until 1874, and pulled HMS *Agincourt* off the Pearl Rock at Gibraltar in 1871. During a gale in 1872 it sustained damage by colliding with HMS *Northumberland*. In 1875–77 it was flagship of the Mediterranean Fleet. After the 1893 modernization *Hercules* was designated as "battleship, third class," and held with the reserve fleet at Portsmouth until 1904, when, renamed *Calcutta*, it went to Gibraltar as depot ship until 1914. Towed back to Portsmouth in 1914, it was used as an engineers' training depot as *Fisgard II*, by then being merely a mastless hulk.

SPECIFICATIONS

DISPLACEMENT: 8,677 tons (8,816 tonnes)

DIMENSIONS: 325 ft x 59 ft x 24 ft (99 m x 18 m x 7.3 m)

RIG: Three masts, full square rig

PROPULSION: Sails, screw propeller, Penn trunk engine, 7,178 ihp (5,353 kW)

ARMAMENT: Eight 10 in (254 mm) MLR, two 9 in (230 mm) MLR guns

SPEED: 14.69 knots (16.9 mph; 27.2 km/h)

CREW: 638

HMS *Hercules*

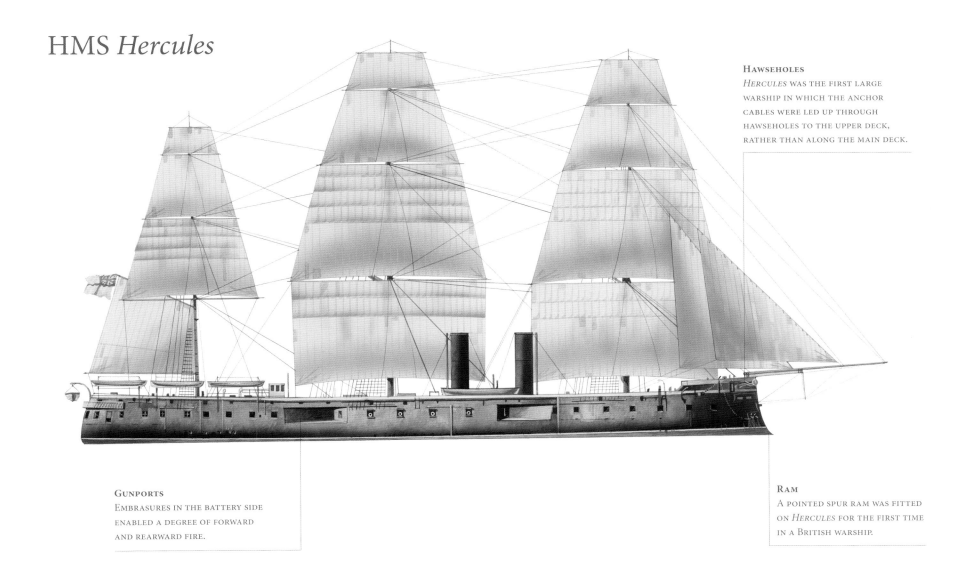

HAWSEHOLES
HERCULES WAS THE FIRST LARGE
WARSHIP IN WHICH THE ANCHOR
CABLES WERE LED UP THROUGH
HAWSEHOLES TO THE UPPER DECK,
RATHER THAN ALONG THE MAIN DECK.

GUNPORTS
EMBRASURES IN THE BATTERY SIDE
ENABLED A DEGREE OF FORWARD
AND REARWARD FIRE.

RAM
A POINTED SPUR RAM WAS FITTED
ON *HERCULES* FOR THE FIRST TIME
IN A BRITISH WARSHIP.

SMS *König Wilhelm* (1868)

CLASSIFIED BY THE PRUSSIAN NAVY AS A *PANZERFREGATTE* OR ARMORED FRIGATE, *KÖNIG WILHELM* WAS FLAGSHIP OF THE PRUSSIAN FLEET, AND AFTER 1871 THE LARGEST BATTLESHIP IN THE NAVY OF THE NEWLY UNIFIED GERMAN EMPIRE. IT RETAINED THAT STATUS FOR 20 YEARS, UNTIL GERMANY'S NAVAL EXPANSION GOT UNDER WAY.

The battleship was originally ordered as *Fatikh* by the Imperial Ottoman Navy from the Thames Ironworks at Blackwall, London, but when the Turks canceled the order, the Prussians bought it on the stocks in February 1867. Launched on April 25, 1868, it was named for King Wilhelm I.

The hull was fitted with the ram-type bow fashionable at the time, although a lengthy bowsprit extended before it, housed in a "cubby" at a lower level than the weather deck. It was a high-sided ship, with 42 ft 5 in (12.94 m) of freeboard. The hull was divided into 11 watertight compartments, and was double-bottomed for 70 per cent of its length.

Steam power came from a Maudslay horizontal two-cylinder engine. Eight boilers were set in two rooms, each with a funnel, and the three masts could mount a spread of 27,986 sq ft (2,600 sq m) of sail. The original armament, which would

quickly become obsolete, was 33 muzzle-loading 32-pounders, smooth-bored.

Service in the German Empire

In 1871 the German Empire was proclaimed, and a new naval building program was put in hand. On May 31, 1878 *König Wilhelm* accidentally rammed and sank one of the new vessels, the turret ironclad *Grosser Kurfürst*.

A complete modernization was undertaken in Hamburg in 1896. The sail rig was taken down and replaced by two new-type naval masts, new boilers and triple-expansion engines were installed, and the ship was completely re-gunned. Twenty-two Krupp 9.4 in (239 mm) and one 6 in (150 mm) rifled breech-loading guns were installed and supplemented by eighteen 3.5 in (88 mm) quick-firing guns. Five torpedo tubes were fitted, above the waterline, and

König Wilhelm was redesignated as an armored cruiser.

From 1893 to 1897 it was flagship of Division II of the Imperial German Navy, at Wilhelmshaven, then relegated to a harbor defense and training role until removal from the active list in 1904. Disarmed, it continued in use as an accommodation ship at Kiel and did not go out of service until 1921, when it was scrapped at Rönnebeck, near Bremen.

SPECIFICATIONS

DISPLACEMENT: 9,603 tons (9,750 tonnes)

DIMENSIONS: 367 ft 5 in x 60 ft x 28 ft 1 in (112 m x 18.3 m x 8.56 m)

RIG: Three masts, square rig (to 1895)

PROPULSION (1869): Sails, screw propeller, Maudslay horizontal 2-cylinder engine, 8,000 ihp (6,000 kW)

ARMAMENT (1869): Thirty-three 72 pounder ML guns (smooth bore)

SPEED: 14.7 knots (17 mph; 28 km/h)

CREW: 730

SMS *König Wilhelm*

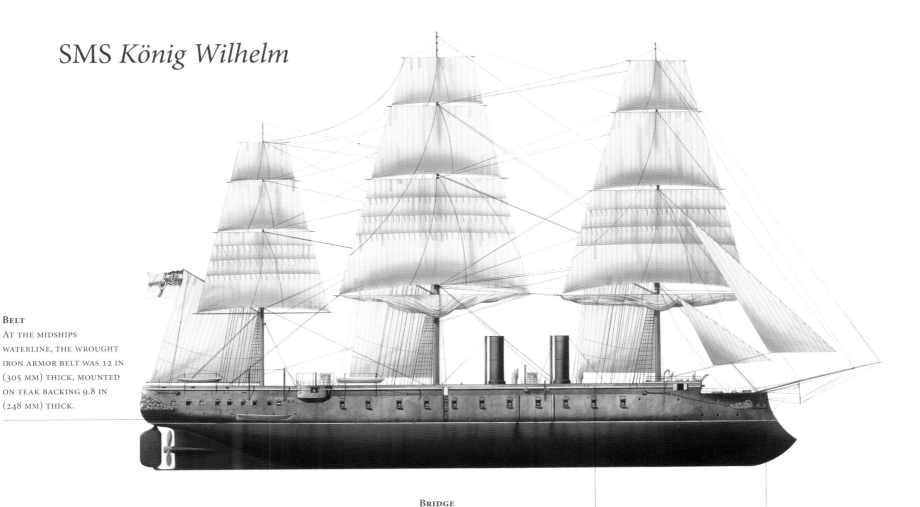

BELT
AT THE MIDSHIPS
WATERLINE, THE WROUGHT
IRON ARMOR BELT WAS 12 IN
(305 MM) THICK, MOUNTED
ON TEAK BACKING 9.8 IN
(248 MM) THICK.

BRIDGE
FROM 1896 A NAVIGATION BRIDGE
WAS INSTALLED AHEAD OF THE
FORWARD FUNNEL.

RAM
REPAIRED AFTER THE 1878 COLLISION,
THE SHIP WAS GIVEN A REINFORCED RAM.

HMS *Monarch* *(1869)*

FOR THE FIRST TIME, THE BIG GUNS APPEARED ABOVE THE LEVEL OF THE WEATHER DECK. THIS WAS THE FIRST SEAGOING WARSHIP WITH GUNS MOUNTED IN TURRETS. AT COMPLETION *MONARCH* WAS THE FASTEST BATTLESHIP AFLOAT AND WAS ALSO A GOOD SAILING VESSEL. ITS LEADING FEATURES CAN BE COMPARED WITH THAT OF THE LESS FORTUNATE HMS *CAPTAIN*, COMMISSIONED AT ALMOST THE SAME TIME.

Sir Edward Reed, Britain's chief naval designer, and Captain Cowper Coles, also an authority on that subject, both agreed that gun turrets should be tried as an alternative to the central battery. But they agreed on little else. Reed designed *Monarch*, which was laid down at Chatham Dockyard on June 1, 1866, launched on May 25, 1868, and completed on June 12, 1869, six months before Coles's *Captain*.

Monarch was provided with the standard armor belt of the time, tapering to the ends of the ships from 7 in (178 mm) to 4.5 in (114 mm). The foremast and mainmast were widely spaced to allow for placing of the gun turrets with the funnel between them. They were protected by a box citadel between the upper and main decks, and an armored control station was positioned in front of the funnel on a raised "hurricane deck": warships were

beginning to acquire a superstructure. Auxiliary power was provided for steering and turret training and for capstan work.

The ship was given a full square rig and carried 27,700 sq ft (2,573 sq m) of sail, although this was reduced when barque rig was adopted in 1872. During a long refit period between 1890 and 1897 new engines were installed and the sailing rig was cut down to the lower masts, with light topmasts and yards.

Service in the Royal Navy

Monarch was with the Channel Fleet until 1872, where it could be under the eyes of its designer and of the Admiralty, conducting trials with *Captain*. Laid up until 1894, it then served again with the Channel Fleet and was next deployed to the Mediterranean Fleet where (with a home refit in 1877) it remained until 1885, taking part in the bombardment of Alexandria in July 1882. From 1885

to 1890 it was again with the Channel Fleet. After modernization *Monarch* was guardship at Simonstown, South Africa, until 1904, when it was converted to a depot ship under the name *Simoom*, but was sold off in 1905.

SPECIFICATIONS

DISPLACEMENT: 8,322 tons (8,455 tonnes)

DIMENSIONS: 330 ft x 57 ft 6 in x 24 ft 3 in (100.5 m x 17.5 m x 7.4 m)

RIG: Three masts, square rig, barque rig (1872–90)

PROPULSION: Sails, screw propeller, Humphreys & Tennant horizontal return engine, 7,842 ihp (5,848 kW)

ARMAMENT: Four 12 in (305 mm), three 7 in (178 mm) MLR guns

SPEED: 10.5 knots (12.0 mph; 19.4 km/h)

CREW: 575

HMS *Monarch*

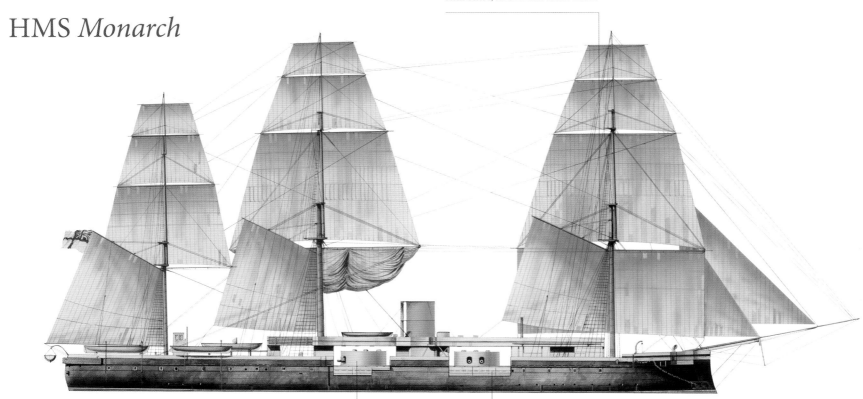

PLATFORMS
Monarch HAD WIDE OBSERVATION
PLATFORMS ON THE FORE- AND
MAINMAST, ABOVE THE MAIN YARD.

TURRETS
THE TURRETS HAD ARMOR PROTECTION
OF 10 IN (254 MM) ON THE FACES AND
8 IN (203 MM) ON THE SIDES.

BULWARKS
HINGED BULWARKS WERE FITTED
ON EACH SIDE OF THE TURRETS,
TO AVOID BLAST DAMAGE.

Cutty Sark (1869)

NAMED FOR THE FLEET-FOOTED WITCH IN A ROBERT BURNS POEM, THIS IS ONE OF THE MOST FAMOUS SHIPS TO SURVIVE FROM THE GREAT ERA OF SAIL. BUILT AS A CHINA TEA CLIPPER, IT ALSO CARRIED MANY OTHER CARGOES BEFORE BECOMING A CELEBRATED WOOL CLIPPER ON THE AUSTRALIA RUN. AFTER A VARIED CAREER IT WAS PURCHASED FOR RESTORATION, SURVIVING A FIRE ON MAY 21, 2007.

Built at Dumbarton, Scotland, and launched on November 22, 1869, *Cutty Sark* was ordered by Captain John Willis for the specialized role of carrying tea from China—an annual race for which a ship came in first with the new season's output, putting a huge premium on its cargo. The hull was of teak planking on an iron frame, and it was hoped that it would be the fastest ship on the run. Although very fast, it did not outrun its great rival *Thermopylae*.

But the opening of the Suez Canal in 1869 soon put an end to the tea races. Facing increasing competition from steamships, *Cutty Sark* was reduced to general cargo service carrying everything from coal to copra.

However, from 1883 it had a renaissance in a new racing game: the annual run to London from Australia with the new season's wool clip. For 12 years it was a prime contender, once making the run from Sydney to London in 69 days. *Cutty Sark* was capable of making 18 knots (20.7 mph; 33.3 km/h), and on one occasion in 1893 it overhauled the P&O mail steamer *Britannia* steaming at full speed on the approach to Sydney.

Later Years

In 1895 *Cutty Sark* was sold to J.A. Ferreira of Lisbon, renamed *Ferreira*, and worked in general trade to the Cape Verde Islands and East Africa. Dismasted by a hurricane in 1916, it was re-rigged as a barquentine. Sold again in 1920, it was renamed *Maria de Amparo*.

In 1922 it was bought by a British sea captain, Wilfred Dowman, returned to Great Britain, and used as a training ship, based at Falmouth, Cornwall, restored to the original rig. In 1936 it was sailed to the River Thames.

Since 1954 it has been preserved as a museum ship at Greenwich, London.

While undergoing restoration it suffered from a fire on May 21, 2007, but fortunately most of the fabric survived.

SPECIFICATIONS

DISPLACEMENT: 2,100 tons (2,134 tonnes)

DIMENSIONS: 212 ft 5 in x 36 ft x 21 ft (64.74 m x 10.97 m x 6.4 m)

RIG: Three masts, full square rig

SPEED: 18 knots (20.7 mph; 33.3 km/h)

CREW: 35

Cutty Sark

SAILS
THE SAIL AREA IS 32,000 SQ FT
(2,973 SQ M).

LODGING
AS ON A WARSHIP, THE CREW BERTHED
IN THE FORECASTLE, THE OFFICERS AFT.

SIZE
WITH A GROSS REGISTERED TONNAGE OF
975 TONS (990 TONNES), IT IS NOT A LARGE
SHIP, BUT WITHOUT MACHINERY ALMOST ALL
OF ITS HULL SPACE WAS AVAILABLE FOR CARGO.

HMS *Captain* (1870)

CAPTAIN WAS A ONE-OFF, DESIGNED TO DISPLAY THE VIRTUES OF THE TURRET SHIP. BRAINCHILD OF CAPTAIN COWPER COLES, IT WAS BUILT IN CIRCUMSTANCES OF CONTROVERSY. AT FIRST IT APPEARED AN EFFECTIVE WARSHIP. BUT, CAUGHT IN A STORM OFF CAPE FINISTÈRE, IT WAS ROLLED OVER AND SANK WITH THE LOSS OF MANY LIVES.

Cowper Coles was a strong advocate of the revolving gun turret and had patented a design for one in the 1850s. The British Admiralty had made some cautious experiments but had not solved the problem of reconciling deck turrets with the rigging of a ship carrying a full set of sails. In 1865 the construction of HMS *Monarch* was authorized, with two turrets. Coles strongly attacked its design and created a public furor until he was authorized to build his own two-turret ship.

Captain, second to bear the name, was ordered in November 1866, laid down by Lairds, Birkenhead, on January 30, 1867, launched on March 27, 1869, and completed in January 1870, only a month after *Monarch*. Superficially the two ships resembled each other, both with a "hurricane deck" to which the rigging was secured so as not to impede the guns' field of fire. *Captain* was ship-rigged. Edward Reed, designer of *Monarch*, was as critical of Captain as Coles had been about his ship, but with better reason.

Design Flaws and Disaster

Captain turned out to be 735 tons (747 tonnes) over the intended weight and consequently sat lower in the water, with a freeboard of 6 ft 6 in (1.98 m) instead of 8 ft 6 in (2.6 m), while its center of gravity had risen by some 10 in (254 mm). If the ship should heel more than 21 degrees, it might roll right over. This was considered a purely theoretical eventuality, and initial trials with *Monarch* appeared satisfactory.

However, on September 6–7, 1870, *Captain* was cruising with 11 ships of the Channel Squadron off western Brittany when the wind rose to gale force and *Captain's* deck was awash. Sail was shortened to only the fore staysail and the fore and main topsails, but the ship rolled increasingly. Shortly after midnight it capsized, taking around 480 men and boys to the bottom, including Cowper Coles himself. Only 18 were saved. The Admiralty's own design, in the form of the more stable *Monarch*, was vindicated, but at a terrible price.

SPECIFICATIONS

DISPLACEMENT: 7,767 tons (7,892 tonnes)

DIMENSIONS: 320 ft x 53 ft 3 in x 24 ft 10 in (97.54 m x 16.23 m x 7.57 m)

RIG: Three masts, square rig

PROPULSION: Sails, two screw propellers, reciprocating engine, 5,400 ihp (4,000 kW)

ARMAMENT: Four 12 in (305 mm) MLR, two 7 in (178 mm) MLR guns

SPEED: 15.25 knots (17.5 mph; 28.2 km/h)

CREW: 500

HMS *Captain*

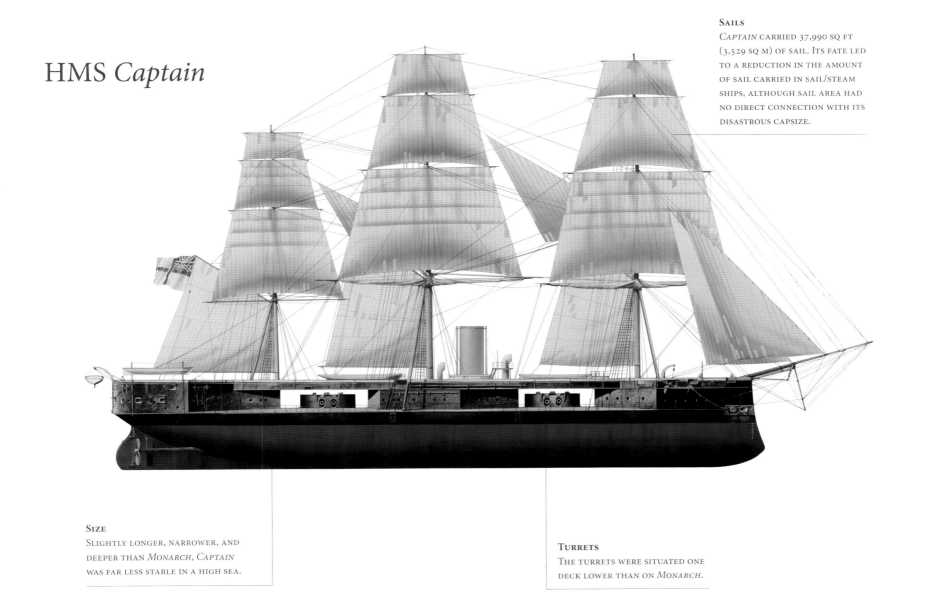

SAILS

CAPTAIN CARRIED 37,990 SQ FT (3,529 SQ M) OF SAIL. ITS FATE LED TO A REDUCTION IN THE AMOUNT OF SAIL CARRIED IN SAIL/STEAM SHIPS, ALTHOUGH SAIL AREA HAD NO DIRECT CONNECTION WITH ITS DISASTROUS CAPSIZE.

SIZE

SLIGHTLY LONGER, NARROWER, AND DEEPER THAN *MONARCH*, *CAPTAIN* WAS FAR LESS STABLE IN A HIGH SEA.

TURRETS

THE TURRETS WERE SITUATED ONE DECK LOWER THAN ON *MONARCH*.

Océan (1870)

THIS WAS THE FIRST OF A CLASS OF THREE FRENCH CENTRAL BATTERY SHIPS, ALL OF WHICH TOOK A LONG TIME TO BUILD AND WHOSE DESIGN WAS CONSIDERABLY ALTERED IN THE COURSE OF CONSTRUCTION. ALTHOUGH PROVIDED WITH IRON TRANSVERSE WATERTIGHT BULKHEADS, AND DESPITE WROUGHT IRON ARMOR PLATING, THEIR WOODEN HULLS REVEALED THE FRENCH NAVY'S DIFFICULTY IN SECURING ENOUGH IRON FOR ALL-IRON HULLS.

Océan was laid down at Brest in July 1865 to the design of Dupuy de Lôme, launched on October 15, 1868, and commissioned hastily on July 21, 1870, at the outbreak of war with Prussia. The wooden hull was obscured by iron, with a waterline belt of 8–7 in (203–178 mm) and 0.6 in (15 mm) above, while the battery was protected by 6.3 in (160 mm) of wrought iron, and the barbettes by 6 in (150 mm), although the barbette armor had to be stripped off because the ship's weight– originally planned to be 7,200 tons (7,315 tonnes)—was becoming excessive.

The design had a pronounced tumblehome that presaged future French capital ships. Océan was completed with a full square rig but this may have been soon altered to barque rig, with a sail area of some 21,000 sq ft (1,951 sq m). The main guns were mounted in four barbettes on the top deck; these 10.8-in (274-mm) guns fired 476.2-pound (216-kg) armor-piercing shells, theoretically capable of piercing 14.4 in (366 mm) of wrought iron at point-blank range.

Service in the French Navy

Océan was part of the squadron dispatched to blockade Prussia's Baltic coast but which returned to France on September 16, 1870, leaving the sea open to the enemy.

Until 1875, Océan was attached to the Evolutionary Squadron for exercises and trials, then lay in reserve until 1879 when it was recommissioned for service in the Mediterranean Sea.

After a refit in 1884–85 it returned to the Northern Squadron at Cherbourg, but was back in the Mediterranean in 1888–91. From that year it was decommissioned, first as a gunnery school and then as an apprentices' training ship, before being stricken and scrapped in 1894.

SPECIFICATIONS

DISPLACEMENT: 7,580 tons (7,700 tonnes)

DIMENSIONS: 282 ft 10 in x 57 ft 6 in x 29 ft 10 in (86.2 m x 17.5 m x 9.1 m)

RIG: Three masts, square rig, later barquentine rig

PROPULSION: Sails, screw propeller, horizontal return connecting rod engine, 3,780 ihp (2,820 kW)

ARMAMENT: Four 10.8 in (274 mm), four 9.4 in (240 mm), twelve 1 pounder revolving guns

SPEED: 13 knots (14.9 mph; 24 km/h)

CREW: 778

Océan

GUNS
THE LATERAL-ONLY FIRING POSITIONS
ON THE MAIN DECK WAS AN OUT-OF-
DATE FEATURE: MANY SHIPS BY NOW HAD
EMBRASURES TO GIVE A WIDE ARC OF
FORE OR AFT FIRE.

TORPEDOES
FOUR 14 IN (356 MM) ABOVE-
WATERLINE TORPEDO TUBES WERE
FITTED, PROBABLY AROUND 1885.

RAM
THE RAM, TIPPED WITH
A 20-TON (20.3-TONNE)
BRONZE CASTING, WAS
9 FT (2.7 M) LONG.

HMS *Audacious* (1870)

BRITAIN'S 1867 NAVAL ESTIMATES PROVIDED FOR FOUR CENTRAL BATTERY SHIPS OF THE SECOND CLASS, PRIMARILY INTENDED FOR SERVICE ON FOREIGN STATIONS, AND ALL WERE IN SERVICE BY JANUARY 1871. *AUDACIOUS* WAS THE FIRST TO BE COMPLETED. THE CENTRAL BATTERY ARRANGEMENT WAS REGARDED AS A PROVEN SYSTEM AT A TIME WHEN WARSHIP DESIGN WAS IN A STATE OF FLUX.

*A*udacious, laid down at Napier's yard, Glasgow, on June 26, 1867, launched on February 27, 1869, and commissioned on September 10, 1870, was the class leader, showing the new features of a two-tier battery, with the upper level extended slightly beyond the beams on sponsons. A waterline armor belt 8 ft (2.4 m) high was 8 in (203 mm) thick amidships, tapering to 6 in (152 mm) at the ends, and the battery area, 59 ft (18 m) long, was also protected by 6-in (15.2-mm) lateral armor, with bulkheads of 5 in (127 mm) fore and 4 in (102 mm) aft.

Muzzle-loading rifled guns were fitted, six in the lower battery and four in the upper tier. The vessel was ship-rigged originally but in a refit in 1871 this was rearranged as a barque rig, with a sail area of 23,700 sq ft (2,202 sq m) and a twin-shaft drive was fitted, with two 2-cylinder Ravenhill engines.

Service in the Royal Navy

Upon completion *Audacious* was guardship of the First Reserve at Kingstown (Dún Láoghaire), Ireland, but was transferred in 1870 to Hull, until 1874. That year it was deployed to the Far East to serve as flagship for the China station. It returned to Hull in 1879, serving there until a lengthy refit, which included new boilers and the addition of a poop deck.

Recommissioned in March 1883 it was again flagship of the China Station later that year, remaining until 1889. On return it was refitted at Chatham, rearmed and de-rigged, with pole masts fitted with fighting tops, then returned to Hull for the third time.

Decommissioned in 1894, *Audacious* was relegated to 4th class reserve until 1902, when the engines were removed and it was hulked at Plymouth as a boys' training ship. In April 1904 it was renamed *Fisgard*, then towed to Scapa Flow in 1914 to be used as a receiving ship, renamed *Imperieuse*. In 1919 it was moved to Rosyth and renamed *Victorious*. On March 15, 1929, it was sold for breaking up.

SPECIFICATIONS

DISPLACEMENT: 6,034 tons (6,131 tonnes)

DIMENSIONS: 280 ft x 54 ft x 23 ft (85.3 m x 16.5 m x 7 m)

RIG: Three masts, square rig (to 1871)

PROPULSION: Sails, twin screw propellers, two 2-cylinder engines, 4,021 ihp (2,998 kW)

ARMAMENT: Ten 9 in (229 mm) MLR, four 64 pounder MLR guns

SPEED: 12 knots (13.8 mph; 22.2 km/h)

CREW: 450

HMS *Audacious*

RIGGING
AS A PRECAUTION, BARQUE RIG
REPLACED THE ORIGINAL RIG AFTER
HMS *CAPTAIN* CAPSIZED IN 1870.

DRAFT
THE CLASS HAD A RELATIVELY SHALLOW
DRAFT FOR OPERATING IN COASTAL
WATERS FROM FOREIGN STATIONS.

BATTERY
THE TWO-LEVEL BOX BATTERY
EXTENDED BEYOND THE SIDES,
PORT AND STARBOARD.

Almirante Cochrane (1874)

NAMED FOR THE RENOWNED BRITISH ADMIRAL WHO HAD LED THE CHILEAN NAVY, THIS CENTRAL BATTERY SHIP GAVE LONG SERVICE, PARTICIPATING IN THE PACIFIC WAR AND THE CIVIL WAR OF 1891. BUILT IN HULL, ENGLAND, ITS COST WAS AROUND ONE MILLION PESOS. SIR EDWARD REED, THE HAND BEHIND MANY WARSHIPS OF THE TIME, WAS A TECHNICAL ADVISOR IN DESIGN AND CONSTRUCTION.

*A*lmirante Cochrane was laid down in 1873 and launched on January 23, 1874. Fear of impending war brought it to Chile in 1874 before completion, and it returned to Earle's yard in Hull for final completion in 1877. A sister ship, *Valparaiso* (later *Blanco Encalada*), was launched at the same yard in 1875.

Iron-hulled, *Almirante Cochrane* carried a waterline belt whose maximum thickness was 9 in (230 mm) at midships, and 4.5 in (115 mm) at the bow and stern. The hull and armor plating were separated by a layer of teak 10 in (254 mm) thick. The battery side, flush with the armored belt, was protected by 7-in (36-mm) armor in the center of the ship, reducing to 2 in (50 mm) fore and aft. Inside, the hull was divided into eight compartments by iron bulkheads. The ram bow had a spur 6 ft 9 in (2 m) long, under the waterline and projecting 7 ft 6 in (2.2 m)

ahead of the stem. Six 9 in (228 mm) Armstrong guns were mounted on pivots in the redoubt.

The Pacific War

In 1878 the Chileans tried to sell *Almirante Cochrane*, without success, but it proved of value on blockade duty in 1879–80 during the Pacific War, and in the Battle of Angamos on October 8, 1879, when the Peruvian monitor *Huáscar* was captured.

In 1889 it went back again to Earle's yard for rebuilding and re-gunning, returning with six 8 in (203 mm) Armstrong BLR, in place of the old 9 in (230 mm) MLR guns, also three 6 pounder Hotchkiss QF guns, six 1.5 in (37 mm) light guns, and three 14 in (356 mm) torpedo tubes, as well as new engines giving a speed of 13.6 knots (15.6 mph; 25.1 km/h). In this form it was by far the most formidable ship on

the west coast of South America through most of the 1890s.

In further modifications between 1897–1900 it was converted as a gunnery training ship, with the fore- and mizzenmasts removed. Hulked by 1908, it was finally scrapped in 1934.

SPECIFICATIONS

DISPLACEMENT: 3,370 tons (3,424 tonnes)

DIMENSIONS: 210 ft x 45 ft 9 in x 21 ft 10 in (64.01 m x 13.94 m x 6.65 m)

RIG: Three masts, barquentine rig

PROPULSION: Sails, two screw propellers, two Penn compound engines, 2,920 ihp (1,230 kW)

ARMAMENT: Six 9 in (228 mm), one 20 pounder, one 9 pounder, one 7 pounder guns

SPEED: 13.6 knots (15.6 mph; 25.1 km/h)

CREW: 300

Almirante Cochrane

DECK
FROM 1899 A TRANSVERSE DECK
WAS FITTED FROM BEAM TO BEAM,
ON EACH SIDE OF AN ARMORED
CONNING TOWER.

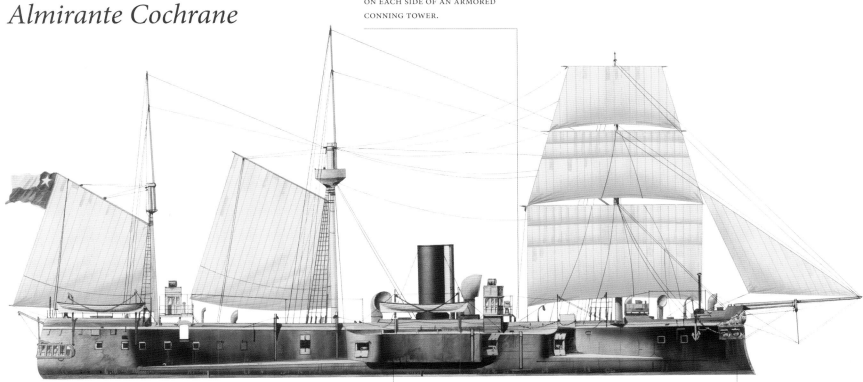

BATTERY
THE BOX BATTERY WAS VERY BOX-LIKE,
NOT FAIRED INTO THE LOWER HULL BUT
PROTRUDING AT 90 DEGREES.

ARMOR
THE ARMORED DECK, ABOVE THE
WATERLINE, WAS 3 IN (75 MM) THICK
ABOVE THE ENGINES, TAPERING TO
2 IN (50 MM) AT THE EXTREMITIES.

Messudieh (1874)

BUILT IN ENGLAND FOR THE IMPERIAL OTTOMAN FLEET, THIS BARQUE-RIGGED
CENTRAL BATTERY IRONCLAD WAS CONSTRUCTED ON A PLAN VERY SIMILAR TO THAT
OF HMS *HERCULES*. IN DECEMBER 1914 IT WAS SUNK IN THE DARDANELLES BY A
BRITISH SUBMARINE.

Messudieh ("good fortune") was laid down in 1872 at the Thames Ironworks, London, and launched on October 28, 1874, as a typical central battery ship of the time. A ram bow, laterally extended battery compartment, and a 9-foot-high (2.7-m) waterline belt armor were among the features. Armor thickness varied from 12 in (305 mm) to 6 in (152 mm). With three masts, the ship was rigged as a barquentine, and a single-screw 8-boiler engine was installed.

Refits and improvements were made at various times. Around 1891, the 7-in (178-mm) guns were replaced by Krupp 5.9-in (150-mm) BL guns, which were much more effective.

Between 1898 and 1903 *Messudieh* underwent a major rebuild at the Ansaldo shipyards in Genoa, Italy. The forecastle and poop deck were cut down and a midships superstructure was added, with a new command post. Armored gun turrets were installed forward and aft of the superstructure, each intended to mount a single 9.2-in (234-mm) Vickers BL gun. But the guns were never installed, and wooden dummies were mounted in their place. However, a secondary armament of twelve 6 in (152 mm) and fourteen 3 in (75 mm) guns was mounted in the battery, supplemented by ten 2.2 in (57 mm) and two 2.75 in (47 mm) guns, all of up-to-date quick-firing type. New engines were installed, with two propellers, and the sailing rig was taken down, to be replaced by a single pole mast with a fighting top placed aft of both funnels.

Torpedoed

Turkey sided with Germany in 1914, and *Messudieh*, by now obsolete, was placed as a stationary guardship at Chanak, at the entry to the Dardanelles Straits, supplementing the coastal forts. On December 13, 1914, the British submarine B11 penetrated the minefield laid across the entrance. Although its periscope was seen, and the shore forts and the ship's secondary guns opened fire, it launched two torpedoes at 800 yards (731 m), both of which hit their target. *Messudieh* began to settle by the stern, capsized, and sank. The submarine escaped. Several Turkish and German officers were court-martialed for neglect as a result, and it was reported that three were executed.

SPECIFICATIONS

DISPLACEMENT: 9,120 tons (9,266 tonnes)

DIMENSIONS: 331 ft 5 in x 59 ft x 25 ft 11 in (101.02 m x 17.98 m x 7.9 m)

RIG: Three masts, barque rig

PROPULSION: Sails, screw propeller, engine 7,431 ihp (5,541 kW)

ARMAMENT: Twelve 10 in (254 mm), three 7 in (178 mm), six 20 pounder guns (1874)

SPEED: 13.7 knots (15.7 mph; 25.3 km/h)

CREW: 700

Messudieh

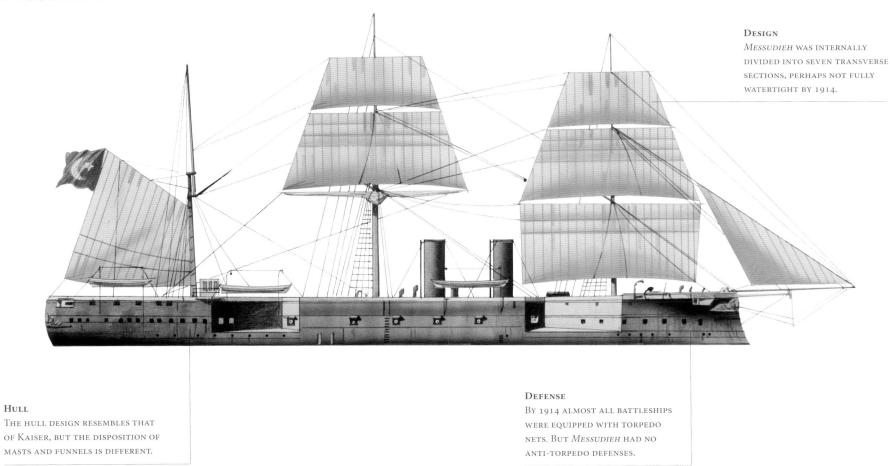

DESIGN
MESSUDIEH WAS INTERNALLY DIVIDED INTO SEVEN TRANSVERSE SECTIONS, PERHAPS NOT FULLY WATERTIGHT BY 1914.

HULL
THE HULL DESIGN RESEMBLES THAT OF KAISER, BUT THE DISPOSITION OF MASTS AND FUNNELS IS DIFFERENT.

DEFENSE
BY 1914 ALMOST ALL BATTLESHIPS WERE EQUIPPED WITH TORPEDO NETS. BUT *MESSUDIEH* HAD NO ANTI-TORPEDO DEFENSES.

SMS *Custoza* (1875)

THE AUSTRO-HUNGARIAN NAVY STARTED BUILDING CENTRAL BATTERY SHIPS AFTER THE BATTLE OF LISSA AND PUT EXCESSIVE EMPHASIS ON THE FUNCTION OF RAMMING, ALTHOUGH THIS HAD THE EFFECT OF ENCOURAGING FORE AND AFT FIRING SO THAT THE SHIP COULD SHOOT FORWARD AT ITS INTENDED RAMMING TARGET. *CUSTOZA* HAD ITS GUNS ENCLOSED IN A CASEMATE.

Laid down at the STT yard in Trieste on November 17, 1869, it was launched on August 20, 1872, and completed in February 1875. The name is from Custoza in Italy, where the Austrians won a land battle in 1866, and it was referred to as a *Kasemattschiff* or casemate ship, and battleship first class. Its lower hull was of iron, and was constructed on what its designer Josef von Romako called the cell-system, which had adapted from the British designs of Sir Edward Reed, dispensing with the traditional keel of the wooden ship, and with a double bottom of iron. High-sided, the casemate was a two-level box whose extended sides met the armored belt above the waterline and enabled the guns at its corners to fire on a near-180-degree arc.

As with other Reed central battery ships, the hull was recessed fore and aft to make forward and rearward firing by the Krupp 10.25-in (260-mm) guns possible,

sacrificing deck space internally and on the top deck. A 9-in (229-mm) armored belt protected the waterline, with 7 in (178 mm) around the casemate.

The appearance was imposing and fortress-like, and although "less speed and fewer guns" was supposed to be the Austrian maxim, combined with high protection, *Custoza* did not lack guns or speed, if indeed it could attain its specified 13.75 knots (15.8 mph; 25.4 km/h). The machinery, built by STT, was the largest engine yet built by the company, and *Custoza* also had a full square rig until 1877, when the yards were cut back except on the foremast, with schooner rig on the main- and mizzenmasts.

Service in the Austro-Hungarian Navy

In 1882, four 14 in (356 mm) torpedo tubes were fitted, with four 47 mm QF guns. *Custoza* was based at Pola, the

main Austro-Hungarian base, and made occasional cruises in the Adriatic Sea. It was withdrawn from active service well before the 1914–18 War; in 1914 it was in use as an accommodation ship, and in 1920 it was ceded to Italy as part of the post-World War I reparations.

SPECIFICATIONS

DISPLACEMENT: 7,609 tons (7,731 tonnes)

DIMENSIONS: 311 ft 9 in x 58 ft x 26 ft (95.03 m x 17.7 m x 7.9 m)

RIG: Three masts, square rig, then barquentine rig

PROPULSION: Sails, screw propeller, 2-cylinder STT engine, 4,158 ihp (3,058 kW)

ARMAMENT: Eight 10.2 in (260 mm) BL, six 3.5 in (90 mm) BL, two 2.7 in (70 mm) guns

SPEED: 13.75 knots (15.8 mph; 25.4 km/h)

CREW: 548

SMS *Custoza*

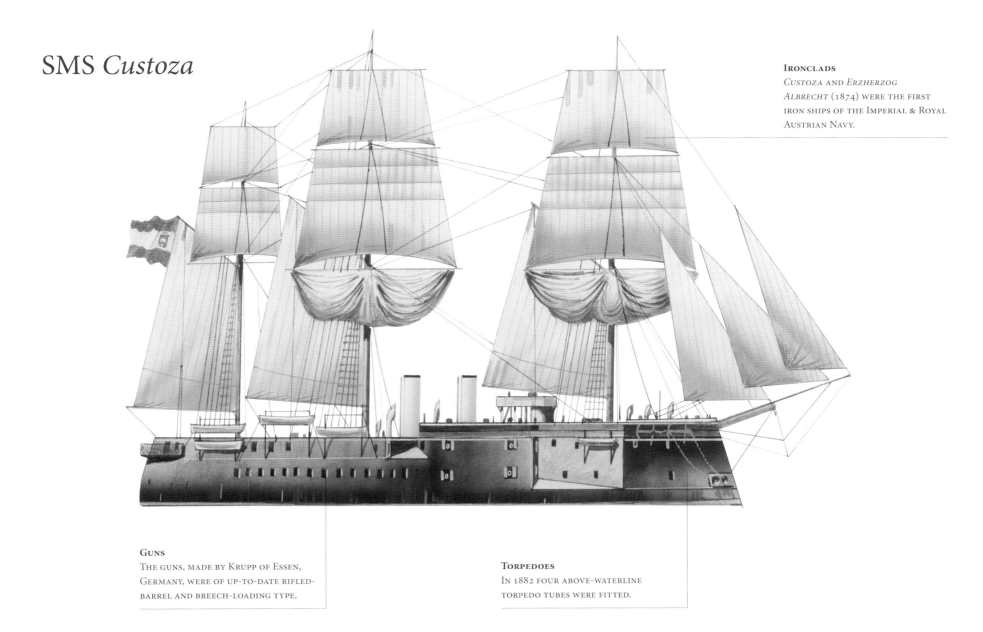

GUNS
THE GUNS, MADE BY KRUPP OF ESSEN,
GERMANY, WERE OF UP-TO-DATE RIFLED-
BARREL AND BREECH-LOADING TYPE.

TORPEDOES
IN 1882 FOUR ABOVE-WATERLINE
TORPEDO TUBES WERE FITTED.

SMS *Kaiser* (1875)

BUILT IN LONDON FOR THE IMPERIAL GERMAN NAVY, TO THE DESIGN OF A BRITISH NAVAL ARCHITECT, *KAISER* UNSURPRISINGLY HAD THE LOOK OF A BRITISH BATTLESHIP. WITH ITS SISTER SHIP, *DEUTSCHLAND*, IT WOULD BE THE LAST GERMAN CAPITAL SHIP TO BE BUILT OUTSIDE OF GERMANY.

The ships were built simultaneously by Samuda Bros., London, to a design drawn up by Sir Edward Reed. *Kaiser* was laid down in 1872, launched on March 19, 1874, and completed on February 13, 1875. It was a typical Reed central battery ship with the casemate extended out on both sides from the hull, enabling forward and rearward fire. Substantial side-armor was applied, with a waterline belt from 10 in (254 mm) to 5 in (127 mm), on teak backing, and 8–7 in (20–178 mm) around the casemate. A 2-in (50-mm) armored deck ran the length of the ship. The engines were also British, built by Penn.

Active Service

Kaiser was based at Wilhelmshaven, Germany's new naval base on the North Sea. Although the fleet was certainly an important instrument of German foreign policy, it was not used in combat at sea prior to 1914 and *Kaiser's* duties were confined to patrols, exercises, and goodwill visits to northern European and Mediterranean ports, with regular spells in reserve as the fleet grew larger. In 1882 it was refitted, with seven 6 in (150 mm) guns replacing the single 8.2 in (210 mm) gun originally mounted.

In 1889 it led the squadron on the Emperor's state visit to Constantinople. Three years later a more complete rebuilding was done at Wilhelmshaven. The rigging was removed, two military-type pole masts were fitted, and it was re-gunned, provided with five torpedo tubes, and redesignated as an armored cruiser.

In this form *Kaiser* was deployed to the Far East as flagship of the East Asia Squadron, and in 1897 led Admiral Diederich's ships supporting the forcible German occupation of Kiachow (Jiaozhou) on November 14. It returned to Germany in 1899.

On May 3, 1904 it was decommissioned for use as a harbor ship, being renamed *Uranus* in 1905. Stricken from the naval register on May 21, 1906, it was used from 1908 as accommodation ship for the torpedo school at the port of Flensburg. It was broken up in 1920.

SPECIFICATIONS

DISPLACEMENT: 8,799 tons (8,940 tonnes)

DIMENSIONS: 293 ft 1 in x 62 ft 8 in x 26 ft (89.34 m x 19.2 m x 7.93 m)

RIG: Three masts, square rig

PROPULSION: Sails, screw propeller, Penn HSE engine, 5,700 ihp (4,190 kW)

ARMAMENT: Eight 10.2 in (260 mm), one 8.2 in (210 mm) guns

SPEED: 14.5 knots (16.6 mph; 26.8 km/h)

CREW: 656

SMS *Kaiser*

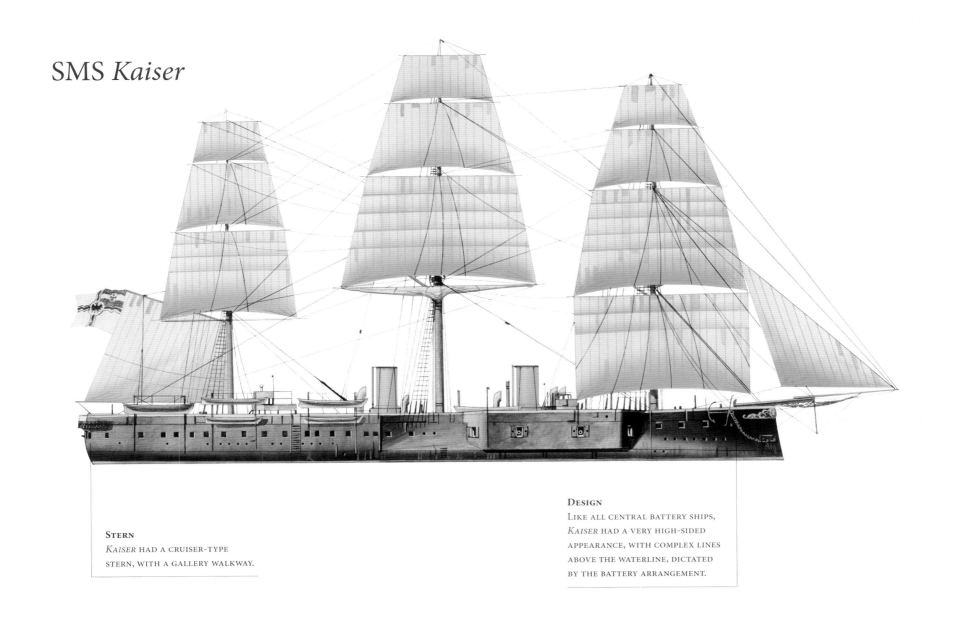

STERN
KAISER HAD A CRUISER-TYPE
STERN, WITH A GALLERY WALKWAY.

DESIGN
LIKE ALL CENTRAL BATTERY SHIPS,
KAISER HAD A VERY HIGH-SIDED
APPEARANCE, WITH COMPLEX LINES
ABOVE THE WATERLINE, DICTATED
BY THE BATTERY ARRANGEMENT.

HMS *Alexandra* (1877)

AS A CENTRAL BATTERY IRONCLAD, *ALEXANDRA* WAS EFFECTIVELY OBSOLETE EVEN WHEN COMMISSIONED, WITH TURRETED WARSHIPS ALREADY AFLOAT. BUT IT ALSO HAD NEW FEATURES, AND SERVED IN THE ROYAL NAVY, FREQUENTLY AS A FLAGSHIP, FOR 23 YEARS, MOSTLY WITH THE MEDITERRANEAN FLEET.

By the mid-1870s the efficiency and power of marine steam engines had greatly improved, but the British Admiralty was not yet prepared to give up the practice of fully rigging the ships intended for blue-water service, and *Alexandra* was rigged as a three-masted barque. Laid down at Chatham Dockyard on March 5, 1873, launched on April 7, 1875, and completed on January 31, 1877, it was regarded as one of the most successful central battery ships.

The iron hull was divided into 115 watertight compartments, with a central longitudinal bulkhead 245 ft (74.7 m) long, and a double bottom. The first Royal Navy ship to have vertical compound engines, making it the fastest large warship of its day, it was also a good sailer, although somewhat slow under sail alone, as all central battery ships seem to have been. An innovation was two 600 ihp (450 kW) auxiliary engines, which kept the screws turning while the ship was under sail. It was the last British battleship to carry its main guns below the top deck, with the typical box-battery arrangement.

Mediterranean Service and Refit

From January 2, 1877 *Alexandra* was flagship of the Mediterranean Fleet and kept the role to 1889. It participated in the show of force off Constantinople in 1878, grounding in the Dardanelles Strait but quickly towed off by HMS *Sultan*; and was one of the ships bombarding Alexandria, Egypt, in June 1882.

Refits were made in 1884 and again on a larger scale in 1889–91 when breech loaders and QF guns replaced the MLR guns in the upper battery level, and four 16 in (408 mm) torpedo tubes were fitted. A control tower, with 12-in (305-mm) armor, was also installed. At this time, too, the rig was cut back with the uppermost masts removed, and light topmasts fitted, with fighting tops on the fore- and mizzenmasts.

From 1891 to 1901, with a reduced armament, *Alexandra* was flagship of the Reserve at Portsmouth. In 1903 it became a training vessel for artificers, and was sold for breaking in 1908.

SPECIFICATIONS

DISPLACEMENT: 9,490 tons (9,642 tonnes)

DIMENSIONS: 344 ft x 63 ft 8 in x 26 ft 6 in (104.8 m x 19.4 m x 8.1 m)

RIG: Three masts, barque rig

PROPULSION: Sails, two screw propellers, vertical inverted compound engine, 8,498 ihp (6,337 kW)

ARMAMENT: Two 11 in (280 mm), ten 10 in (254 mm) MLR guns

SPEED: 15.09 knots (17.3 mph; 27.9 km/h)

CREW: 674

HMS *Alexandra*

SAILS
ALEXANDRA'S BARQUE RIG GAVE
A SAIL AREA OF 27,000 SQ FT
(2,508 SQ M).

BATTERY
DESPITE THE EXTENDED BATTERY SIDES,
AHEAD AND ASTERN FIRING FROM A
BATTERY WAS RESTRICTED BY THE
DANGER OF BLAST IMPACT ON THE HULL.

ARMOR
AN ARMORED BELT 10 FT 6 IN (1.26 M)
HIGH AND FROM 12–6 IN (305–152 MM)
THICK, WITH TEAK BACKING, PROTECTED
THE WHOLE WATERLINE LENGTH.

Redoutable (1878)

FRENCH NAVAL DESIGNERS COULD ALWAYS BE RELIED UPON TO BE ORIGINAL IN THEIR APPROACH, AND *REDOUTABLE* WAS A VERY DISTINCTIVE SHIP OF THE CENTRAL BATTERY TYPE, IN APPEARANCE AND DIMENSIONS, BUT ALSO REVOLUTIONARY IN CONSTRUCTION MATERIAL, AS THE FIRST WARSHIP TO BE BUILT LARGELY OF STEEL. IT SAW MUCH SERVICE IN ASIAN WATERS IN THE COURSE OF ITS CAREER.

Laid down at Lorient naval yard in August 1873 and launched in September 1876, *Redoutable*, a celebrated name in the French Navy, was completed in December 1878. Its designer was the engineer Louis de Bussy. France led the world in steelmaking with the Siemens process at that time, and only the bottom plates of the vessel were of iron, the rest of the hull being steel, with consequent improvement in structural strength and reduction in weight. Compared to other central battery ships, it was of wider beam and with a shortened battery, holding only four main guns, corner-mounted. The armor belt, 9 ft 10 in (3 m) high, was of wrought iron and completely enclosed the hull, which had a marked tumblehome.

The ship was full-rigged at first, with 24,000 sq ft (2,229.7 sq m) of sail, but was later altered to barquentine rig. Its service was mostly with the Mediterranean and Indo-China squadrons, based at Toulon and Saigon respectively. *Redoutable* had 15 captains from 1879 to 1909.

Refit and Active Service

In the mid-1890s a major modernization and reconstruction was done, with new guns, new boilers, and a revised superstructure. Electric circuits were installed. The rig was dismantled and replaced by two military masts, and torpedo defense netting was fitted.

From 1894 it carried seven 10.6 in (270 mm) and six 5.5 in (140 mm) breech-loading rifled guns, as well as Hotchkiss machine guns, four of these being mounted on a platform running around the outside of the funnel. Four torpedo tubes were mounted, two on each side.

In the early 1900s the ship was in the Far East during a period of high international tension, with war between Japan and Russia. In 1909 *Redoutable* completed its final tour of service at Saigon, Vietnam. Stricken in 1910, it was broken up in 1912.

SPECIFICATIONS

DISPLACEMENT: 9,224 tons (9,372 tonnes)

DIMENSIONS: 318 ft 8 in x 64 ft 6 in x 25 ft 7 in (97.13 m x 19.6 m x 7.8 m)

RIG: Three masts, square rig, later barquentine rig

PROPULSION: Sails, screw propeller, horizontal compound engine, 6,200 ihp (4,560 kW)

ARMAMENT: Eight 10.8 in (274 mm), six 5.5 in (140 mm), twelve 1 pounder guns

SPEED: 14.7 knots (16.9 mph; 27.2 km/h)

CREW: 705

Redoutable

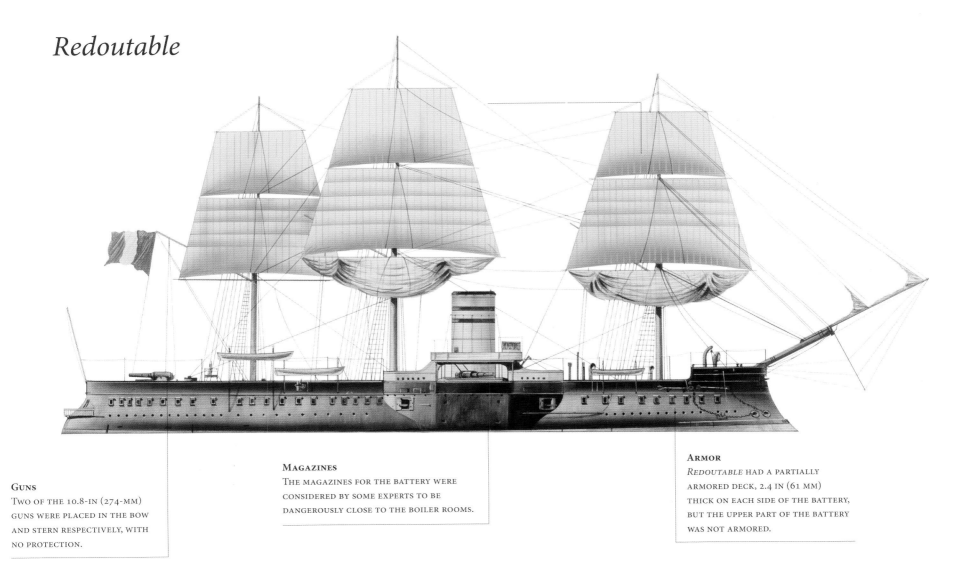

GUNS
TWO OF THE 10.8-IN (274-MM)
GUNS WERE PLACED IN THE BOW
AND STERN RESPECTIVELY, WITH
NO PROTECTION.

MAGAZINES
THE MAGAZINES FOR THE BATTERY WERE
CONSIDERED BY SOME EXPERTS TO BE
DANGEROUSLY CLOSE TO THE BOILER ROOMS.

ARMOR
REDOUTABLE HAD A PARTIALLY
ARMORED DECK, 2.4 IN (61 MM)
THICK ON EACH SIDE OF THE BATTERY,
BUT THE UPPER PART OF THE BATTERY
WAS NOT ARMORED.

Herzogin Cecilie (1902)

HERZOGIN CECILIE ("Duchess Cecilie") was named for a German duchess, and operated as a sail training and cargo carrying ship between 1902 and 1936. A much-admired four-masted barque of fine appearance, it was wrecked off the coast of South Devon in June 1936.

Constructed at Rickmers Reismühlen Reederei & Schiffbau, Bremerhaven, Germany, in 1902, this was a purpose-built sail training ship, ordered by the Norddeutscher Lloyd Steamship Co., and intended to combine the training aspect with carrying commercial cargoes. The hull was of steel, with shapely lines, and below the weather deck it held accommodation for a professional crew plus 63 cadets. In 1912 the poop deck was lengthened by 19 ft (5.8 m) to make room for 90 cadets.

Sailing mostly from Bremerhaven, it carried mixed cargoes of manufactured goods out to South American or Australian ports, returning with bulk loads of nitrates, grain, or timber. *Herzogin Cecilie* was an excellent sailer and made fast passages. During World War I it was interned in Chile, leaving only as late as 1920, carrying a cargo of nitrates to Ostend. On arrival it was passed to France as part of Germany's postwar reparations.

The French government sold it to Gustaf Erikson of Mariehamn, in the Finnish Åland Islands, famed as owner of the last fleet of windjammers. No longer a training ship, *Herzogin Cecilie* carried cargoes for Erikson between Europe and Australia, coming back with grain from Port Lincoln, making regular passages of Cape Horn. Although able to charge less than steamship prices, the slump in demand during the Depression years of the early 1930s made it hard to run the ship economically.

Grounded

Its last voyage to Australia was from Copenhagen, Denmark, leaving on October 15, 1935. In only 86 days it was back from Port Lincoln, reaching Falmouth, England, on April 23, 1936, carrying 4,295 tons (4,364 tonnes) of grain. Leaving Falmouth for Ipswich, and sailing too near the cliff-bound coast, it grounded on rocks. Much of the cargo and other gear was offloaded, and the ship was refloated on June 19, but ran aground again off Salcombe harbor, South Devon. Salvage attempts this time failed, and although the wreck was sold for £225, most of it still lies in Starhole Bay. Numerous relics are preserved in the seafaring museum at Mariehamn.

SPECIFICATIONS

DISPLACEMENT: 2,786 tons (2,830 tonnes)

DIMENSIONS: 310 ft x 46 ft x 24 ft 7 in (94.5 m x 14 m x 7.4 m)

RIG: Four masts, barque rig

SPEED: 20 knots (23 mph; 37 km/h)

CREW: c. 26, plus cadet

Herzogin Cecilie

MASTS
THE MAINMAST ROSE TO 175 FT 6 IN
(53.49 M) ABOVE THE WATERLINE.

SPEED
THE *DUCHESS*'S SAIL AREA WAS 38,000
SQ FT (3,530 SQ M), CAPABLE OF DRIVING
IT AT 20 KNOTS (23 MPH; 37 KM/H).

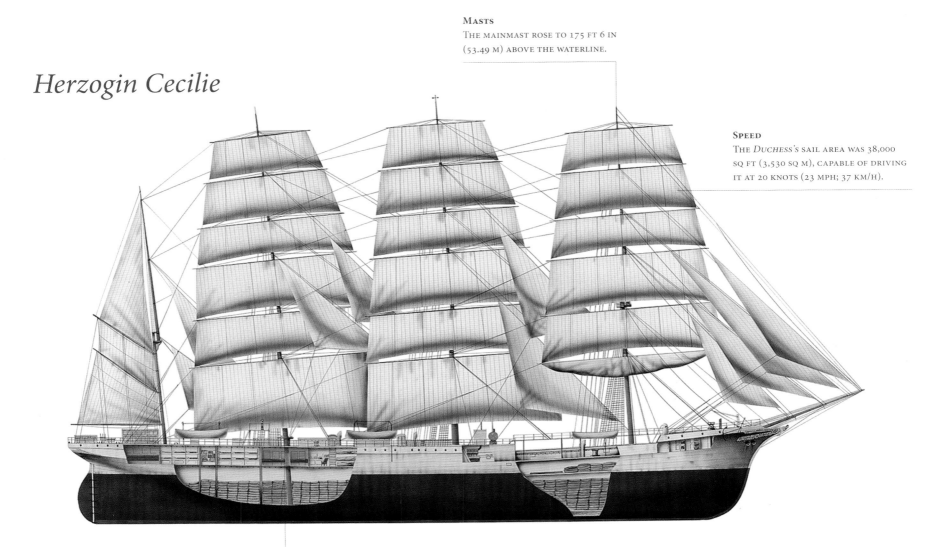

DECKHOUSE
BECAUSE OF ITS LARGE CADET CREW,
THE SHIP HAD A LONG DECKHOUSE FROM
QUARTERDECK TO STERN. THIS ENABLED IT
TO CARRY SOME PASSENGERS IN THE 1930S.

Preussen (1902)

PREUSSEN ("PRUSSIA") WAS ONE OF ONLY FOUR FIVE-MASTED SQUARE-RIGGERS EVER BUILT. IT WAS THE SECOND OF THE NAME TO SAIL FOR THE REEDEREI F. LAEISZ "FLYING P-" SHIPPING LINE OF HAMBURG, GERMANY, AND MADE MANY FAST PASSAGES BETWEEN SOUTH AMERICAN AND NORTHERN EUROPEAN PORTS.

All Laeisz ships had names beginning with P. *Preussen* was ordered in November 1900, laid down at the J.C. Tecklenborg Shipyard, Geestemünde, Germany, in August 1901, launched on May 7, 1902, and was ready for service by July 31, when it left Hamburg on its maiden voyage to the nitrate port of Iquique, Chile. The ship was designed by Dr. Georg Claussen. Its hull was built of steel, as were the lofty masts and the yards, and most of the fixed rigging was of steel cable. A central island was built between the second and third masts, providing crew accommodation.

It was a pure sailing ship, but with a relatively small crew, labor-saving devices were needed and numerous winches were fitted, as well as sliding shoes for the yards. Two donkey engines provided power for winching, loading, and pumping. All five masts were fully rigged, and the total sail area was claimed as 73,260 sq ft (6,806 sq m): a total certainly never exceeded, and perhaps rarely mounted, although *Preussen* was certainly a very fast ship, capable of 20 knots (23 mph; 37 km/h) in good conditions.

Speed and Capacity

A five-masted ship needed a larger crew than a four-master (it is interesting to compare *Preussen's* dimensions with those of its contemporary, *Archibald Russell*), but could offer much more cargo capacity: some 8,000 tons (8,100 tonnes), which made a big difference in commercial terms. *Preussen* made many fast passages, perhaps the fastest being 55 days from Land's End, England, round Cape Horn to Iquique, in 1903, running in ballast to pick up a cargo of nitrates.

Its career came to an end not off the Horn but in the English Channel in November 1910. Outward bound for Chile, it rammed the cross-Channel steamer *Brighton*, cutting across its path in defiance of the rules. With its bows stove in, *Preussen* was taken in tow, but in bad weather the towlines parted, the anchor chains broke, and the ship grounded on a reef in Crab Bay, off Dover. All efforts to pull it off failed, and the wreck had to be abandoned.

SPECIFICATIONS

DISPLACEMENT: 3,150 tons (3,200 tonnes)

DIMENSIONS: 482 ft x 53 ft 8 in x 27 ft 1 in (147 m x 16.4 m x 8.26 m)

RIG: Five masts, full square rig

SPEED: 20.5 knots (23.4 mph; 38 km/h)

CREW: 46

Preussen

PREUSSEN

RIGGING
IN ALL, THE SHIP CARRIED A SUIT OF 47 SAILS, AND THE STANDARD SAIL AREA WAS AROUND 59,848 SQ FT (5,560 SQ M). THE MASTS WERE DESIGNATED AS FORE, MAIN, MIDDLE, MIZZEN, AND JIGGER.

DISPLACEMENT
FULLY LOADED, THE SHIP DISPLACED 11,150 TONS (11,330 TONNES).

WHEEL
PREUSSEN'S DOUBLE WHEEL WAS 6 FT 6 IN (2 M) IN DIAMETER. TACKING IN NEAR-GALE WINDS, IT MIGHT TAKE SIX MEN TO HOLD IT AGAINST THE RUDDER'S TENDENCY TO SWING AWAY FROM THE COURSE SET.

Archibald Russell *(1905)*

BY THE 1900S, MOST SHIPPING COMPANIES CONCENTRATED ENTIRELY ON BUILDING UP A STEAMER FLEET, BUT A FEW CHOSE TO REMAIN IN SAIL. ONE OF THESE WAS JOHN HARDIE & SON, OF GLASGOW, WHO ORDERED THIS FOUR-MASTED BARQUE IN 1904 AS AN ADDITION TO A FLEET CONSISTING ENTIRELY OF IRON- OR STEEL-HULLED SAILING SHIPS.

Built by Scott's of Greenock, and launched on January 23, 1905, at a cost of £20,750, *Archibald Russell* was the last big square-rigger to be launched on the Clyde. It was steel-hulled, and fitted with two 120 ft (36.5 m) bilge keels to reduce rolling.

Barque-rigged with four masts, *Archibald Russell* was a fine and fast sailer and participated in the Chilean nitrate and Australian wheat traffic, also carrying coal, case oil, and timber; on one occasion making it back from Australia to England in 93 days. Its cargo capacity related to the density of the load, but it regularly carried around 4,000 tons (4,064 tonnes) of wheat.

It continued to sail through World War I, but Hardie's then moved on to steamships and in December 1923 *Archibald Russell* was sold, like *Herzogin Cecilie*, to Gustaf Erikson (who already had two ex-Hardie sister ships).

Cargo Carrier

In 1925 or 1926 *Archibald Russell* was refitted to carry cadets again, but still ran in commercial traffic, mostly carrying wheat. It continued to make fast passages, such as Copenhagen to Port Lincoln in 93 days between September 19 and December 31, 1930. In 1934 it made a rare visit to its home port of Mariehamn in the Åland Islands, probably for refitting, before taking another general cargo from Copenhagen to Port Lincoln. It continued on the same routes until its arrival at Hull with a cargo of wheat on August 27, 1939, when it was detained by the British government because of the German occupation of Poland, which had closed the Baltic Sea.

In 1941 Finland joined Germany in war against Russia but the ship was not formally claimed by Britain. Through World War II it was used for food storage at the port of Goole. It was released back to Erikson in 1948 but its condition had deteriorated past the point of economic restoration and it was sold for scrapping at Gateshead in 1949.

SPECIFICATIONS

DISPLACEMENT: 2,385 tons (2,423 tonnes)

DIMENSIONS: 291 ft 4 in x 43 ft x 24 ft (88.8 m x 13.1 m x 7.3 m)

RIG: Four masts, barque rig

CREW: c. 30

Archibald Russell

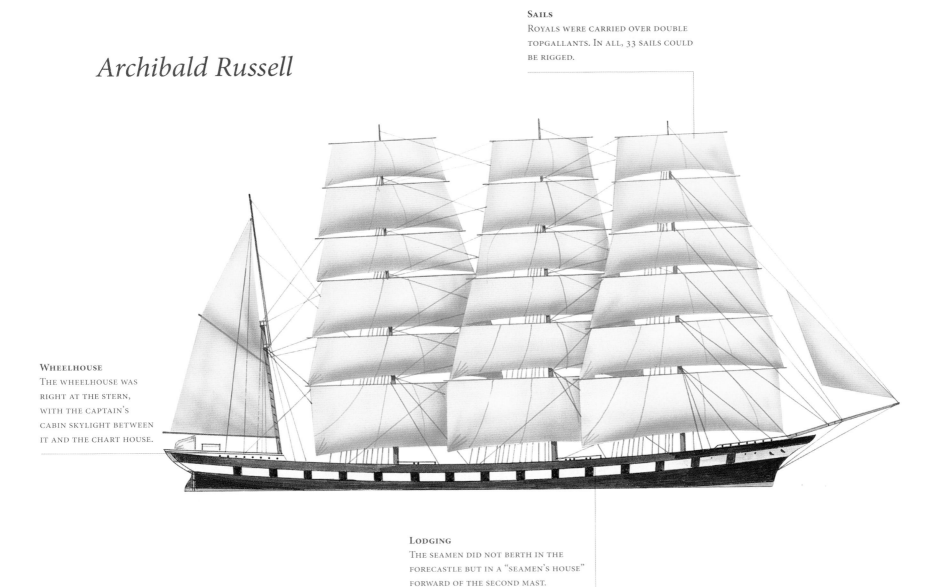

SAILS
ROYALS WERE CARRIED OVER DOUBLE TOPGALLANTS. IN ALL, 33 SAILS COULD BE RIGGED.

WHEELHOUSE
THE WHEELHOUSE WAS RIGHT AT THE STERN, WITH THE CAPTAIN'S CABIN SKYLIGHT BETWEEN IT AND THE CHART HOUSE.

LODGING
THE SEAMEN DID NOT BERTH IN THE FORECASTLE BUT IN A "SEAMEN'S HOUSE" FORWARD OF THE SECOND MAST.

Amerigo Vespucci (1931)

IN 1925, THE ITALIAN NAVY ORDERED TWO SAIL TRAINING SHIPS. UNUSUALLY FOR SUCH VESSELS, THEY WERE BUILT ON THE MODEL OF A LATE 18TH CENTURY 74-GUN SHIP OF THE LINE, SPECIFICALLY THE SPANISH-NEAPOLITAN *MONARCA* (1794), DUPLICATING ITS SOMEWHAT BUXOM LINES, ALTHOUGH INCORPORATING SUCH ANACHRONISTIC FEATURES AS A STEEL HULL AND MASTS, AND AUXILIARY ENGINE POWER.

Their designer was General Francesco Rotundi, who made a remarkably effective job of replicating an 18th century design in a hull of modern materials. The first, *Cristoforo Colombo*, was put into service in 1928. After World War II, it was handed over to the USSR as part of war reparations and was shortly afterwards decommissioned. *Amerigo Vespucci*, named for the explorer who gave his name to the Americas, was laid down in 1930 at the Naval Shipyard of Castellammare di Stabia, Naples. Launched on February 22, 1931, it entered service in July of that year. With *Cristoforo Colombo* it was used by the Italian Navy until 1943, both ships often making joint cruises, and recommissioned after World War II.

The ship carries no guns other than two 6 pounders for saluting purposes, and the interior provides cadet accommodation very different from 18th century standards. The sail suit consists of 26 canvas sails, including main courses, staysails, and jibs.

The rig uses traditional hemp ropes; only the mooring lines are synthetic, to comply with port regulations. Under sail with a good following wind it can reach 12 knots (13.8 mph; 22.2 km/h). The hull is painted black with two white stripes, harking back to *Monarca's* two gun decks. The deck planks, of teak wood, had to be replaced every three years.

STILL IN SERVICE

Amerigo Vespucci is the last sail-based naval training ship still in active use. Other than in the war years and the period immediately afterwards, the ship has been continually active, and still makes regular cruises with midshipmen of the Naval Academy as well as other cruises and participation in such events as the annual Tall Ships Race. Training cruises are usually in European waters, but it has also sailed to North and South America, and navigated the Pacific. In 2002, *Amerigo Vespucci* undertook a voyage around the world.

SPECIFICATIONS

DISPLACEMENT: 4,146 tons (4,212 tonnes)

DIMENSIONS: 331 ft x 51 ft x 23 ft (101 m x 15.5 m x 7 m)

RIG: Three masts, full square rig

PROPULSION: Sails, screw propeller, auxiliary diesel electric engine, 1,900 ihp (1,417 kW)

SPEED: 12 knots (13.8 mph; 22.2 km/h)

CREW: 276, plus 174 cadets

Amerigo Vespucci

RIGGING
THE MASTS ARE OF STEEL, 164 FT
(50 M), 177 FT 2 IN (54 M), AND
141 FT (43 M) HIGH; THE SAIL
AREA IS 30,140 SQ FT (2,800 SQ M).

ANCHOR WINCH
THE RIGGING HAS TO BE WORKED
BY HAND; POWER IS APPLIED ONLY
TO THE ANCHOR WINCH.

WHEELHOUSE
AN ENCLOSED WHEELHOUSE REPLACES THE OPEN
COCKPIT OF FORMER TIMES. EITHER MANUAL OR
POWER STEERING CAN BE EMPLOYED.

Glossary

Barbette: Open-topped armored enclosure, protecting a gun.

Beam: Width of a ship.

BL: Breech-loading.

BLR: Breech-loading, rifled barrel.

Bonaventure mast: A fourth mast sometimes found on galleons.

Bowsprit: The forward-pointing spar at the bow.

Bumpkin: A boom pointing over the stern.

Burthen: Expression of a vessel's carrying capacity.

Careen: Tilting of a ship to repair and maintain its bottom.

Carrack: A late medieval merchant ship, carvel-built, with a square sail.

Carronade: A short-barrelled, large-bore short-range gun, effective in close fighting.

Carvel-built: Hull planks attached edge-on, giving a smooth finish.

Casemate: An armored area set in the hull, where guns are mounted.

Citadel: An armored area in the center of a ship.

Clinker-built: Hull planks attached with overlapping edges.

Coppering: The protective cladding of a wooden hull with copper plates.

Course: The lowest sail on a mast carrying more than one level of sails.

CSS: Confederate States' Ship—used to designate all ships of the Confederate states during the American Civil War.

Displacement: A measure of the actual weight of a ship and its contents, excluding cargo.

Embrasure: An angled opening in the hull side, enabling a gun to fire fore and aft.

Gaff: A spar used to support the head of a fore-and-aft sail.

HDMS: His/Her Danish Majesty's Ship (in Danish, *KDM*), the ship prefix for Denmark's Royal Danish Navy.

HMS: His/Her Majesty's Ship. Used to designate all ships in the British Royal Navy from the mid 18th century.

Hogging: Sagging of the forward and after parts of a ship's hull.

Howitzer: A short-barrelled gun firing a heavy shell at an elevated angle and relatively low muzzle velocity.

Hulk: The hull of a vessel with all rigging and equipment removed.

Lay up: To place in a reserve mooring. (See also *Ordinary*.)

Magazine: Secure storage room for gunpowder and explosive shells.

ML: Muzzle-loading.

MLR: Muzzle-loading, rifled barrel.

Obus: A howitzer shell.

Ordinary: A ship "in ordinary" was in reserve, with guns and masts removed.

QF: Quick-firing: guns firing projectiles that combined the shell and the firing charge.

Quarterdeck: The upper deck aft of the mainmast.

RB: Rifled bore (gun barrel).

Reserve: Temporary removal from active service. (See also *Ordinary*).

SB: Smooth bore (gun barrel).

Skysail: A topmost sail, mounted above upper topgallants and royals.

SMS: *Seiner Majestät Schiff* ("His Majesty's Ship"). Ship prefix used by the Prussian, Imperial German, and Austro-Hungarian navies.

Spanker: Originally a sail set above the mizzen course but often used to refer to the mizzen course itself.

Spar-deck: A deck (originally temporary) laid across the well between forecastle and quarterdeck.

Sponson: A gun-platform extended beyond the side of the upper deck.

Spritsail: A square sail fitted on a yard below the bowsprit.

Staysail: A sail mounted between two masts.

Stem: The foremost member of the hull, fixed to the forepart of the keel.

Studding sail: Additional square sails set from extensions to the yards.

Stunsail: Another name for a studding sail.

Topgallant: The uppermost section of the mast, mounting the topgallant yard.

Transom: A squared-off stern form.

Tumblehome: Inward angling of a ship's sides.

Turret: An armored construction containing a gun or guns, able to revolve in a partial or complete circle.

USRC: United States Revenue Cutter Service. Established in 1790, the USRC served as an armed maritime law enforcement agency in US coastal waters until replaced by the US Coast Guard in 1915.

USS: United States Ship, referring to ships of the United States Navy.

Weather: Direction from which the wind (and so the weather) is coming from.

Weather deck: The upper deck, open to the sky.

Ships Index

General Index

Select Bibliography

Chapelle, Howard I. *History of American Sailing Ships.* New York, 1936.

Davis, Gerard Charles. *American Sailing Ships.* New York, 1984.

Donnelly, I.A. *Chinese Junks.* Shanghai, 1930.

Gardiner, Robert. *Warships of the Napoleonic Era.* Barnsley, 2011.

Greenhill, Basil. *Evolution of the Sailing Ship.* London, 1988.

_____. *Sail's Last Century.* London, 1993.

Ireland, Bernard. *Naval Warfare in the Age of Sail.* London, 2000.

Landström, Björn. *The Ship.* London, 1961.

Malcomson, Robert. *Warships of the Great Lakes.* London & Annapolis, 2002.

Marcus, Geoffrey. *The Age of Nelson.* London, 1961.

Naval History & Heritage Command. *Dictionary of American Naval Fighting Ships,* Vols 1–8. Washington, D.C., 1959–81.

Paine, Lincoln. *Ships of the World: An Historical Encyclopedia.* London 1998.

_____. *Warships of the World to 1900.* New York, 2000.

Warrington-Smyth, A. *Mast and Sail in Europe and Asia.* London, 1929.